Soviet Involvement in the Middle East: Policy Formulation, 1966-1973

Soviet Involvement in the Middle East: Policy Formulation, 1966-1973
Ilana Kass

Using a systematic comparative analysis of the Soviet press organs' attitudes toward a specific issue, Ilana Kass examines Soviet foreign policy formulation and the activities of policy-relevant groups in the stages preceding and following the formal adoption of decisions. Soviet involvement in the Middle East in the crucial period 1966-1973 is used as a case study; it was assumed that an issue with such wide political, economic, strategic, and ideological ramifications would involve a broad array of policy groups and thus serve to pinpoint their divergent attitudes.

Kass focuses on four official groups close to the locus of Soviet decision making—the CPSU, the governmental bureaucracy, the military, and the trade union—and delineates and analyzes the attitudes of these groups toward the Soviet involvement in the Middle East. She explores the possibilities of opposition to the official policy line, and illustrates the respective roles of each group in the decision-making process.

This study provides evidence of the broadening basis of elite participation in the formulation of foreign policy and the gradual emergence of polycentricity in the Soviet political context. Having shown that the spectrum of opinion among Soviet decision makers is relatively diversified, Kass calls for a more discriminative, less restrictive approach to the study of Soviet policy.

Ilana Kass is an analyst with the Soviet and East European Research Center of the Hebrew University, Jerusalem, and a research fellow at the Davis Institute of International Relations. Dr. Kass is editor of a bimonthly bulletin on the Soviet Union and the Arab-Israeli conflict, and her articles on the Soviet Union and the Middle East have appeared in *Soviet Union, Ost Europa,* and *Soviet Studies.*

To Nori

Soviet Involvement in the Middle East: Policy Formulation, 1966-1973
Ilana Kass

Westview Press • Boulder, Colorado

Dawson • Folkestone, England

This volume is included in Westview's Special Studies on the Soviet Union and Eastern Europe.

Copyright © 1978 by Westview Press, Inc.

Published in 1978 in the United States of America by
  Westview Press, Inc.
  5500 Central Avenue
  Boulder, Colorado 80301
  Frederick A. Praeger, Publisher

Published in 1978 in Great Britain by
  Wm. Dawson and Sons, Ltd.
  Cannon House
  Folkestone, Kent CT19 5EE

Library of Congress No.: 77-8279
ISBN (U.S.): 0-89158-349-1
ISBN (U.K.): 0-7129-0857-9

Printed and bound in the United States of America

Contents

Preface

Most books originate as essays of limited scope or as doctoral dissertations whose findings await a receptive audience. Although this study passed through both these metamorphoses, it owes its birth to a mere coincidence. As a graduate student in the Political Science Department of The Hebrew University and a junior research fellow at the university's Soviet and East European Research Centre, I was responsible for documenting pronouncements relevant to the USSR's Middle Eastern policy that appeared in the CPSU organ *Pravda.* Within a few months I was assigned the task of analyzing excerpts from the Trade Union's organ *Trud,* only to discover that the two newspapers adopted diametrically differing attitudes toward some crucial issues. Trained as I was to view the Soviet system as a totalitarian, cohesive entity and the Russian media as a centrally controlled, monolithic means of mass manipulation, I was rather bewildered by my findings. An attempt to assess and rationalize this empirical reality resulted in two essays, each dedicated to the analysis of a policy group as represented by the press organ officially declared to be its platform. Special thanks are due to Professor Roger Kanet of the University of Illinois, editor of the journal *Soviet Union,* and to the editorial board of *Soviet Studies,* whose valuable suggestions and probing queries helped transform these crude attempts at systematic analysis into publishable papers, unwittingly laying the foundation for a doctoral thesis and, subsequently, for this book.

I would like to express my deepest gratitude to all those who helped me along the way, making the lonely process of academic endeavor a meaningful experience. I could hardly exaggerate the debt I owe to Professor Shlomo Avineri of The Hebrew University, teacher, friend, and spiritual father, who assisted me at every stage of my work. Heartfelt thanks are due to Dr. Jonathan Frankel, my doctoral adviser at The Hebrew University, for his stimulating counsel and guidance.

A three-year stay at Columbia University, made possible by a fellowship from the British Friends of The Hebrew University, added a new dimension to both my research and academic personality. The staffs of the Middle Eastern and Russian Institutes and, especially, Professor Charles Issawi and Professor Oles Smolansky spared neither time nor effort in offering help and advice. Most of all, I owe thanks to Professor J. C. Hurewitz, whose scholarly expertise and invaluable guidance were matched only by his kindness and willingness to assist, support, and encourage. Without his inspiring criticism, wise counsel, and perceptive judgments, this work might never have been completed.

I would be remiss were I to overlook the efficiency and high level of professional competence exhibited by Westview Press in handling the manuscript.

No words can suffice to express my gratitude to my husband Norman. A dear friend and fellow Sovietologist, he helped me through every stage of this research. To him, for his readiness to shoulder every burden, for his brilliant mind and loving heart, this book is dedicated.

Soviet Involvement in the Middle East: Policy Formulation, 1966-1973

1. Introduction: A Framework for Analysis

The Soviet Political System:
From Totalitarianism to Creeping Pluralism

Analysts have vacillated between two major explanations of foreign policy behavior. Theorists of international politics have generally adopted a macroanalytic approach, in which the internal dynamics of a state's behavior—including such factors as the particular political structure of the polity, the perspectives and personalities of the decision makers, and the articulated attitudes and demands of the citizenry—are "black boxed" in the name of analytic parsimony. These scholars anthropomorphize the state, treating it as a unitary, rational decision maker whose behavior is explained largely as a response (1) to the anarchic quality of politics in an international arena devoid of international government, (2) to changes in the structure of the international system, or (3) to calculated moves by rival states.

In contrast, those whose interest in international politics has developed out of a comparative politics or area studies concern, have shown themselves more prone to adopt microanalytic approaches to foreign policy analysis. These scholars view foreign policy as the result of the interplay of phenomena particular to the state in question. According to these analysts, policy attributes may grow out of entirely nonhuman factors, such as the state's geopolitical position or its natural resources endowment. Or they may stem from domestic forces, such as the state's national character, "modal personality," political culture, belief system or ideology, or social structure. Or they may originate in factors that shape the effective structure of a state, factors ranging from the state's formal constitutional framework on the one hand to structural impacts on information flows within the state on the other. Finally, according to the microanalysts, foreign policy attributes may be thought to originate in the idiosyncrasies of particular decision makers—their anxieties, their aspirations, and their perceptions. In short, the microanalysts have tended to regard the nature of the individual components of a polity, rather than the situationally induced general propensities of a state, as providing the most important clues to a proper understanding of any state's foreign policy. This has been particularly true in Western analysis of Soviet foreign policy.[1]

The Cold War created an atmosphere conducive to stressing the extent to which Soviet policy differed from that of other states in its conduct, goals, and instrumentalities. Until the early 1960s, Soviet studies remained somewhat divorced, conceptually and methodologically, from the mainstream of comparative politics and international relations inquiry.[2] Students of Soviet affairs developed a unique form of "blackbox" approach, perceiving the Soviet "leadership" as a homogenous entity and denying the existence of conflict—usually regarded as the central feature of all political systems—within the Soviet regime. The totalitarian model set forth by Brzezinski and Friedrich emerged as the only valid means of analysis of the Soviet political system.

Although there has been by no means general agreement on the meaning of totalitarianism, it has been common in the West to treat it as a phenomenon unique in world history, sharply distinguished not only from Western democracies, but also from traditional authoritarian regimes. It has usually been accepted that totalitarianism involves the widest possible extension of state power over society, thus tending to annihilate all boundaries between the two and destroying any associations or groups between the individual and the state.[3] It has been further argued that totalitarianism entails an unavoidable compulsion on the part of the ruling elite to absorb or destroy all social groups obstructing its complete control of society.[4]

The concept of totalitarianism that has dominated the analysis of communist systems in the West, at least until the late 1950s, has seemed to preclude the possibility that interest groups could challenge or affect the single ruling party as the fount of all power. The uniqueness of the totalitarian system has been deemed to lie in the very totality of its power, excluding, as if by definition, any area of autonomous behavior by groups other than the party and, still more, preventing serious influence by them on the process of decision making.[5]

The totalitarian concept also often implied a certain changelessness in the nature of communist politics. Even after the death of Stalin, the likelihood of a decline of totalitarianism was doubted by some; if anything, argued Friedrich and Brzezinski, communist societies would become more totalitarian.[6]

The model of communist politics implicit in most Western analyses appeared to be exclusively concerned with "outputs," i.e., the imposition of binding decisions, and to be entirely lacking in "inputs." Unlike all other systems, the Soviet system was depicted as one in which struggles over ideas and interests, or conflicts among rival groups, are absent. Issues requiring decisions are raised not by society or social groups, but presumably by the party, or better, by its topmost leaders, without regard for the values and interests of other entities. The monolithic party has been regarded as the only interest group, itself undifferentiated in its thinking and behavior.[7]

Interestingly enough, the totalitarian concept of a single, monolithic party claiming and exercising absolute authority was corroborated by communist theory. Marxist theorists have assumed that the single ruling party, the organization of the proletariat, best knew the "real" interests of the people as a whole and they have thus denied the possibility of fundamental conflict of interest within the working class. Conflict within and among other social classes and between them and the proletariat was depicted in terms of "class struggle," from which the proletariat was historically determined to emerge victorious. Thus, Soviet theory (and practice, at least under Stalin) regarded any aggregation or articulation of particularistic interests as an antisystemic, and therefore illegitimate, challenge to the hegemony of the proletariat and the party ruling in its name.

Even under the inhibiting burden of Stalinist dictatorship, however, the Soviet Union was being transformed into a complex industrial society, one that was divided into a number of functional groupings and that was developing a vast bureaucracy. It came to include several institutions with strong loyalties and parochial interests. After Stalin's death, an accelerated loosening of political controls over society took place, and the divergent institutional claims, hitherto suppressed, became publicly articulated and advocated with various degrees of vigor.[8] Perhaps the best analysis of this process is Alexander Dallin's:

> Creeping pluralism invades totalitarian life as it must invade all developing politics. The growing complexity of society and economy are bound to produce greater functional specialization, greater multiplicity of role conflicts, a greater awareness of divergent group interests, and at least their incipient aggregation. At the same time, political articulation and participation tend to increase while the pressures of forcible social, political and economic mobilization are somewhat relaxed; while the system has more material resources to spare from its all-out mobilization and survival needs; and as important choices among alternative strategies need to be made. Different elite elements tend to opt for different priorities in resource allocation, reflecting different values with different political implications. As terror tends to recede at this stage, dissenting voices may be heard with greater impunity, precisely at a time when the regime must make great efforts to manufacture a genuine consensus. The more modernized society must rely more heavily on "experts" who in turn tend to press for better information and greater rationality and often seek access to policy-makers, thus introducing notes which clash with the repetitive refrains of the ideologues and the timid, conservative bureaucrats.[9]

In addition, the fear of a return to one-man rule supports

"collective" decision making at the highest level, which requires the adjustment of conflicting opinions and preferences —or else stalemate and inaction. Collective leadership invariably creates a situation in which outside influences can more effectively be brought to bear on the narrow circle of decision-makers.[10] Conversely, in a collective leadership in which no individual is automatically assured of predominance, each person must secure his position by first winning and then maintaining the support of a combination of sociopolitical groups. Actual and potential rivals, on the other hand, can build their own power bases by identifying themselves with elements discontented with current policy. Under conditions of leadership conflict, unresolved disputes may lead some of the participants to broaden the conflict by involving political groupings that may shift the balance in their favor.[11]

As a result of the changes that occurred since Stalin's death and the shifting perspectives of both Western and communist analysts, a new version of communist politics slowly began to emerge. "The concept of a totalitarian system in which a single party, itself free of internal conflict, imposes its will on society, and on all social groups, was challenged by an approach that took account of the conflicting groups that exert an influence on the making of policy by the party."[12]

There is a marked controversy in the standard texts as to the functioning of Soviet interest groups.[13] Differences of interpretation center on (1) the kinds of groupings that do exist, (2) the rules of the game governing the articulation of their interest, and (3) the degree of influence groups may have on policy outcomes. Brzezinski and Huntington,[14] Azrael,[15] Kolkowicz,[16] Erickson,[17] and others see policy relevant groups as forming principally along occupational lines, such as the military, the state bureaucracy, and party *apparatchiki.* Meyer,[18] cautioning against any attempt at an a priori listing, suggests that interest groups may form around issues or individual leaders in addition to occupations. Barghoorn[19] and Leonhard[20] argue that the major policy groups do not form along occupational lines but cut across these to coalesce around issues, namely, modernizers versus conservatives, revisionists versus dogmatists, and the like.

Skilling and Griffiths similarly conclude that groupings most frequently form around issues, but, unlike Barghoorn and Leonhard, they see a greater multiplicity of viewpoints.[21]

Writers appear to divide roughly into two camps when assessing the informal rules governing group activity. Though all tend to agree that some kind of articulation of perceived group interests can and does occur in the USSR, differences arise over the limits imposed on such activity. One line of interpretation stresses the illegitimacy of group action and the high risks involved in crossing the line from "advocacy to pressure."[22] The others tend to emphasize the much greater freedom of discussion, even on "vital" issues, that in their view came to characterize Soviet political life after Stalin's death.[23]

Assessments of the extent of group influence on policy outcomes are as diverse as those on the rules of the game. Brzezinski, Azrael, and Barghoorn stress the Party's formal monopoly over decision making and the weakness of interest groups. At the same time, they suggest that groups having a relatively high institutional cohesion may occasionally act as "veto groups," successfully resisting Kremlin pressures.[24] Meyer, while pointing out our serious lack of knowledge of Soviet policy processes, suggests that the interests of a wide variety of groups are considered by the Soviet decision-makers. At the same time, he concludes, such interests usual- ly "do not count very heavily."[25] Griffiths, Skilling, and Meissner, on the other hand, argue that certain kinds of "stra- tegic" groupings may indeed count heavily in Soviet decision making.[26]

The foregoing summary clearly suggests that the issue is by no means resolved. Moreover, systematic empirical re- search on this problem is still in embryonic form. Perhaps the main reason for this "state of affairs" is the fact that "the style of interest groups is always strongly influenced by the entire political culture within which they operate."[27]

Thus, in a system in which decision making is highly cen- tralized, where several parties or genuine elections do not exist, where the communication media are controlled, and where unity of action is considered the supreme principle, policy groups will take on forms appropriate to this setting. Specifically, in the USSR, public articulation of dissenting opinion and aggregation of "constituencies" may be carried out only in a veiled, almost clandestine, manner.

The tediousness and frustration involved in attempts to penetrate the elaborate smoke screen around the inner workings of the Soviet political processes may account for the somewhat elusive character of most Western commentary on Soviet decision making and the activity of policy groups.

With the exception of one pathbreaking research project, sponsored and edited by Skilling and Griffiths, the main thrust of Western research has centered in recent years upon analysis of individual institutional groups, their makeup, career patterns, professional attitudes, and role in Soviet society.[28] Addressing themselves to the problem of the role these groups may play in the decision-making process, these analyses pointed to the formal points of contact between the various institutional hierarchies, assuming that "these institutional arrangements serve as channels of input into policy."[29]

To give but one example: the military has access to the decision-makers through the Defense Council (formerly referred to as the Higher Military Council), composed of military leaders and Politburo members; through the Council of Ministers, of which the Minister of Defense is of course a member; and through the Central Committee (CC) of the Communist Party of the Soviet Union (CPSU), on which thirty-six military officers at present serve as full or candidate members. In May 1973, with the promotion of Marshal Grechko to the Politburo, the military gained direct access to the highest decision-making body. By the same token, other political interest groups may attempt to impress their opinion upon the decision-makers through direct approaches at the key points of authority.

Here, however, a seemingly insurmountable difficulty is encountered. The activity of Soviet policy groups in the decision-making forums is an unknown quantity to the student of Soviet affairs. We have no direct evidence about the relative effectiveness of the formal channels of communi-

cation and means of access. We do not know what opinion
was argued, whether it was unanimously presented by the
representatives of a given group, and, perhaps most crucially,
whether it was heeded and acted upon by the decision-
makers. Equally obscure to the Western observer is the
probable utilization by policy groups of indirect channels of
approach, such as personal connections and clique activity.

In the realm of Soviet foreign policy, these obvious problems appear to be compounded by the fact that "overt
dissent over foreign policy issues is even less permissible than
public differences on internal affairs."[30] Consequently, the
actual process of Soviet foreign policy formulation remains,
even today, terra incognita and a subject of more or less educated guesswork.

Far from being in a position to offer solutions to these
problems, I propose a somewhat tedious and time-consuming,
yet rewarding and illuminating, method of analysis. Namely,
I propose to examine Soviet foreign policy formulation and
the activity of policy groups in the stages before and after the
formal adoption of a decision by the topmost leaders by
means of a systematic, comparative content analysis of the
Soviet press organs' attitudes toward specific policy issues.

This study does not attempt to present a full and complete analysis of the dynamics of Soviet foreign policy
making. However, by focusing attention on a specific, though
admittedly limited, case study, I do hope to shed some new
light on Soviet foreign policy decision making. Furthermore, the proposed research method may prove relevant
to the analysis of other policy issues in both foreign and
domestic affairs. To cite Arthur Bentley, "the most useful
approach to the study of a political process is to look for the
way in which interests clash and coalesce and to ascertain
which interests are expressed in the policy that emerges."[31]

The Research Method: Its Advantages and Pitfalls

The present study uses the compound problem of Soviet
involvement in the frontline Arab states in the crucial period
of 1966-1973 as a case study of Soviet foreign policy formulation. This case study was chosen with the hope that an issue

with such wide political, economic, strategic, and ideological ramifications would involve a relatively wide array of policy groups and serve to pinpoint their divergent approaches.

The central assumption underlying this study is that in the more than twenty years since Stalin's death the Soviet political system has been passing through a period of transition, characterized, inter alia, by the increased activity of political interest groups and the presence of group conflict. Although decision making in its final stage still remains in the hands of a relatively small group of leaders at the top of the party hierarchy, there has been, it is assumed, a broadening of group participation in the crucial preliminary stages of policy deliberation and in the subsequent phase of implementation.[32]

It should be emphasized that the present study does not focus on the shared characteristics of any given group, but rather on the actual attitudes and claims voiced by a politically active group through its press organ. Moreover, it should be pointed out, since this study examines a foreign policy issue, it centers upon four "official" groups, which are presumably close to the strategic locus of decision making and which may therefore be relevant to the process of foreign policy formulation.[33] These groups possess, in varying degrees, official authority, may have their own occupational group interests or their own views of the general public and national interest, and may press these on the ultimate decision-makers. Moreover, these groups are presumably often consulted by the topmost leaders and may consequently exert serious influence on decisions. In addition, the "official" groups enjoy easy access to the media of communication. The four strategic groups examined in this study are, at least officially, represented in and responsible for four of the USSR's central daily newspapers.

By choosing four official groups only, namely, the CPSU, the government bureaucracy, the military, and the trade union, we do not intend to imply that other groups, both official and nonofficial, do not form and articulate opinions on any given foreign policy issue. Specifically, the broad issue of Soviet policy toward and involvement in the Middle East may concern and therefore involve certain national groups (e.g., Muslims, Jews, Ukrainians), certain "intellectual" groups (e.g., Middle East experts in various scientific institutes), or even such strategic groups as the KGB. Limitations of time and space alone are responsible for the exclusion of these groups from the present study.

Four operational hypotheses underlie the current research project:

1. In the Soviet political context, the aggregation and articulation of group interests assume a unique form of public debate on policy issues; the discussion takes place not on the floor of a parliament but rather on the pages of professional magazines and newspapers. In other words, it is hypothesized that the Soviet press organs serve as additional channels of input through which the relevant groups impress their point upon the decision-makers and affect the general climate of opinion.

2. Interest groupings form primarily on the basis of similarity of viewpoints on one or more issues. These groupings may be found within a single bureaucratic structure (institution) or they may cut across organizational lines.

3. The press organ officially serving as the mouthpiece of a given institution provides the platform for expression of that group's opinion.

4. Leaders identified with key institutions may use these institutions as the sources or bases of their power. Consequently, they may employ the press organ of this institution as a means to articulate their own opinions and interests.

Pursuant to these hypotheses, the following research method was elaborated. Four central Soviet dailies were selected as representative of four political groupings: *Pravda,* the organ of the Central Committee of the CPSU; *Izvestiia,* the organ of the Soviet Council of Ministers; *Krasnaia zvezda,* the organ of the Ministry of Defense; and *Trud,* the trade union organ. These four press organs were screened day after day over the period of January 1966–July 1971 for articles, news items, and other references to the Middle East.[34] The roughly fifteen thousand items (an average of two items a day per newspaper) were subjected to a comparative content analysis and to a comparative quantitative analysis in an attempt to assess the divergent opinions and alternative policies these organs advocated.

This study will attempt to delineate and analyze the attitudes of the broad policy interest groups, which were presumably represented in these press organs, toward the various aspects of the USSR's involvement in the frontline Arab states in the period 1966-1973; to explore in these views the possibility of divergence from and opposition to the official policy line; and, most crucially, to illustrate the role of each group in the decision-making process.

It should be emphasized that our main concern is the reaction of the Soviet press organs and the groups they might represent toward the evolution and development of the situation in the Middle East. Consequently, the study does not attempt a detailed history of the Middle Eastern problem or Soviet relations with the Middle Eastern states. Nevertheless, background information will be provided whenever deemed relevant.

The main advantage of using the Soviet press as a means of examining Soviet political processes is that the researcher is dealing with written material, which easily lends itself to analysis. However, the advantage is also a pitfall. Although there is a confirmed relationship between language and thought patterns, this does not necessarily apply to language (i.e., communication) and action. In other words, we know that what one communicates has an impact on others and is an expression of one's thought patterns; we do not know whether one's political communication discloses what one is doing or intends to do.[35] Moreover, there is a seemingly perpetual discrepancy between what any person or group would like to do and what he or the group may actually decide to do or be capable of doing. Since Soviet leaders appear particularly committed to the perfection of man and his environment and hence promote high hopes about the future, such a discrepancy may be especially acute. Accordingly, textual analysis of the Soviet elite's descriptive or prescriptive communications presents a major methodological challenge to the student of the Soviet political system.[36]

Furthermore, because of the very nature of the Soviet regime, groupings and individuals may articulate their opinions and interests only in an oblique form. The internal debates reach the observer mainly through controlled communication media, with appropriate emendations and omissions. What appears in the press may reflect only to a limited degree the actual sharpness of the debate conducted in closed forums. Differences of opinion must often be deduced by interpreting seemingly semantic nuances, subtle emphases, or even by detecting what has not been said on a certain issue.

Since the issues at stake are rarely stated explicitly and since the "deciphering" of official Soviet publications is far from being an exact science, the interpretation of any differences discerned among the Soviet organs must be undertaken very cautiously. It is necessary, first of all, to attempt to eliminate the possibility that the differences discovered are insignificant variations or a result of a division of labor. As far as the first possibility is concerned, the rule of thumb is recurrence. The elimination of the second possibility (existence of a division of labor), though more complicated, is connected with the former. It seems unlikely that a central Soviet organ would be assigned the role of consistently opposing the official policy. Only when these possibilities are eliminated (as far as possible) may one assume that he is presented with a veiled—yet meaningful—dissenting opinion.

No less problematic is the task of assessing the level or degree of the divergences discerned. Robert Levine and others differentiate between systemic and marginal elite cleavages.[37] While the former relate to fundamental differences over policy objectives, the latter describe conflicts over alternative ways of achieving shared goals. Methodologically, this distinction raises particular difficulties in the Soviet context. Not only is overt dissent over foreign policy even less permissible than public differences on internal affairs, but even when couched in indirect, esoteric argument, systemic differences—if voiced at all—must be cloaked in marginalist terms.[38] For example, differences over the effectiveness of Soviet military aid to Egypt may or may not reflect (or veil) more profound differences over Soviet policy objectives.

Furthermore, one is examining organs that are official mouthpieces of such vast and heterogeneous institutions as the CPSU Central Committee or the Soviet Council of Ministers. It is hardly probable that this intrinsic heterogeneity would allow the elaboration of a uniform line on any controversial issue, let alone on an issue of such wide ramifications as the Soviet involvement in the Middle East. Yet each of the press organs investigated did present a unified line vis-à-vis the lines promulgated by the organs of other institutions. Hence, it is possible that a press organ is not controlled by and does not serve as mouthpiece for an institution as a whole, but rather for the group currently in ascendancy within a given institution. In other words, it is plausible that the group currently in power uses the institution's press organ as its exclusive platform, denying it to intrainstitutional opposition. Isolating such a group and establishing its probable composition is one of the main problems encountered in this study. Factual data point only to the existence of divergences. The attribution thereof becomes a matter of educated guesswork.

The problems of attribution and identification are further aggravated by the crisscrossing lines of institutional affiliation and representation; thus, for example, every Soviet official in a position of responsibility is almost inevitably a Party member. Moreover, functionaries associated with one institution participate in forums representing other institutions or groups. For example, the military is represented in both the government structure (in the Council of Ministers) and the Party structure (in the Politburo and the Central Committee).

These methodological problems impose the following mode of presentation. The first part of the study will center on the questions of "what," "why," and "how." What is being advocated by the four organs under investigation and on what ground? What are the points of divergence, how are they presented, and what are their probable reasons? For the sake of clarity, in this part the reference will be to broad categories, with "party," "military," "trade union," and the like serving as symbols of the conflicting groups. Once the horizontal divisions, i.e., differences among institutions, have been established and analyzed, a more differentiated approach will be adopted in the final section of the study. An attempt will be made to explore the possibilities of vertical divisions, i.e., differences within institutions and among personalities.

Before entering into discussion of the issues at hand, a few remarks about the press organs with which this study is concerned might be in order.

All four papers examined here are central organs, that is to say, they are under the direct control of the Propaganda Department of the CPSU Central Committee.[39] However, while *Krasnaia zvezda* and *Trud* are intended mainly for internal consumption, *Pravda* and, perhaps to a somewhat lesser extent, *Izvestiia* are also directed at readers outside the Soviet Union. Moreover, the latter two are considered abroad as the official mouthpieces of Soviet policy. Clearly, this fact may well influence both the tone and content of *Pravda* and *Izvestiia.* Conversely, *Krasnaia zvezda* and *Trud* may well take the liberty of printing opinions that could not be voiced by the main organs of the Party and the Council of Ministers.

Interestingly enough, the existing division of areas of interest (evident especially in *Krasnaia zvezda,* whose main concern is with military matters) is not reflected in reports or commentaries on international affairs. There is, in fact, a ratio of 2:1 between *Pravda* and *Izvestiia,* on the one hand, and *Krasnaia zvezda* and *Trud,* on the other, in articles and news reports on foreign affiars. Bearing in mind that *Pravda* and *Izvestiia* usually have six to eight pages and *Trud* and *Krasnaia zvezda* only four pages each, one may say that all four organs are almost equally concerned with foreign affairs in general and with those of the Middle East in particular.

Part 1
At the Crossroads

2. The Syrian Coup d'Etat of February 1966: A Turning Point?

Soviet foreign and military policy immediately after World War II concentrated largely on the West. The Third World remained a region of marginal interest to the USSR at least until the mid-fifties.

Stalin considered the leaders of the former colonial areas as undependable bourgeois of marginal utility in the zero-sum game of international politics.[1] The emergence of the so-called neutral countries did not change his basically negative attitude toward national liberation movements and their leaders. The prevailing "two camps" concept of the international situation made it difficult for the Soviet Union to co-operate with the countries that had only recently acquired independence from the West. Stalin's rigid categorization held that any noncommunist country was, by definition, capitalist or capitalist-controlled, i.e., a member of the adversary camp.

The years following Stalin's death saw a perceptible change in Soviet attitudes toward the Third World, a change that eventually developed into a clear departure from previously established patterns.

The new, positive attitude toward neutral countries and their national leaders and movements became detectable in Soviet official publications as early as 1954. Subsequently, Moscow's enthusiastic support of the Bandung Conference of April 1955, as well as the Khrushchev-Bulganin visit to India, Burma, and Afghanistan signified the emergence of a new political line.[2] In September 1955, the first arms deal between the USSR and a Third World country was made public. In retrospect, the decision to supply arms to Egypt was the beginning of a major breakthrough of Soviet influence into the Third World in general and into the Arab East in particular.

At the Twentieth Congress of the CPSU in February 1956, Khrushchev introduced a new ideological approach toward the underdeveloped countries, one that replaced the Stalinist concept of "two camps" with the concept of "two zones." Khrushchev depicted the world as being divided into the "zone of war," composed of the capitalist-imperialist West, and the "peace zone," composed of the socialist states as well as nonsocialist, "peace-loving" countries. Thus was formulated the ideology that enabled the USSR to develop new forms of relations with regions situated beyond the immediate proximity of the Soviet borders.

Clearly, the change in Soviet policy and the concomitant emergence of the USSR as a global power were precipitated and conditioned by the progressive improvement of the USSR's strategic capabilities, particularly by the development in the mid-1950s of a thermonuclear and ICBM delivery system. In addition, the new Soviet global policy developed and gathered momentum in response to actual or perceived weaknesses of the West, as well as in response to opportunities created by Western political blunders.

Scholars have written extensively about the USSR in the Middle East, particularly about the Soviet Union's entry into the Middle East region. Since the Soviet foreign policy in the Khrushchev era has been so thoroughly explored, we shall limit ourselves to only a brief reassessment.

Khrushchev's initial thrust into the Third World in general and into the Arab East in particular appears to have been motivated by political considerations reinforced by military-strategic and ideological motives—he was endeavoring to curtail Western influence and to neutralize the potential threat to the USSR emanating from the Baghdad Pact and the deployment of US land-based aircraft and MRBMs.

In the early 1960s, with the appearance of the Polaris submarines, which seemed to provide the United States with a significant lead in second-strike capability and, in so doing, seriously affected Soviet chances of quickly reaching nuclear parity with the United States, Soviet motivations took on a new dimension. Any hope of eventual neutralization of the Polaris threat (and the impressive nuclear striking force assembled in the Sixth Fleet in the Mediterranean) depended in part on Moscow's ability to establish and maintain a naval and air presence there. However, this task was greatly complicated by the fact that after the loss of the Albanian bases in 1962 the USSR had no such facilities available to it in the Mediterranean. This consideration alone helps explain Khrushchev's refusal to break with Syria and Egypt even in the face of occasionally strong provocations. Confronted with the choice of extricating himself from the political turmoil in the Middle East or persisting in his course of action in disregard of the mounting difficulties that his initiatives entailed, Khrushchev not only chose the second alternative but actually sought to expand Soviet activities.[3]

Khrushchev's successors, facing a choice between continuing or discarding his Middle East policy, initially opted for a modified, low-profile version of his approach. The basic policy of cooperation with the Arab clients remained intact, and the buildup of the Soviet Mediterranean squadron continued; but there was a temporary decline in Soviet initiatives.[4]

The new Kremlin leaders' line of least resistance was soon brought to its test. On February 23, 1966, after a bitter internal struggle, a radically leftist faction of the Ba'th party assumed power in Syria.

The Soviet Union did not greet the new regime with joyous banner headlines. Rather, its attitude was one of caution and reserve. The gist of the laconic TASS reports on the events in Syria was the "quickly normalizing situation" and "broad national support for the new regime."[5] It seems as though Moscow initially viewed the Zu'ayyin-Atasi coup d'etat as one of many such upheavals that had shaken Syria in recent years, as a mere change of personalities, which would not involve any substantial changes in policy.[6]

By the end of February 1966, two main Soviet newspapers moved apart on this question. *Izvestiia,* the press organ of the Soviet Council of Ministers, suddenly began providing broader coverage of leftist declarations voiced by the new Syrian leadership. On March 1, 1966, for example, *Izvestiia* quoted *al-Thawra's* editorial (it may be mentioned that in Soviet practice, quoting without criticizing is tantamount to endorsing) to the effect that "the present Syrian government is closest to the socialist countries, and [it] intends to do everything in its power to assure the success of socialism in Syria." For almost a week *Izvestiia* was the only Soviet paper to give publicity to such pronouncements. On March 8, 1966, *Krasnaia zvezda,* the press organ of the Ministry of Defense, joined *Izvestiia* in publishing Atasi's statement that "Syria's main objective is the implementation of socialism." It took *Pravda,* the press organ of the Central Committee of the CPSU, another day to publish this same declaration.

Apparently, a tacit consensus to give de facto recognition to the new regime was achieved in the Soviet leadership. On March 10, 1966, telegrams of greeting were sent to Atasi and Zu'ayyin by Podgornyi and Kosygin, respectively. Brezhnev's abstention from greeting the new Syrian leaders seems to indicate that, at least for the time being, relations were to be maintained strictly on the interstate, intergovernmental levels.

Yet, the controversy between the government and party organs continued. *Izvestiia's* reports on Syria struck a note of exuberant optimism. "The Syrian regime has *already* undertaken real steps toward the attainment of its goals—socialism and friendship and cooperation with the USSR."[7] *Pravda,* on the other hand, though attaching "importance" to the Syrian "radicalism" (which, in communist parlance, may or may not be a positive attribute) and to the "clearly defined program of the new government" (again, a noncommittal reference), played up the precarious position of the new regime: "The skies above Syria are not clear. . . . There is the danger of subversive activity coupled with internal rivalries."[8] Interestingly enough, even such a "progressive" act as the inclusion of communists in the Syrian government, an act hailed by *Izvestiia,* received a cold shoulder from *Pravda,* which rather obliquely reported the inclusion of "progressive elements, other than Ba'th members, in the Syrian government."[9]

The Soviet press debated the significance and ramifications of the Syrian coup d'etat for another month, with the controversy ending only on the eve of the Syrian prime minister's arrival in Moscow on April 19, 1966. The joint communiqué published at the end of the visit seems to imply that the *Pravda* line prevailed. With the statement "the Syrian Ba'th sets as its aim the creation of conditions necessary for development on the noncapitalist path," Syria was officially relegated to the same ideological category as the UAR, Algeria, Mali, and others.[10] No advanced standing was awarded.

With this, the ideological dispute ended. Hereafter, the Soviet press organs referred to Syria as a "revolutionary," "progressive" regime but stopped short of bestowing socialist epithets.

The internal Soviet dispute over the evaluation of the Syrian coup may perhaps be best explained against the background of preceding events, specifically the ousters of such "progressive" and avowedly pro-Soviet leaders as Ben-Bella in Algeria, Sukarno in Indonesia, and Nkrumah in Ghana. The 1965 setbacks could have been interpreted as harbingers of a mounting wave of anticommunist sentiment in the Third World. Moreover, the events in Algeria, Ghana, and particularly in Indonesia, where tens of thousands of real and alleged communists had been murdered or imprisoned, accentuated the inherent weakness of both the Soviet position in the Third World and the so-called national liberation movement.

Against this background, *Pravda*'s caution toward the Atasi-Zu'ayyin regime in Syria appears logical and politically judicious. Those responsible for *Pravda*'s line presumably concluded that ideological endorsement of the new regime might entail the assumption of an unnecessary risk by the USSR, limiting its options in an unstable, volatile situation. This low-risk, noncommittal approach was challenged by *Izvestiia*. *Izvestiia*'s proposal to award Syria the status of a "candidate member" in the socialist community could have been designed to break the impasse in Soviet policy toward the Third World and perhaps to reestablish the

Khrushchevian pattern of forward, aggressive foreign policy.

As we have seen, the more moderate line prevailed, at least as far as ideological endorsement was concerned. Nevertheless, the USSR extended its economic and military aid to Syria and decided to embark upon such a costly and risky aid project as the construction of the Euphrates High Dam.[11]

The April 1966 decision to grant extensive economic and military aid to the Syrian Arab Republic while denying it recognition as a country building socialism might have been a compromise between the cautious approach advocated by *Pravda* and the more aggressive policy advocated by *Izvestiia.*

The decision to commit the USSR to the construction of the Euphrates High Dam, preceded as it was by the signing in February 1966 of a protocol implementing a $277 million loan to Egypt (promised by Khrushchev in May 1964 and frozen since), may indicate that at least in the sphere of political-economic relations with the "progressive" countries, a trend away from caution was beginning to appear.

The new trend was further reflected in the May 28, 1966, TASS announcement expressing the USSR's concern and alarm about the "imperialist intrigues" against the Syrian regime. Moreover, the announcement stated, "the Soviet Union cannot remain indifferent to attempts to undermine peace in a region immediately adjacent to its southern borders." Thus, for the first time since Khrushchev's ouster, direct Soviet interest in a Middle Eastern country was explicitly and officially stated.

The compromise presumably achieved in April 1966 did not put an end to divergent approaches toward the Syrian regime and its policy. Throughout 1966, *Pravda* consistently ignored Syria's militancy on the Palestinian problem. *Izvestiia,* on the other hand, though faithful to the agreement to refrain from ideological endorsement, gave publicity to the Syrian leaders' bellicose statements. The width of the gap between *Pravda* and *Izvestiia* on this issue may perhaps be inferred from the following example. On October 19, *Izvestiia* quoted Zu'ayyin's statement that "the central goal of Syrian policy in the Middle East is the liberation of Palestine." *Pravda* ignored this statement. In a later article, entitled "Clear Choice," it unequivocally stated its opinion: the Arab states and especially Syria had made a clear choice in favor of "the path of peace, cultural development, and [industrialization] and rejected the policy of military adventures into which the imperialists try to drag them."[12] The article pledged all-out Soviet aid in this "peaceful construction."

Pravda's disaffection with Syrian militancy may be further inferred from its consistent emphasis upon the necessity of Syrian-Egyptian rapprochement and from its subsequent enthusiasm about the signing of the Syrian-Egyptian agreement.[13] It might well be that the hope that Nasser would be able to exert a moderating influence on Syria was the underlying factor in *Pravda's* exuberance. *Izvestiia,* apparently much less concerned about Syrian bellicosity, viewed the rapproachement with cool aloofness.[14] Perhaps the fear that the events of 1958 would be repeated lay behind *Izvestiia's* reservations.

The proceedings of the December 1966 CC CPSU Plenum may also attest to the existence of debate within the Soviet leadership concerning its policy toward Syria and the Arab world. The central theme of the Plenum, convened on December 12, 1966, was Brezhnev's lecture "On the International Policy of the USSR and the Struggle for Consolidation of the Communist Movement." This lecture took the entire first day of the Plenum. The second and final day was dedicated to "debate" on Brezhnev's report, with the participation of thirteen Central Committee members. Neither Brezhnev's lecture nor the subsequent debate was ever made public. The Plenum resolution, published on December 14, contained no reference whatsoever to the Middle East. Nor was the Middle East mentioned in the lengthy editorials summarizing the results of the Plenum.

It seems doubtful that the situation in the Arab world, especially the rapidly escalating Israeli-Syrian border conflict, would be totally ignored at a forum convened to deal with Soviet foreign policy, particularly after numerous indications of Soviet concern about these events. Thus, the omission of the Middle East from a resolution intended to represent the participants' unanimity may well be explained by a failure to achieve unanimity on this particular issue.

Apparently, the Soviet leadership was at a crossroads. Taken by surprise by the emergence of an avowedly leftist and extremely militant regime in Damascus, Moscow failed to develop, in the course of 1966, any clear-cut, uniform posture.

3. The Lingering Debate

USSR's Role in the Prewar
Escalation as Mirrored in the Soviet Press

The period November 1966–February 1967 witnessed a substantial development of Soviet-Syrian relations on both the interparty and interstate levels. Delegations traveled back and forth between Moscow and Damascus, engaging in "fruitful exchanges of theoretical and practical experience."[1]

At the same time, taking advantage of the new regime's declared radicalism and its growing political, economic, and military dependence on the Soviet Union, Syrian communists increasingly penetrated the governmental apparatus and public institutions. In March 1967, probably with Moscow's blessing, the Syrian Communist party started pressing for the formation of a "progressive national front."[2]

These developments must have had a significant impact on the USSR's interest in preserving the leftist regime in Damascus.

The campaign, which was initiated by the Soviet Union immediately after the February coup d'etat and which claimed that the existence of the Syrian "progressive" regime was in danger, gathered momentum by the beginning of 1967. The prevalent tone of Soviet commentary became one of concern and alarm. The Soviet newspapers pointed to the existence of a well-coordinated plot against Syria, a plot prompted by the "imperialists'" fear that Syria's independent progressive policy might prove contagious."[3] The scheme, as depicted in the news media, was to operate as follows. Israel was supposed to provoke border incidents, thereby luring the Syrian army into concentrating on the armistice line. Thus, the Syrian hinterland would be unprotected and vulnerable to fifth-column activity. At an unspecified moment, an émigré civilian government would be imported from Jordan and established in power in Damascus. The American Sixth Fleet would, according to this plan, patrol offshore and intervene if anything were to go wrong.[4]

It is difficult to determine to what extent the Soviet leadership really believed in the existence of an "imperialist conspiracy" threatening the Syrian regime. Without entering into a lengthy discussion of the role that ideology plays in Soviet politics, I would venture the assumption that Leninist theory is more than hollow rhetoric for the Soviet leaders and that it shapes, at least to a certain extent, their world outlook. Thus, for example, the doctrine of "hostile capitalist encirclement," of imperialism fighting its "last-trench struggle against the national liberation movement" in order to safeguard its monopolistic interests, is in all probability an integral part of the Soviet conceptual framework. Furthermore, the period under discussion had witnessed a rapid escalation of the Syrian-Israeli border conflict. An endless chain of raids and counterraids brought the situation to the verge of open war. A series of increasingly vehement statements was issued by Israeli leaders, threatening Syria and its regime. All these, particularly when seen against the background of the Sixth Fleet's maneuvers, probably contributed to Moscow's alarm. The precarious position of the Atasi regime, which was shaken by a wave of political unrest in spring 1967, might have been another factor underlying Moscow's concern.[5] Soviet leaders might have assumed that another blow against Syria might easily have led to the overthrow of the "progressive" regime and a serious setback to leftist forces in Syria and elsewhere.

The Soviet propaganda campaign, accompanied as it was by "intelligence" reports transmitted to Cairo and Damascus and claiming that an Israeli offensive against Syria was imminent, could have also been designed to evoke a change in the UAR's position. Moscow might have hoped that Abdel Nasser, already under virulent Arab criticism for his "absenteeism," would not be able to ignore a direct threat against his ally's capital city, and would concentrate his army on the Israeli border, thus deterring Israel from attacking Syria. It seems plausible that, apart from being interested in bringing relief to Damascus and deterring Israel, the USSR's activity could have been motivated by a desire to preserve Nasser's prestige and position in the Arab world. Moscow probably viewed with dismay the pronounced contempt voiced by Jordanian, Syrian, and Saudi leaders, scorning Nasser for "hiding behind the skirts of the UN Emergency Forces" and failing to come to his brethren's aid."[6]

One may assume that these evaluations were communicated to the Egyptian parliamentary delegation, which, arriving in Moscow on April 27, spent more than two weeks in the Soviet Union. Upon the delegation's return on May 14, Egyptian armed forces were placed on alert, and official orders were issued for mobilization and movement of troops. On May 15, the Egyptian army began to move through Cairo into the Sinai in a demonstrative fashion. Soviet press reports of those "glorious" days sound as though they were providing the cadence for the Egyptian march: "Ready to Rebuff Aggression,"[7] "Standing Shoulder to Shoulder Against Any Surprise,"[8] "Nasser Ready to Act Against Israel if Syria Is Attacked."[9]

So far the situation was well under control. A potential threat was checked by counterthreats. If Israel had seriously contemplated an attack on Syria, it would now know that this would precipitate hostilities with Egypt as well and would no doubt be deterred. The Soviets had shown themselves wise counselors and Nasser a loyal ally. At this point, the matter might have gone no further, save for two factors: Arab public opinion and the presence of the UN Emergency Force. The Syrian cry for help and the Egyptian military demonstration set off throughout the Arab world a wave of emotion such as could hardly have been predicted and that was to have considerable influence on the course of events. The whole Arab world suddenly seemed united and looked to Nasser for action. This swelling support, the confidence Nasser derived from it, and the realization that if he did not exploit it others would, explained Nasser's actions over the next two weeks.[10]

Moscow viewed the escalating crisis with cool aloofness and virtually fatalistic resignation. The Soviet press organs limited themselves to short TASS dispatches that objectively and laconically reported the steps undertaken by the parties to the conflict. Only the large headlines announcing the "escalation" and "alarming severity of the situation" might have indicated Soviet concern.[11]

Nasser's request on May 16, for the immediate withdrawal of the UNEF did not receive any commentary from either *Pravda* or *Krasnaia zvezda*. *Izvestiia* provided some support, albeit qualified. "The UN Emergency Force was stationed on Egyptian territory with Egypt's consent. Now that this consent has ceased to exist, continued presence of [the UNEF] would constitute a violation of Egypt's sovereignty."[12] This notion was echoed in the Soviet government's announcement on May 24.

On May 21, Nasser closed the Straits of Tiran to Israeli and Israeli-bound ships, thus creating a clear casus belli. The Soviet press reported the blockade with some delay: *Krasnaia zvezda* and *Izvestiia* on May 24 and *Pravda* on May 25. An interesting fact, ignored by virtually all Western analysts, is that the Soviet Union did comment on Nasser's action. A commentary in *Pravda* on May 26 stated:

> The closing of the Gulf of Aqaba to Israeli ships and also to ships bringing strategic materials to Israel is dictated by need, stemming from Israel's preparation to attack Syria. At the same time, these are measures necessary for the final liquidation of the consequences of the Tripartite aggression . . . of 1956. As is known, before November 1956, Israel was not able to use the Gulf of Aqaba. In this, Israel was hindered by Egyptian troops stationed at the entrance to the Gulf, which, by not even a single decision of the UN, can be considered as territorial waters of Israel. . . . Egyptian troops have now returned to their previously held positions.

This statement does not conclusively show that the Soviet Union had encouraged Nasser to close the Straits.

It constitutes, however, an *ex post facto* endorsement of the Egyptian cause in the Gulf of Aqaba.[13]

At this point, the Soviet newspapers diverged in their attitudes toward the evolving situation, presumably reflecting an internal debate within the leadership. *Izvestiia* and *Krasnaia zvezda* adopted a cavalier, even adventurous, posture. *Izvestiia* emphasized the high level of Arab preparedness, claiming that "the Egypt of 1967 is different from the Egypt of 1956, when it fell victim to the Tripartite aggression. Today the Republic is strong enough to defend its own cause."[14] *Krasnaia zvezda* went even further, stressing that "Israel does not have any chances against the united Egyptian and Syrian armies."[15] On June 3, 1967, *Izvestiia* spoke about "the polarization of international forces" prompted by the Middle Eastern crisis. The Soviet stand in this polarized situation was clear: "The Soviet Union and the socialist countries helped and *will help* the Arab countries *in every way* in their struggle against imperialism and aggression. The Soviet all-out support is being manifested in the course of the current crisis. . . . The Soviet peoples are confident that the Arab cause will prevail." It is noteworthy that this commentary was entitled "A Test of Sincerity."

During the same period, *Pravda* was preoccupied with and alarmed by the United States, more specifically, by Sixth Fleet activity in the region. *Pravda*'s articles brimmed with virulent criticism of American and British "aggressive activity in the area," and upheld the theory of "imperialist conspiracy aimed at securing the interests of American and British oil monopolies."[16] This campaign may well have been an expression of genuine concern that the West would interfere on Israel's behalf, thus leaving the Soviet Union very little room to maneuver. In view of Soviet naval inferiority, the embarrassment of a retreat as in Cuba was by no means a remote possibility. Concurrently, *Pravda* mounted a last-minute effort to minimize the proportions and significance of the crisis; the Arab-Israeli confrontation was depicted as "tension along the borders," which is "a recurrent phenomenon in this region."[17] Egypt's "steps" were defined as "clearly defensive measures aimed *only* at sheltering Syria from an Israeli attack."[18] Since in any event "only 2-4 Israeli ships pass through the Straits of Aqaba every twenty-four hours," Israel need not resort to war because of this.[19] On June 1, *Pravda* elaborated upon Egypt's "peaceful intentions," asserting that "Egypt had submitted proposals for a truce with Israel as early as 1956." All these commentaries repeatedly stressed the interest of "the nations of the world" (generally a euphemism for the Soviet bloc) in the preservation of peace and the prevention of an armed conflict. This interest was reiterated in another commentary, which appeared on the very day that the war erupted.[20] Throughout this period, *Pravda* refrained from any explicit pledges of support to either Egypt or Syria.

All these divergences seem to indicate the existence of a debate within the Soviet leadership. It is difficult, however, to pinpoint the issues actually at stake. In my opinion, in spite of their cavalier attitude, neither the government lobby (presumably represented by *Izvestiia*) nor the Ministry of Defense (represented by *Krasnaia zvezda*) contemplated a direct Soviet intervention on the Arabs' behalf. On the contrary, by expressing confidence in the Arabs' superiority and by stressing the Arabs' ability "to defend their own cause," they in fact obviated any need for such intervention. On the other hand, these two groups were apparently carried away by the Arabs' enthusiasm and considered the eruption of an armed clash as inescapable. If this analysis is correct, the government's and military's pressure for a more prominent expression of Soviet support seems a very reasonable policy. What is more expedient than supporting a sure winner?

The posture taken by *Pravda* is less clear. Was the belief (or hope) that the war could still be averted a sincere one? Or was it a smoke screen intended to lull the world's vigilance? My guess would be that the *Pravda* group was really alarmed by the swift escalation, by the fact that the avalanche touched off by the USSR was no longer under its control. This premise appears to be corroborated not only by *Pravda's* attitude on the eve of the war, but also by its consistent adherence to and advocacy of a moderate, cautious line throughout 1966.

To take this speculation one step further, it may be argued that the Soviet role in the prewar escalation reflected the temporary predominance of hard-liners, presumably represented by *Izvestiia* and *Krasnaia zvezda*. As we have seen, these two organs, particularly the former, advocated throughout 1966-1967 a more forward and aggressive policy in the Middle East. Up to early spring 1967, official Soviet policy appeared to reflect a compromise between the two conflicting approaches. As of April 1967, presumably under the impact of regional developments, the hard-liners were in ascendancy. However, during the last week of May, the *Pravda* group appeared to bow out of the temporary coalition with the *Izvestiia* and *Krasnaia zvezda* groups and returned to its earlier, low-risk approach.

The Israeli preemptive strike on the morning of June 5, 1967, cut the debate short. The fact that Israel struck first served to unite the Soviet press organs in one mighty chorus of indignation. However, as we shall see, the overtones of the preceding debate could still be traced.

The Outbreak of Hostilities: Unity and Divergence

The Main Strands in the Soviet Propaganda Web

The outbreak of the Six-Day War brought an unprecedented proliferation of Soviet commentaries on the subject. Any attempt to present in detail the few hundred articles published between June and September, 1967, would exceed the limits of this research project. In the following three chapters, therefore, I shall present only the main currents of the Soviet analysis, paying special attention to opinions and views that may be cited as inconsistent with the commonly shared attitudes.

The Soviet analysis of the Middle Eastern events may be divided into several main themes:

1. Israel was condemned as the aggressor and its strike as "a surprise attack." Israel's claim that it was fighting for its existence was rejected as a sheer lie.

2. The idea of an "imperialist conspiracy" against the "progressive" regimes of Egypt and Syria and against the Arab

national liberation movement in general was pursued throughout. The raison d'être of "imperialist activity" in the area was to thwart the national liberation movement, topple the "progressive" regimes, and restore colonial rule. Within this scheme, Israel served as the imperialists' tool, as the spearhead aimed at the hearts of the "progressive" regimes.

3. Since the Arabs were both victims of aggression and a "progressive" community threatened by "imperialism," their struggle was a just struggle, and it was the Soviet Union's "internationalist duty" to support them. Thus, the Arab-Israeli confrontation and the Soviet championing of the Arab cause were given an ideological underpinning.

4. Very early, even before the cessation of hostilities, the idea of Israel's expansionism was introduced. Numerous articles elaborated on this theme in its historical perspective. At the same time, the Soviet press organs demanded the "immediate, unconditional withdrawal of the aggressor's forces to the 1949 armistice lines." The "elimination of the traces of the Israeli aggression" was presented as the *conditio sine qua non* for future peace in the area. Soviet support was pledged for the Arabs' "just struggle" to achieve this goal.

5. Numerous articles pointed to the atrocities allegedly committed against the Arab population in the occupied territories. Israeli treatment of prisoners of war and the Arab population was equated with Nazi savageries. The Soviet press organs went on to threaten that the Israeli "invaders" may well meet the same fate as the Nazis did.

6. Most articles pointed to "a clear connection" between the Israeli aggression against the Arabs and the American "barbarous war" in Vietnam. The former was said to create convenient conditions for the latter. The Soviet press, however, failed to explain how and in what sense such a correlation existed.

It should be stressed that the above categorization is arbitrary and made only for the sake of convenience. It is, however, a fairly complete presentation of the main strands in the Soviet propaganda web during this period. These were the main ideas recurring, in varying combinations, in Soviet press reports[21] and official pronouncements.[22]

Three Variations on the Common Theme

There were, however, three interesting variations on the common theme. Significantly enough, in all three instances, *Izvestiia* and *Krasnaia zvezda* diverged from *Pravda*'s line.

Vested Soviet interest in the Israeli withdrawal. Several articles and editorials in both *Izvestiia* and *Krasnaia zvezda* reiterated the idea that Israel should not be allowed to continue its occupation of Arab territories and that the world should not condone its aggression, for "this creates a dangerous precedent that could help countries like West Germany, which base their policy on aggression, intervention, and revanche."[23] A subsequent commentary was even more specific, stating that "to allow Israeli annexation . . . is to whet the appetites of those who have claims to their neighbors' territories, who want to change the order upon which . . . the freedom of nations is based" (a clear euphemism for Eastern Europe).[24]

This unvarnished manifestation of the historic Russian fear of Germany is interesting in itself. No less interesting, however, is the context in which this sentiment was articulated. Apparently, the governmental and military organs attempted to exploit Soviet interest in preserving the postwar order in Europe to buttress their demand for a more resolute Soviet stand on the question of Israeli withdrawal. Consequently, *Izvestiia* and *Krasnaia zvezda* were the most militant and unequivocal in demanding the "elimination of the traces of the Israeli aggression." "Such is the demand of millions. And they will *force* the bunch of aggressors to reckon with their request."[25]

Both *Izvestiia* and *Krasnaia zvezda* were also the most unequivocal in pledging unqualified political and military support to the Arabs in their struggle for the Israeli withdrawal: "Indignantly condemning the Israeli invaders and their [imperialist supporters], the Soviet nation and its *armed forces* are resolved to do everything to curb the aggressors."[26]

Negation of direct involvement on the Arab side. This deviation seems somewhat mysterious. At least at first sight, it seems inconsistent with *Izvestiia*'s and *Krasnaia zvezda*'s manifest militancy and support of the Arab cause.

The theme appeared only twice in *Izvestiia* and once in *Krasnaia zvezda*. In all three instances, the implications and frames of reference were vague and ambiguous. Consequently, the analysis offered below is largely conjectural.

On June 13, 1967, *Izvestiia* published a lengthy commentary signed by V. Petrov. Analyzing "the Israeli aggression and its aftermath," the correspondent mentioned and indignantly rejected a Chinese offer "to send 700 million men to fight on the Arab side." Explaining that such an undertaking was totally impractical because of geographical, military, and logistic considerations, Petrov asserted that the Chinese "magnanimity" reflected Peking's "lack of faith in the deterministically inevitable victory of the liberation movement." This was tantamount to stating that anybody suggesting military intervention on the Arab side was guilty of heresy and deviation from the Marxist doctrine of historical determinism. Was Petrov here referring only to Peking? Or was he poking at the "terrified petite bourgeoisie" in his own capital, who, instead of placing their trust in the inevitable course of history, were suggesting direct involvement in the Arab-Israeli war?

In this example, a direct military intervention was rejected on ideological grounds, but in two later instances the reason was more practical, namely, the danger of a nuclear holocaust.

In an editorial of July 4, 1967, *Krasnaia zvezda* stated: "In the nuclear age, any spark can set the whole globe afire. The world is grateful to the Soviet Union for thwarting the Israeli aggression, thus saving humanity from devastation." *Krasnaia zvezda* appeared to be referring to the past, i.e., to the Soviet position during the hostilities. Thus, the above statement may have echoed an internal debate that could have occurred during the war and may have been an *ex post facto* public disclosure of the military's position in that debate. What this position might have actually been is more difficult to determine. For one, *Krasnaia zvezda* expressed awareness of the danger of a nuclear confrontation and relief that the danger was averted. On the other hand, however, the statement may have indicated Soviet readiness to risk a major confrontation over the Middle East in case the Israeli offensive could not be thwarted. Thereby, the Soviet military may have been setting some line beyond which the USSR would not allow Israel to go, intervening, if necessary, to stop the Israeli advance. One may speculate that if, during the Six-Day War, Israel had continued its advance beyond Qunaytira, the Soviet military might have advocated direct intervention to save Damascus. This line of thought may be projected further, into the more recent past. During the War of Attrition, the Soviet military could have argued that Israeli encroachments upon the vicinity of Cairo and the Aswan High Dam were the line at which Israel would have to be stopped, by force if necessary. During the October War, the Soviet military might have urged Soviet action were Israel to have advanced any further on the road to Cairo.

Perhaps it should be stated again that the preceding analysis is highly speculative and based, at best, on circumstantial evidence.

The third reference to the problem of Soviet intervention appeared in *Izvestiia* on July 26, 1967. It was perhaps the most ambiguous and circumspect of all three. *Izvestiia* recalled the "tragic results that the policy of appeasement had for tens and hundreds of millions of people," adding that "today such a policy is fraught with even greater danger. Not a single country can ignore the fact that the nuclear age has created a new reality in questions of war and peace, placing a tremendous responsibility on all states."

At first sight, there appears to be an obvious contradiction between the two parts of *Izvestiia*'s statement, for a condemnation of a "policy of appeasement" is tantamount to an appeal for action. On the other hand, however, *Izvestiia* drew attention to the dangers inherent in and stemming from the nuclear balance of terror.

Its ambiguity and contradiction notwithstanding, *Izvestiia*'s statement may be plausibly interpreted as an appeal for action within the limits imposed by the nuclear reality. Moreover, in stating that "today [a policy of appeasement] is fraught with an even greater danger," *Izvestiia* may have been

introducing the opinion that timely action against an aggressor might prevent a worldwide tragedy. Insofar as the frame
of reference is concerned, *Izvestiia*'s statement may be seen
both as an echo of an earlier debate and as a declaration of a
future position. Seen against the background of *Izvestiia*'s unequivocal references to the vested Soviet interest in an Israeli
withdrawal, it may be further interpreted as a warning to
both Israel and the United States.

*The Middle East crisis necessitates the strengthening of
Soviet military might.* As may be inferred from the title, this
deviation was characteristic mainly of *Krasnaia zvezda.*

Krasnaia zvezda perceived Israeli aggression as a "link
in the chain of the imperialist offensive against the forces of
socialism and progress." The existence of such an offensive
was, in *Krasnaia zvezda*'s opinion, evidenced by events not
only in the Middle East but throughout the globe, particularly in Vietnam, Greece, Africa, and Latin America.[27] In the
face of this imperialist assault, the USSR and its armed
forces, cast in the role of the "guardians of the peace and
security of nations," could not but increase their "vigilance
and military preparedness."[28] At times, *Krasnaia zvezda*
expressed its opinion in even more specific terms, explicitly
demanding the "strengthening of the Soviet Army and
Navy."[29]

The rationale behind the demand to devote particular attention to the development of the Red fleet was presented in
an essay by Admiral Kasatonov in *Krasnaia zvezda* on July
30, 1967. Kasatonov, the first deputy commander of the
Soviet navy, predicted that the Soviet navy would play "a
primary role in a future war"—for "military actions in the
vast naval theaters will be of growing significance" in the
forthcoming years. Kasatonov's opinion was echoed in numerous articles in *Krasnaia zvezda* and *Morskoi sbornik,* the
press organ of the Soviet navy.[30]

Thus, the Soviet Ministry of Defense appeared to be using
the Arab-Israeli war as a means to advance its own parochial
interests, namely, to secure a high level of resource allocation
for the armed forces in general and the navy in particular.
Conscious of the fact that its claim upon the nation's re-

sources and, to an extent, its political role were in direct proportion to the level of international tensions, the Soviet military tended, throughout the period under discussion, to portray the global situation entirely in black.

It may be added that the extremely militant tone in *Krasnaia zvezda* may have been designed not only to impress
upon the decision makers the urgency and importance of the
military's role in securing the welfare and interests of the
socialist motherland, but also to restore the international
prestige of the Soviet armed forces and the credibility of the
USSR's commitments to "allies and friends":

> If it becomes necessary to defend the motherland, its allies, or
> its friends, we shall fulfill our military duty and smash any ag-
> gressor. We say that, since recently there was a pronounced in-
> tensification of barbarous military adventures [such as the
> American aggression in Vietnam and the Israeli aggression in
> the Middle East], which threaten world peace. The contem-
> porary aggressors, who adopt Hitler's ideas of global domina-
> tion, will suffer an even more devastating crash. It is not 1941
> or 1945 now! The year is 1967. The mighty Soviet Armies are
> guarding world peace, and they have ample means to smash
> the imperialist robbers. [31]

The foregoing analysis appears to attest to a lingering
debate in the Soviet leadership. Uncertainty and oscilla-
tion, promoted by the emergence of a leftist and extremely militant regime in Damascus, were evident
throughout the period preceding the outbreak of hostilities, and their reverberations could be traced even in the
seemingly uniform line adopted in the wake of the Six-
Day War. Moreover, it is suggested that the Syrian coup
d'etat and ensuing events might have produced a division
within the Soviet leadership between the advocates of an
aggressive policy and the proponents of moderation.

Before dealing with the crystallization and evolution of this division in the ensuing period, it might be
interesting to examine two issues that held the attention
of the Soviet press in the period immediately following
the cessation of hostilities, namely, the analysis of the

causes and effects of the Arab defeat and the propaganda campaign aimed at establishing the USSR as the Arabs' faithful ally.

Moscow Analyzes the Causes and Effects of the Arab Defeat

It is difficult to avoid the impression that the USSR was as surprised as its Arab clients were at the swiftness and thoroughness of the Israeli victory and that, at least in the short run, Moscow did not benefit from the Six-Day War. The stunning defeat of the Arab armies, trained by Soviet military advisers and equipped with Soviet armor, and Moscow's unwillingness and inability to intervene militarily in favor of its allies dealt a blow to the Soviet position and prestige and subjected it to virulent criticism. In the wake of the war, Moscow had two alternatives: (1) to throw its weight behind the Arabs, to rearm and rebuild their armies, attempting thereby to recoup its losses and secure its position in the Arab world; or (2) to abandon the Arabs in a state of ruin. The second alternative seemed utterly unrealistic in view of Soviet strategic, political, and ideological postures.

The Soviet reaction was twofold. On a practical level, Moscow embarked, in the immediate aftermath of the war, on a large-scale program of military, economic, and political support, a program that made Egypt the cornerstone of Soviet Middle Eastern policy. This was accompanied by a vast propaganda campaign aimed at rationalizing the causes of the Arab defeat, recouping and elevating Soviet prestige, and providing the basis and justification for the increased commitment. This chapter will deal with the second level of reaction: a propaganda exercise in turning a military defeat into a political victory.

The Soviet military press appeared to be the most preoccupied with analyzing the military showdown and providing the rationale for continuing and enlarging the military assistance program. This preoccupation seemed logical, for the Arab defeat had dealt a blow to the reputation of Soviet training and Soviet military equipment and probably rendered those Soviet military institutions responsible for foreign military aid subject not only to Arab, but also to Soviet and Western criticism and derision.

Appearing very early[32] and evident throughout the period under discussion was the notion of Israel's technological superiority, its "mastering of the science of war" (not better training but greater adaptability to training), and its capability to mobilize "to the limit" its human and material resources.[33] Conversely, the Arabs' "lack of success" was said to be caused by their placidity, by the fact they "were caught by surprise before having time to complete their mobilization."[34] Furthermore, the Arab air defense proved ineffective and insufficient in the face of the "decisive air superiority of the enemy."[35] The implication is clear: in the opinion of the Soviet military, in this particular battle the Arabs fought against superior odds, against an enemy whose strength and tactics they had underestimated.[36]

The Soviet military press tended to dwell only upon those causes of the Arab defeat that were clearly subject to the time factor, i.e., those that could be eliminated with the appropriate Soviet assistance. By blaming shortcomings in discipline, military professionalism, planning, coordination, and intelligence, the Soviet military press saved face and prepared the ground for the virtual take-over of those spheres by Soviet advisers later in the year (1967). Pointing specifically to the inadequacy of air defense, the Soviet military set the pattern for the future buildup, centering on the air force and antiaircraft missile systems.

In order to counter possible (internal Soviet) criticism as to the profitability of continuing the military assistance, the Soviet military press organs recurrently emphasized the inherent positive qualities of the Arab soldier. This was tantamount to saying that a healthy substratum for continued Soviet activity did in fact exist, and a continuous effort to train and equip the Arabs was therefore not necessarily throwing good money after bad.

Much as the military pointed out the temporary shortcomings and emphasized the healthy nucleus, the party and government organs drew the same distinction, though along different lines. Both *Pravda* and *Izvestiia* held the Egyptian

military command, and the officer corps in particular, directly responsible for the defeat. Egypt's senior military leaders
were depicted as a fifth column, as a bunch of turncoats, who
knowingly worked for the defeat of their country.[37] The
alleged treachery of the Egyptian military command was attributed to the fact that it had a vested interest in the overthrow of Nasser and in putting an end to his "progressive"
measures that endangered the military's privileges. "Those
generals and high-ranking officers looked upon the socioeconomic transformation undertaken by the Nasser regime as
. . . an axe that strikes that juicy branch of material well-
being on which they sat, either in the trade-industrial or in
the agricultural spheres."[38]

The political unreliability and lack of loyalty of the
Egyptian officers were directly linked to, and in fact
stemmed from, the deep socioeconomic factors underlying
the Arab defeat. "The lost battle in the Sinai is first and foremost the result of the still existing remnants of the colonial
past: economic and technological backwardness, the existence of privileged castes, the activity of forces hostile to the
revolution."[39]

By blaming rightist bourgeois elements for the defeat, the
Soviet political leadership attempted to achieve several goals:
(1) to support Nasser against the so-called American lobby,
which reportedly claimed that "too much talking about
socialism and attempts to transplant alien ideologies" caused
the defeat; (2) to evade any Soviet responsibility for the
defeat; and (3) to secure and accelerate the "progressive"
trend in the UAR, which was essential for preserving the
USSR's position.[40]

The remedy that the Soviet political leadership suggested
to Egypt was more wide-ranging than what military assistance
could provide. What was required was a thorough reorganization of the military and government apparatus, the promotion of "young, enthusiastic [and apparently Soviet-trained]
experts to command posts,"[41] and above all the continuation
and acceleration of the "socialist transformation in the political, economic, and social spheres."[42]

These programs opened wide horizons for Soviet activity

and influence, and their successful implementation would strengthen and secure the Soviet position in Egypt. However, since revolutions cannot be fomented in a vacuum, both *Pravda* and *Izvestiia* took pains to emphasize the "increasing revolutionary activity of the masses," their "rising conscious- ness," and consolidation behind "the ideas of the revolu- tion."[43] In communist parlance, this meant that the necessary prerequisites for a revolutionary change had taken root. Con- comitantly, there was an emphasis on the viability and stabil- ity of the Egyptian regime as well as on its willingness and ability to preside over the socialist transformation.[44]

What we are faced with here is an elaborate ideological justification for the Soviet aid to and support of Egypt: the Egyptian nation was promoted to the lofty category of a national liberation movement struggling for socialism and against an imperialist threat, and, if only on the basis of this ideological affinity, it was entitled to full Soviet support. "The Soviet Union, the motherland of socialism, is safe- guarding and serving as the arsenal for the heroes of Vietnam and the national liberation movement in the Middle East."[45]

Much as the Soviet military stressed the inherent positive elements within the Egyptian armed forces as a basis for con- tinued and expanded military assistance, so too did Moscow's governmental and party organs extol the viability of the Nasser regime and the receptivity of the Egyptian people to Soviet-orchestrated revolutionary change. In this sense, the outcome of the June 1967 war was seen as a catalyst and a means of purification, purging Egypt of vestiges of its coloni- al past and charging the impulse for socialist change. Certain- ly, such a situation could not but promote Soviet interests in the Middle East.

The positive results of the June 1967 war (in terms of Soviet interest in the area) were perceived not only on the internal Egyptian level but also on the inter-Arab and global levels.

On the inter-Arab level, the defeat promoted a strong movement toward unity, one based upon antiimperialism and implacable hatred toward the West. Antiimperialistic trends were evident even in countries considered "silent" by Western politicians. "The West succeeded in antagonizing even the feudal Arab countries."[46] The antiimperialist trend was reflected inthe Arab oil boycott, in demands to dismantle Western bases (specific references to Wheelus Field in Libya and Aden), and in severing diplomatic relations with Great Britain and the United States.[47] "The Western powers have sowed the seeds of hatred, which will continue to bear fruit for many generations to come."[48] The Arabs now realized that only "through reliance upon the Soviet Union and other socialist countries can they abolish completely imperialist influence in the Middle East and achieve an Israeli withdrawal from the occupied territories."[49]

In terms of the global balance of power, it was a zero-sum game: the loss of prestige and position by the West was considered, ipso facto, a Soviet gain. Thus, three months after the cessation of hostilities, the Soviet Union could confidently claim: "The position of the USSR, in spite of the fact that its allies suffered a military defeat, has been strengthened and its influence in the Middle East has spread."[50]

The Aftermath:
The USSR as the Sole Champion of the Arab Cause

In the preceding section we have analyzed the Soviet press campaign aimed at turning the Arabs' military defeat into a political victory. In the following remarks an attempt will be made to examine yet another aspect of the postwar propaganda effort, namely, the establishment of the USSR as the Arabs' faithful and, more crucially, only ally. These two sections attempt to provide some insights into the modus operandi of the Soviet propaganda machine and its employment as a tool of foreign policy.

In striving to establish the Soviet Union as the sole champion of the Arab cause, Soviet propaganda depended upon two main techniques: (1) amplification to enormous proportions of favorable facts and (2) minimization of unflattering data or the complete omission thereof.

On June 9, 1967, a meeting of East European leaders was convened in Moscow. In the subsequently published resolution, Israel was condemned as the aggressor, and solidarity with the Arabs' "just cause" was expressed. The resolution included a rather vague pledge of the socialist countries' support for the Arab "struggle."

However, the vagueness of the declaration did not prevent the Soviet press from claiming that it "was received with great satisfaction in the Arab capitals [since] it included a serious warning to the aggressors."[51]

In the following days, the Moscow Declaration was blown up to even greater proportions. *Pravda* stated on June 12, "The Declaration demonstrates the mighty support on which the Arab states can rely in their struggle to eliminate the traces of Israeli aggression." *Izvestiia*'s editorial of June 13 went even further: "The socialist states demonstrated their resolve to aid the Arabs to conduct *to the end* their struggle for independence and territorial integrity. The Declaration brought about an outburst of Arab enthusiasm, stemming from the assurance that their achievements *will be defended.* . . . Nobody will be allowed to restore colonial rule in the Arab lands."

In a commentary of June 16, *Pravda* labeled the Moscow Declaration as the "epitome of Leninist international policy." The Soviet support for the Arabs was thereby provided with an ideological underpinning. The Declaration of the Soviet-bloc leaders became the cornerstone in the construction of the Soviet image as the Arabs' faithful ally.

On June 9, the same date on which the Moscow Conference was convened, a wave of "spontaneous" demonstrations swept the Soviet Union. The demonstrators demanded the "condemnation of the Israeli aggressor" and a prompt "cleansing" of the Arab lands from occupying forces. The Soviet press dedicated whole columns to these "popular manifestations," under such banner headlines as "The Soviet Union—a Loyal Friend of the Arab Countries."[52]

Subsequent Soviet political actions received a similar treatment. The severance of diplomatic relations with Israel by the Soviet Union and the East European countries (with the exception of Romania); Fedorenko's appeal to the Security Council to condemn Israel and require its immediate withdrawal; Gromyko's letter to U Thant demanding the con-

vocation of the General Assembly; Kosygin's appearance at
the Assembly, introducing a new demand that Israel make
restitution to the Arabs for the damages it caused; the Resolution of the June 22 CC CPSU Plenum repeating these
demands; the Budapest Declaration of East European socialist countries—all were subsequently presented, individually
and collectively, as ultimate proof of the unqualified Soviet
support of the Arab cause.

> The Soviet Union is on the Arab side! The Soviet Union de-
> mands the condemnation of the aggressor in the Security
> Council! The Soviet Union demands a cease fire! The Soviet
> Union resolutely warns Israel of its responsibility for the
> crimes committed! The Soviet Union severs diplomatic rela-
> tions with Tel Aviv! The Soviet Union and other socialist
> countries sign the Moscow Declaration and participate in the
> Budapest Conference. They fully support the Arab countries
> fighting against Israeli aggression and demand immediate with-
> drawal of the invaders' armies!
>
> These words express the concrete actions undertaken by the
> Soviet Union and other socialist countries in support of the
> Arab nations and against the aggressor. These are the practical
> steps undertaken by the CPSU and the Soviet Government in
> the name of peace in the Middle East, already in the first hours
> of the Israeli *blitzkrieg*.[53]

The noble Soviet stand in support of the Arabs was
contrasted with the "treacherous schemes of the imperialists," who unequivocally supported Israel. Thus, the Soviet
Union was presented not only as a faithful ally but also as the
only ally.[54]

Perhaps the main characteristic of this propaganda campaign was its repetitiveness. The idea of Soviet friendship
with and support for the Arabs was presented as an indis-
putable fact and virtually hammered into the reader's mind.

Another interesting aspect of the Soviet postwar propaganda campaign was its treatment of Arab criticism of the
Soviet role during the war. In dealing with Arab criticism,
the USSR employed a technique of diminution. The point of
criticism was minimized in both scope and significance and

actually drowned in extensive references to the positive counter-opinion. Interestingly, the Soviets preferred to use "authentic" Arab pronouncements to counter Arab criticism. The following example may illustrate this point: *Pravda*'s commentary of June 14, referred to

> two little articles [the diminutive form appears in the Russian original] by a certain Muhammed al-Tabi, whose name did not appear in the columns of the Egyptian papers in recent years. We know very well who paid him for his appearance. Such out-bursts obviously do not express in any way the UAR's true attitude toward the sincere, friendly aid the Soviet Union is providing to it. *Al-Ahram*'s editorial, which is considered to express the official view of the Egyptian leadership, dealt today with Soviet-Egyptian relations.

Then comes a lengthy quotation from this editorial, extolling the Soviet position and the unqualified Soviet support for "the just demands of the Arab nation." This quotation was accompanied by no less lengthy citations from other Arab sources to the same effect.

With the Soviet Union established as the Arabs' faithful ally and the Arab criticism of the Soviet role rebuffed, Soviet propaganda proceeded further. The USSR was given credit for thwarting Israeli aggression, for nipping it in the bud.[55] *Izvestiia* and *Krasnaia zvezda* went on to imply that were it not for "the resolute Soviet steps," the outcome of the war might have been even more disastrous.[56] No further elaboration was provided. The Soviet support was further de-picted as the guarantee and shelter against the renewal of Israeli aggression.[57] Reliance upon the Soviet Union was pre-sented as the only way to bring about the Israeli withdrawal and secure the "lawful" rights of the Arab nation.[58] Thus, the Soviet-Arab alliance was presented as being in the Arab na-tional interest. Whoever harbored any doubts about the necessity of this alliance "plays into the hands of the imperial-ist enemy, drastically undermining his country's security and well-being."[59]

Needless to say, verbal declarations of friendship and po-litical support were only one facet of the Soviet postwar effort. The propaganda campaign was accompanied by a swift airlift of military matériel and a vast program of economic support. All these efforts were aimed at recouping Soviet prestige and its position in the Arab world. The Arab countries, defeated and humiliated, eagerly reached for the hand extended to them and drew closer and closer to the only power openly supporting their cause. Desperately needing Soviet assistance, they had to accept the strings attached to it. In the short run, Moscow scored a clear gain and entrenched its position in the Arab world. However, the ever-growing Arab dependence on the Soviet Union increased the latter's commitment to its clients' cause. Thus, Moscow found itself with few options and less room for maneuver and, if necessary, retreat. Seen this way, the Soviet decision to side with the Arab cause, initially dictated by the need to recover lost prestige, became, in the long run, a shackle that materially affected Moscow's Middle East policy.

Part 2
Divergences Intensify within the Framework of Involvement

4. Debate over Problems of Conflict and Settlement

Divergent Perceptions of the
Arab-Israeli Dispute: A Basis for Debate

The preceding chapters indicated that a lingering debate can be seen in the seemingly uniform line promulgated by the Soviet press organs. The ensuing chapter will attempt to analyze the evolution and intensification of the aforementioned differences.

In the period of June-October 1967, the dispute among the three organs under investigation focused on the nature and origins of the Arab-Israeli conflict and, subsequently, on its solution.

Pravda brought the debate into the open, publishing in July and August a series of articles by two of its senior commentators, Beliaev and Primakov. The articles, which presumably reflected the perception of the group represented by *Pravda* and responsible for its line, presented an extremely interesting and unique analysis.

Pravda set forth the notion that the Arab-Israeli conflict was essentially a dispute between extremist governments on both the Arab and the Israeli sides, rather than a conflict based on "racial or nationalistic prejudices."[1] Moreover, it asserted, the enmity was harmful to the interests of both the Arab and the Israeli nations.[2]

In an unprecedented attempt at an objective analysis, *Pravda* expressed the opinion that "extremists on both sides bear the brunt of guilt and responsibility for the existing animosity." Thus, the Israeli "hawks" were blamed for their "territorial seizures *after* the Palestinian war of 1948-1949. Israel's unwillingness even to negotiate the fate of the Palestinian refugees did not help to normalize the situation. The Tel Aviv leaders justified the annexation with the argument that these lands were included in the boundaries of the old Jewish state during the rule of Czar David."[3] The Israeli leaders exacerbated the conflict even more by "conducting an actively aggressive policy, resorting to territorial occupation, and executing imperialist assignments in opposing the Arab national liberation movement."[4]

Pravda's criticism of Israeli policy was relatively mild, particularly when seen against the background of the unusually vehement censure of the Arab postulates.

The Arabs were blamed for "seriously aggravating" the situation by refusing to accept the "famous UN resolution on the partition of Palestine," which was intended to allow "the thousands of Jews living in Palestine to establish peace and their right to national existence."[5] At the same time, *Pravda* condemned "the chauvinistic, nationalistic current" in the Arab world for its "declarations of plans to annihilate the state of Israel."[6] Stressing that the slogan calling for the liquidation of Israel was unrealistic and infeasible, *Pravda* warned that "the Arabs will turn the whole world against them if they continue to present [their] struggle as an intention to create a bloodbath."[7] Pronouncements by several "progressive" Arab journalists were cited to reinforce the point that "nobody in the world—neither friend, nor enemy, nor neutral —agreed to the annihilation of the state of Israel."[8]

The disavowal of Arab extremism was further reinforced by recurrent references to the Soviet support for the establishment of the state of Israel. Moreover, *Pravda* stated explicitly that its support of the Arab demand for the withdrawal of Israeli troops is limited to "territories occupied during the *recent* conflict."[9]

Pravda's unique position seemed to be closely correlated with the notion it set forth virtually on the morrow of the 1967 cease-fire, namely, that the Arab-Israeli dispute could and should be solved by political means.[10] This notion was further reinforced by *Pravda's* refusal to give publicity to the

Arabs' militant rhetoric and by recurrent statements to the effect that "the USSR supports the Arab struggle aimed at safeguarding their liberty and independence," i.e., statements refraining from pledging support for attempts to recover "territorial integrity."[11]

Thus, the unequivocal and unprecedented condemnation of Arab extremism appeared to be an integral part of *Pravda*'s position that the Arab-Israeli dispute could and should be solved through political rather than military means. The presentation of the conflict as rooted mainly in a dispute over territories, as a conflict between extremist governments rather than between nations, seemed to convey the same idea. By minimizing the conflict, *Pravda* underlined its solvability.

Furthermore, by criticizing extremism on both the Arab and Israeli sides and by refusing to side with Arab bellicosity *Pravda* may have been introducing the Soviet Union as an objective, even-handed arbitrator. This may be further inferred from *Pravda*'s evident effort to explain, justify, and exonerate Soviet policy in the region. Thus, the Soviet pro-Arab position was explained in terms of magnanimous support for the victims of aggression.[12] Concurrently, *Pravda* went to great pains to refute "accusations that those who condemned the Israeli aggression were motivated by anti-semitic sentiments":

> This is a crude falsification, an attempt to portray the petit-bourgeois ideo-political Zionist movement—analogous in its nature to other chauvinistic movements in the capitalist world —as the synonym of everything Jewish. The unmasking of the class content of Zionism is referred to as anti-Semitism! . . . The USSR opposes only Zionist expansionism. It has nothing against the Israeli nation or Judaism as such.[13]

Pravda's position contrasted sharply with the line presented by *Izvestiia* and *Krasnaia zvezda*. Refraining from any attempts to minimize the seriousness of the Arab-Israeli conflict or from criticism of Arab extremism, these two organs unequivocally sided with the "Arab national cause," stressing the "Arab nations' resolve to fight for the liquidation of the traces of Israeli aggression."[14] Moreover, they specifically pledged Soviet "all-around" aid and support for the Arab struggle against the "Israeli occupiers."[15]

The discrepancy between the positions of *Izvestiia* and *Krasnaia zvezda* on the one hand and of *Pravda* on the other hand can also be illustrated by their commentaries on Nikolai Podgornyi's visit of June 21-24 to Egypt. On June 24, 1967, *Izvestiia* and *Krasnaia zvezda* cited the Cairo *al-Ahram* to the effect that the visit of the Soviet president "arouses new hopes and new resolve in the fighting nation." *Pravda*, also citing *al-Ahram*, omitted this point, reporting only the Cairo daily's opinion that "the visit . . . is an expression of the deep friendship between the Soviet and Egyptian nations."

Pravda's emphasis on a political solution may be further contrasted with statements such as: "Supported by its friends, the Egyptian nation is resolved to fight for the liquidation of the consequences of the Israeli aggression"[16] or the pledge included in Colonel Leont'ev's *Krasnaia zvezda* commentary of September 29:

> The resolute Soviet support and the USSR's readiness to resort to sanctions against the aggressor forced Israel to cease its military activity. Today, the Soviet Union demands a swift withdrawal of the Israeli troops from all the Arab land occupied by Israel. Our nation has sworn allegiance to the toilers of the world and bears the standard of internationalism. . . . We shall keep our allegiance, and, if necessary, do everything to defend the revolutionary achievements of the workers, the liberty and security of nations.

The disagreement between the *Pravda* group on the one hand and the *Izvestiia* and *Krasnaia zvezda* groups on the other hand appeared to stem from and reflect divergent perceptions of the Soviet position in the Arab East. *Izvestiia*'s and *Krasnaia zvezda*'s support of Arab militancy and maximalism may have originated from the assumption that the Soviet position in the frontline Arab countries was not as yet strong enough to warrant attempts to channel Arab politics along Soviet lines. Moreover, the *Izvestiia* and *Krasnaia zvezda* groups might have argued (in closed forums) that criticism of certain Arab postulates might result in a rift in the fragile Soviet-Arab alliance.[17] Conversely, *Pravda*'s advocacy of moderation and its overt criticism of Arab extremism may have reflected its confidence that the then existing strength of the Soviet position and the Arabs' dependence on the Soviet Union were a sufficient basis for attempts to channel Arab politics along Soviet lines.

The differences between *Pravda* and *Izvestiia* were further crystallized in their respective attitudes toward the Arab summit in Khartoum and the resolutions made there.[18]

Throughout August 1967, *Izvestiia* published numerous informative TASS dispatches, citing Arab pronouncements and emphasizing the importance of the forthcoming meeting. No commentary was provided. *Pravda*, on the other hand, accompanied the TASS reports with several detailed commentaries, the main gist of which was to reiterate its opinion that the conflict should be solved by political means.[19] Emphasizing the importance of Arab unity, it pointed to the "vital necessity of establishing [this] unity on an antiimperialist basis." "A united antiimperialist Arab front can become an important *political* tool for the task of elimination of the consequences of the Israeli aggression."[20]

On September 2, 1967, *Pravda* published a partial text of the Khartoum resolution. *Izvestiia* followed suit, publishing an identical citation on September 3. In subsequent commentaries both expressed "satisfaction" on the part of "the progressive community" with the results of the conference.[21] Both agreed that the mere convening of the summit "in the existing conditions" was in itself a success.[22]

Here, however, the similarity ended. *Izvestiia* played up the fact that Syria did not sign the Khartoum resolution because "the Syrian leaders consider military means the only way of liquidating the consequences of the Israeli aggression."[23] *Pravda*, on the other hand, attempted to gloss over Syria's abstention, stressing instead that Syria "supports all the positive steps outlined in the Khartoum resolution."[24] Though admitting that the conference manifested its participants' "resolve to eliminate the consequences of the Israeli aggression,"[25] *Pravda* made a great effort to draw attention to the "sober attitude manifested at the conference, underlining the necessity to exhaust all means and ways, including political and economic, in the struggle for the elimination of the results of the Israeli aggression." Furthermore, it claimed, "this attitude replaced the former [attitude] that renewal of war is the only way out." Agreeing that "the demand for withdrawal was and is paramount, and [is] supported by the Soviet Union," *Pravda* repeated its opinion that the line of withdrawal was "the demarcation line existing up to June 5, 1967."[26]

Izvestiia's commentary, published on the same day and signed by senior correspondent V. Kudriavtsev, did not mention the Arab "realism" or "soberness" allegedly manifested in Khartoum. *Izvestiia* stated that "the struggle against imperialism is a many-faceted one, necessitating the mobilization of ALL means and resources." In contrast with *Pravda,* *Izvestiia* did not go on to explain that "all" connoted political and economic means. In fact, the bold print and the capitalization of the word "all" in *Izvestiia*'s commentary might have been meant to convey the opinion that military means were not and should not be excluded. In the same article, *Izvestiia* cited the Khartoum resolution to "liquidate the consequences of the Israeli aggression and to strive for the withdrawal of Israeli forces from Arab territories occupied after June 5, 1967," adding, however, that "the conference stressed that it is the Arabs' task to continue to struggle for the rights of the Palestinian nation to its motherland, i.e., [rights] to an independent state that should have existed, according to the United Nations resolution of 1947."[27]

This statement, striking in its support of Arab maximalism, stood in sharp contrast with *Pravda*'s recurrent criticism of and dissociation from extremism. More important still, *Pravda* and *Izvestiia* were apparently at odds not only over the means of struggle (political versus military) but also over the ultimate goal of the Arab struggle. *Pravda* interpreted the slogan calling for the liquidation of the results of the Israeli aggression as a reference to territories occupied during the Six-Day War, but *Izvestiia* apparently had in mind the "aggression" that had occurred nineteen years earlier.

This seemed to be the climax of the postwar divergence. A gradual convergence of the lines pursued by *Pravda* and *Izvestiia* subsequently became apparent. Thus, *Izvestiia*'s commentary of September 13 (also by Kudriavtsev) underlined the "necessity to exhaust the political means in the struggle for liquidation of the results of the Israeli aggression."

In an article published on September 12, *Izvestiia* stated that the Arab countries expected the UN to put an end to the Israeli provocations and to liberate the occupied territories. With *Izvestiia* modifying its militancy, *Pravda* came closer to *Izvestiia*'s line. Thus, *Pravda*'s commentary of September 25 stated that "there is no chance of a political trade off as far as the Arab territories are concerned." Another article on October 11 stressed, along with the importance of a political solution, that "a settlement should not be achieved at the expense of Arab national interests." On November 2, *Pravda* sided for the first time with the line consistently pursued by *Izvestiia* and *Krasnaia zvezda,* which claimed that allowing Israel to retain the occupied territories would be tantamount to creating "a precedent and excuse for other aggressive forces [such as] the West German revanchists."

This convergence was also evident in Brezhnev's November 4 speech as well as in commentaries following Ali Sabri's visit later in November. Brezhnev's opinion that in supporting the Arab states politically, diplomatically, economically, and militarily the USSR was "restraining imperialism, . . . defending the peace and security of nations and defending the socialist cause"[28] was a significant departure from his and *Pravda*'s previous stand that ideological affinity was the sole basis of the Soviet-Arab alliance. (*Izvestiia* and *Krasnaia zvezda* asserted all along that strategic interests were the raison d'être of this alliance.)

Brezhnev's and *Pravda*'s realization or perhaps their readiness to admit that relations with the Arabs had as their basis more practical considerations than ideology was further reflected in the festive celebration of the anniversary of the October Revolution. Ali Sabri, chairman of the Egyptian Arab Socialist Union, was invited to deliver his speech ahead of such senior communist activists as Khalid Bakdash and other Middle Eastern communist leaders. Furthermore, on November 10 Sabri held a "friendly meeting" with Brezhnev. According to Soviet press reports,[29] Brezhnev pledged "comprehensive aid for the heroic struggle of the Egyptian nation against Israeli aggression. . . . The USSR assumes that peace and security in the Middle East are impossible without the full elimination of the consequences of the Israeli aggression, liberation of the occupied territories, and compensation for the damage. The Soviet Union opposes any settlement that will aim at rewarding the aggressor."[30]

Thus, on the eve of the UN Security Council's session, unity was achieved in Moscow.

The convergence in the three press organs under discussion may have reflected the establishment of a coalition among the groups they represented. It appears plausible that the *Pravda* group became aware that in insisting on a political settlement and overtly condemning Arab militancy, it was dissociating itself from the mainstream of Arab politics. Such awareness might well have been prompted by the "three no's" line adopted in Khartoum, as well as by Arab criticism of the Soviet refusal actively to intervene on their side during the Six-Day War. Thus, presumably for reasons of political expediency, *Pravda* aligned itself, at least for the time being, with the line supporting Arab militancy.

Izvestiia's, and, to a lesser extent, *Krasnaia zvezda*'s temporary adherence to the line advocating the exhaustion of political means, may perhaps be explained by the logic of the give and take that characterizes coalitionary processes in every political context. Another explanation, one that does not necessarily exclude the former, is that in view of the forthcoming Security Council session on the situation in the Middle East, these two organs deemed it proper to modify or veil their position as staunch supporters of Arab bellicosity. For in international forums, the Soviet posture is always expressed in terms of interest in the preservation of world peace.

The Short-Lived Compromise

On November 22, 1967, the UN Security Council, convened to discuss the situation in the Middle East, adopted the British draft proposal, the vagueness and ambiguity of which were sufficient to unite all the permanent members in an affirmative vote.

The Soviet media made it clear that they would have preferred the Security Council to adopt a more "unequivocal" resolution.[31] Nevertheless, all Soviet organs tended to agree that "Security Council Resolution 242 may become, in spite of the vague formulation of the demand for Israeli withdrawal, the first step on the path toward reduction of tension in the Middle East."[32] *Pravda, Izvestiia,* and *Krasnaia zvezda* stressed again and again that "the essence, the gist of the British draft proposal is an appeal for Israeli withdrawal from territories occupied during the recent conflict":

> The adopted resolution includes further stipulations concerning the recognition of sovereignty, territorial integrity, and political independence of all the states of the region, as well as provisions concerning freedom of navigation, just solution of the refugee problem, and other issues. Undoubtedly, however, the solution of these problems . . . is possible only as the result of elimination of the traces of the Israeli aggression, that is to say, pursuant to withdrawal of all Israeli forces from all the occupied Arab territories. This is the first and indispensable step.[33]

There was only one dissonant voice in this chorus. In the same commentary stating that the Security Council resolution "may become the first step toward relaxation," *Pravda*'s senior correspondent Vishnevskii lauded "Arab soberness and political wisdom [as manifested in their] effort to liquidate the consequences of Israeli aggression through political means." Concurrently, he criticized "hotheads in certain Arab countries [presumably Syria, Iraq, and Algeria] and hasty press declarations, which in existing circumstances only help Western propaganda and [which] are, in fact, utilized by the Tel Aviv extremists."[34] No similar comment was published by *Izvestiia* or *Krasnaia zvezda.*

On December 23, the Soviet press carried the communiqué issued at the end of a meeting of European socialist states' foreign ministers. The communiqué constituted the official endorsement of Security Council Resolution 242 by the Soviet Union and its European allies. It asserted that "the undelayed withdrawal of Israeli troops from all occupied Arab territories is the basic element" of the resolution. Moreover, "any interpretations aiming at weakening this basic element contradict the letter and the spirit of the Security Council resolution."[35] Typically, the Soviet interpretation of reality was presented as the sole and absolute truth.

The Soviet vote in the Security Council in support of the British proposal and the subsequent endorsement of the resolution by the Warsaw Pact nations established a common parameter of analysis for the Soviet press organs, or, conversly, imposed a certain limit on their debate. In accordance with the principles of democratic centralism, debate is legitimate only up to the moment of decision and precluded thereafter. However, as we shall see, the general adherence to the principle of political settlement, as embodied in the Security Council resolution, left sufficient margin for controversy and debate. In fact, an ever growing gap seemed to emerge between the position of the *Izvestiia* and *Krasnaia zvezda* groups and that adopted by the *Pravda* group.

Divergences Reemerge: Focus on the Peace Initiatives

Throughout 1968 *Pravda*'s commentaries invariably stressed the urgency of achieving a political settlement of the Arab-Israeli conflict. They indicated that the settlement ought to be based on the Security Council resolution of November 22, 1967, which was "the only way to peace in the Middle East."[36] Concurrently, *Pravda* also emphasized the USSR's "resolve to fight for the implementation of the Security Council resolution, utilizing all [Soviet] international power and authority."[37] Moreover, the Soviet vested interest in a political settlement of the Middle East crisis was repeatedly voiced. Thus, for example, *Pravda*'s article of April 13 (signed "Observer"—this title is customarily signed to important editorial statements) declared that the Soviet nation demands a political settlement of the Middle East crisis and an immediate implementation of Security Council Resolution [242] . . . . As a country situated in *direct vicinity* of the area of conflict and as a state supporting the just cause of the Arab nations, the USSR is fulfilling its obligations deriving from United Nations' resolutions on the Israeli aggression.[38]

Pravda's attempt to portray the Soviet Union as the staunch supporter of a political settlement was accompanied by an effort to present the Arab, especially the Egyptian, position in a similar light. *Pravda* reiterated the opinion that Egyptian policy was "realistic and flexible" and that "the UAR is consistently striving for a political settlement of the Middle East problem, recognizes the November 22, 1967, Security Council resolution, and cooperates positively with the UN secretary general's special representative, Dr. Gunnar Jarring."[39]

Egypt's "realism" and "political wisdom" were constantly juxtaposed with Israel's "intransigence" and "stubbornness":

Any objective observer can see that the UAR is doing everything possible to solve the Middle East problem peacefully. . . . Israel, on the other hand, ignores the Security Council resolution and stubbornly refuses to comply with its central demand— to withdraw its forces from the occupied Arab territories.[40]

This line received further impetus following the May statements by the Egyptian Foreign Minister Mahmud Riyad. (Riyad came to the Soviet Union on April 18 and held talks with Brezhnev and Gromyko. En route to Cairo, he gave two statements to the Paris newspaper *Le Monde*,[41] declaring that the UAR accepted the Security Council resolution as a whole and did not insist on Israeli withdrawal as a precondition.) On May 13, *Pravda* printed an article entitled "Cairo's New Initiative" and subtitled "remarks of a political observer." The "observer" greeted the UAR's "important initiative aimed at searching for ways to implement the [November Resolution]," explaining that:

In a letter to the UN Secretary General's Special Representative . . . Riyad stressed the importance of elaborating a timetable for the implementation of the Security Council resolution and suggested that Jarring himself prepare one. Cairo's
suggestion undoubtedly opens new chances for a quick political solution of the Middle East problems. The . . . resolution
stipulates, besides [the demand for] Israeli withdrawal from
occupied territories, several additional measures aimed at
securing a lasting peace in the Middle East. The UAR government's initiative is another testimony to its goodwill and
striving for a political settlement. Such a position increases the
UAR's authority in the international arena and strengthens the
support for its just policy on the part of international public
opinion.

Following the Egyptian initiative, *Pravda* indulged in
stepped-up efforts to persuade Israel of Egypt's sincerity.

The UAR does not pose any preconditions. It sees the Security
Council resolution as one entity. Israel's claims that Egypt dis-
sociates the question of withdrawal from that of termination
of the state of war are simply not true. Demonstrating flexibility, Egypt declared that it is ready to terminate the state of
war even in the initial stage of Israeli withdrawal, pending an
Israeli obligation [statement of intention] to withdraw its
forces from all the occupied territories. The UAR accepts the
. . . resolution as a whole, including the provision for free navigation, but demands that Israel fulfill its obligations concerning withdrawal and settlement of the refugee problem. If Israel
fulfills its obligations, the UAR will fulfill its [obligations],
and peace will be attained. . . . Israeli declarations that it wants
to retain part of the occupied territories [such as the Gaza
Strip and Jerusalem] contradict the letter and the spirit of the
Security Council resolution.[42]

Employing a stick-and-carrot technique, *Pravda* warned
that if Israeli intransigence continued, "the Arabs will be left
with only one way to liberate their land."[43] "Israel should
not interpret the Arabs' readiness to work for a political solution as a sign of weakness. If worse comes to worst, they will
be able to defend their liberty and territorial integrity."[44]

However, no Soviet aid or support was promised for the military solution.

The Israeli counterproposals, specifically the so-called Dayan and Allon plans, were unequivocally rejected by *Pravda* as "attempts to perpetuate the occupation and gain a prize for aggression."[45] Israel's demand to conduct direct negotiations with the Arab states was termed "an unrealistic demand, totally infeasible within the context of continued occupation."[46] In short, asserted *Pravda*, the "Israeli counterplans and insistence on direct negotiations are nothing more than attempts to evade responsibility to comply with the Security Council resolution, to torpedo the Jarring mission, and to force the Arabs to accept a "peace" suiting the interests of the Israeli extremists and their imperialist supporters."[47]

Izvestiia, by contrast, was less optimistic than *Pravda* about the prospects of achieving a peaceful solution of the Arab-Israeli conflict. Though agreeing with *Pravda* that the November Resolution "constitutes the sole basis for a political settlement," *Izvestiia* stressed that the chances for the realization of the Resolution were very slight because of Israel's "ill will."[48]

In fact, *Izvestiia* presented the Middle East situation as a vicious circle, resulting from a clash between irreconcilable positions. On the one hand, claimed *Izvestiia*, "Israel does not even dream about withdrawing its armed forces behind the June 5, 1967, lines."[49] On the other hand, it reiterated that "Arab borders violated by the Israeli aggression are not a subject of trade," i.e., in plain terms, there was nothing to negotiate.[50] Such statements were in and of themselves a departure from *Pravda*'s stress on Arab flexibility.

In contrast to *Pravda*'s stick and carrot, *Izvestiia* employed only the stick. Time and again it pointed out that "Israel's fate as a state and as a nation is at stake. . . . Israeli leaders, recklessly playing with their country's destiny, brought Israel to the verge of national catastrophe."[51] "Israel should withdraw its troops and the sooner the better for Israel itself."[52] Many of *Izvestiia*'s articles had the words "serious warning" in their title. Several times *Izvestiia* published "echoes from abroad" to these pronouncements. Thus, for example, it published on March 30, 1968, the Algerian and Pakistani reactions to its article of March 26, which "was a serious warning to Israel and underlined the Soviet resolve to fight together with the Arabs for the liquidation of the consequences of the Israeli aggression." Interestingly enough, the article itself was less unequivocal than the reaction to it.

On April 27, 1968, *Izvestiia* printed a commentary by Demchenko, its Middle East correspondent, entitled "Serious Fallacy." The article asserted that Israel's refusal to comply with the Security Council resolution and its sabotaging of the Jarring mission were a "political blunder" and that Israel was "oblivious" to the "significant changes that have occurred both in the Arab world and in the international arena."

> The Arabs have rebuilt their armies, and the Israeli officers have had a chance to witness the improved military capability [of the Arabs]. The Arab resolve to liberate their lands and to liquidate the results of the Israeli aggression has increased. The [Palestinian] partisans' infiltration is gathering momentum, and repression will not be able to stop the resistance movement. ... In these circumstances, if the Israeli leaders are genuinely concerned with the future of their nation, they should, for their own good, withdraw the troops.

Another commentary declared, "Israel should subordinate itself to the Security Council resolution's demand for a total withdrawal of its forces from all the occupied territories. Otherwise, a bitter fate awaits it."[53]

Izvestiia did not even try to present the Arab position in terms of "flexibility" and "striving towards a political settlement." Nor did it voice any Soviet interest in peace in the Middle East. The only instance when Arab policy was referred to in these terms was *Izvestiia*'s report of "the UAR's important initiative," i.e., Riyad's May pronouncements.[54] However, *Izvestiia* hastened to add that chances for progress were scant because of "Israel's refusal to agree to indirect negotiations" and its "insistence on border adjustments."[55] Instead of lauding and supporting the UAR's "flexibility and realism," the organ of the Soviet government made do with a rather vague statement to the effect that "the UAR's initiative met with warm approval in the *political* circles of countries striving for détente in the Middle East."[56] No further references to the Egyptian initiative appeared in *Izvestiia*.

Throughout this period, *Krasnaia zvezda* pursued a line very similar to *Izvestiia*'s. In broad terms, it referred only infrequently to the various attempts to achieve a political settlement of the Arab-Israeli conflict and, like *Izvestiia*, it refrained from playing up Arab "flexibility" and "resolve to work toward peace." Perhaps the best illustration of *Krasnaia zvezda*'s manifest lack of interest in the "struggle for peace" in the Middle East was the fact that Riyad's May initiative was mentioned for the first and only time in November 1968 —some six months after the proposals had actually been set forth.

In an article printed on November 15 and bearing the signature of Lieutenant-Colonel M. Ponomarev,[57] *Krasnaia zvezda* stated that

> It is known that the basis for solving the Middle East crisis is the Security Council resolution of November 22, 1967. The Arabs *are agreeable to such a presentation of the issue.* In order to accelerate the implementation of the resolution, the UAR proposed [to elaborate] a *so-called* timetable for a stage-by-stage realization of all the provisions of the November resolution concomitantly with the *solution of other problems connected with the conflict.* However, Israel undermined this proposal. The point is that the November resolution foresees the withdrawal of Israeli troops from occupied Arab lands. The Israeli extremists [however] wish to eternalize the results of their aggression.

Krasnaia zvezda's language was strikingly vague, particularly in view of the long time span that had elapsed since the Riyad proposals were originally presented.

But *Krasnaia zvezda* did far more than merely ignore the Arabs' "striving for peace." In a commentary by Lieutenant-Colonel Popov, it actually pointed out the "hardening of the Arab position." The Arab "toughness and resolve to fight and never to capitulate" were seen as originating from "the increased defense capabilities of the Arab states":

> The hotheads in Tel Aviv should ponder the changes occurring
> in the Arab world. They should remember that in creating the
> menace of a new war they assume heavy responsibility before
> their own nation as well as before the whole world.[58]

Like *Izvestiia, Krasnaia zvezda* tended to threaten Israel
instead of attempting to persuade it that it was in Israel's best
interest to agree to a political settlement. At times, *Krasnaia
zvezda*'s threats were as unequivocal as *Izvestiia*'s, warning
that "Israel's policy of defying the Security Council resolution . . . can bring disaster on Israel itself."[59] At times, it
employed a milder tone, expressing confidence that "nothing
can stop the Arab nations . . . [and therefore] Israel's hopes
of enjoying the fruits of its aggression are doomed to be
futile."[60] These fluctuations in *Krasnaia zvezda*'s tone did not
form any set pattern; nor did they correlate with political
events. Thus, their underlying reason (if any) remains inex-
plicable.

Like *Izvestiia, Krasnaia zvezda* perceived the Middle East
situation as a clash between irreconcilable demands. Therefore, attempts to achieve a political settlement of the Arab-
Israeli conflict were, in its opinion, bound to wind up in a
blind alley. "Israel refuses even to hear about complying with
the Security Council resolution, which foresees the withdrawal of Israeli forces from all the occupied territories."[61]
On the other hand, "the Arabs will not surrender even one
inch of their territory"[62] and are resolved "to fight for their
legal rights."[63] Moreover, Israel, knowing "very well" that the
Arabs would never agree to direct negotiations, insisted on
this point "in order to drag the issue out and preclude a settlement."[64]

Like both *Izvestiia* and *Pravda, Krasnaia zvezda* frequently pledged Soviet "all-around aid" to and support for the
Arabs' "just struggle." But *Pravda* generally justified this aid
on ideological grounds, while *Izvestiia* justified it in terms of
Soviet strategic interest. *Krasnaia zvezda* preferred a still
different and somewhat curious explanation: in its editorial

of March 29, 1968, it declared that "in view of Israel's ties with imperialism, it is the Soviet Union's *right* to support the Arab nations. Moreover, it is the USSR's *obligation, derived from the Charter of the United Nations.*"[65]

It is interesting to indicate that, in contrast to the alignment on the eve of the UN Security Council session in November 1967, there was no convergence in the positions of the three organs on the eve of President Nasser's visit in July 1968.[66] Assuming that differences among the press organs reflect, at least to a certain degree, differences within the leadership, it is possible that Nasser met with a disunited Soviet leadership. It is also possible that the lack of agreement among Soviet leaders themselves was at least partially responsible for the failure to arrive at a clear-cut joint Soviet-Egyptian position.

Nasser arrived in Moscow on July 4, 1968. The visit, originally scheduled to last until July 7, was prolonged until July 10. According to a TASS announcement of July 5, Nasser "accepted the invitation of the Soviet leaders to postpone his departure." A joint communiqué was published on July 10, according to which "frank" views were exchanged regarding "the development of comprehensive cooperation between the USSR and the UAR, the Middle East situation, and methods of eliminating the consequences of the Israeli and imperialist aggression."[67] According to the communiqué, both sides reiterated "the need to settle the Middle East crisis on the basis of the Security Council resolution of November 22, 1967." "The UAR," it was stated, "has declared its readiness to implement the resolution as soon as possible and to take important and practical steps toward doing so, because of its belief in its commitment to peace." The subsequent formula, however, did not bear out agreement on the substance of the settlement to be reached. Instead, the communiqué made do with voicing joint support for Jarring's efforts and appealing to "all interested parties to aid his mission."

Hasanayn Haykal, who accompanied Nasser to the USSR, wrote from Moscow that "there was one and only one subject that figured prominently . . . this was the Middle East

crisis and the continuing aggression against Arab territory."
Within this framework, one point "took precedence . . . : what
if the political solution fails and if it does not achieve a result
to which the Arab nation can agree?" Haykal said that Nasser
told the Soviets at the "first public session of the talks" that
the UAR would give "ample opportunity for a political solution. . . . I am aware that a military solution offers many ad-
vantages, particularly as concerns the Arab nation's morale."
Yet, Nasser said, he gave "priority to the basic goal: to eliminate the consequences of the aggression. . . . But if I fail to
do this politically, then war will not be an option, but will be
necessary." Nasser went on to say that "concerning the political solution we are not intransigent. . . . But there are . . .
impossibilities." Among these were, according to the UAR
president, the concession of "an inch of occupied Arab territory," agreement to negotiate with Israel, the signing of a
peace treaty with Israel, and recognizing Israel.

Haykal was unable to answer the question he had posed
as the main issue, for "while the open sessions [of the talks]
were devoted to probing the prospects remaining for the political solution," the closed session, "which was devoted to
the critical and important question: what if the political solution fails," was attended only by Brezhnev, Podgornyi,
Kosygin, and Nasser.[68]

The *Daily Telegraph* reported on July 13 that "a time
limit has been set at the talks for obtaining definite results
from the peace moves and both Egypt and Russia will review
the situation in further talks at a later date." This assessment
seems plausible, particularly in view of the fact that the divergence between *Pravda,* on the one hand, and *Izvestiia* and
Krasnaia zvezda, on the other hand, continued. Assuming that
in Soviet politics the principle of "democratic centralism" is
paramount, discussion may be allowed only up to the moment of decision. Subsequently, after a decision has been
adopted, unity of action is obligatory.

Thus, following Nasser's departure, *Pravda* continued to
play up Arab "flexibility" and "political realism," contrasting them with Israel's "intransigence."[69] At the same time, it
stepped up its efforts to persuade Israel that peace would suit

Israel's best interests, especially since there was a chance that, following the presidential elections in the United States, "there will be a change in the American policy of support for Israel."[70] It seems, however, the the main reason behind *Pravda*'s increased efforts to appeal to Israel's "political reason" was the escalation of clashes along the Suez Canal, culminating with an Israeli raid deep into Egypt's heartland and the destruction of the power station in Naj' Hamadi on October 31, 1968.

Interestingly enough, *Pravda*'s response to the raid, which hit a target not far from the Aswan High Dam, was relatively mild. More interesting still, only a few days after the raid *Pravda* published a lengthy article explaining the Soviet position in apologetic terms. Rejecting the Israeli "accusations" that the USSR "bears the blame for the escalation of tension in the area," *Pravda* stated:

> The Soviet Union strives for the unconditional implementation of the Security Council resolution of November 1967, which foresees an Israeli withdrawal from occupied territories. *The USSR does not have any vested, parochial interests in the Middle East,* yet it is seriously concerned with the protracted conflict. The Soviet Union does whatever is in its power to bring about a political settlement.[71]

It took the Israeli defense minister's declaration that an attempt to introduce ships into the Suez Canal would result in a Soviet-Israeli confrontation to provoke *Pravda* to a more strident response: "We were terribly scared by Dayan's threats. We spent sleepless nights contemplating the grave fate Dayan was preparing for us. Truly, one cannot but recall Krylov's fable about the barking Mos'ka."[72] Thus, even here, *Pravda* was scornful and derisive rather than threatening.

In contrast to *Pravda*'s mild and virtually apologetic response, *Izvestiia* and *Krasnaia zvezda* reacted with bursting indignation, terming the Israeli raid "a barbarous crime," and threatening "severe punishment."[73]

Interestingly enough, however, very little of this indignation appeared in the official Soviet response, published on November 7 in the form of a TASS announcement. In general, the document followed *Pravda*'s mildness. No threats were made. Moreover, the gist of the announcement was to stress the vital importance of a political settlement. Concurrently, in what may be considered a concession to the demands of the *Izvestiia* and *Krasnaia zvezda* groups, the announcement pointed to the proximity of Naj'Hamadi to the area where "the UAR, in close cooperation with the USSR, and with the participation of Soviet workers and experts, is building the Aswan hydroelectric complex." Moreover, in an obvious reference to the USSR, it was indicated that Israel was "harming the political and economic interests of . . . states situated in close proximity to the [Middle East]."

On November 24, 1968, *Pravda* printed an article by two doctors of jurisprudence, F. Kozhevnikov and T. Blishchenko, an article that appears to be the epitome of *Pravda*'s moderate line. The article presented a long list of the benefits Israel could draw from the restoration of peace, such as freedom of navigation and guarantees for its security and territorial integrity. Israel's attention was called to the fact that "the Palestinian resistance is gathering momentum. In these conditions, swift withdrawal in accordance with the Security Council resolution [242] is the only solution." Furthermore, the article flatly pointed out that the "Arab *states* do not have any territorial claims against Israel."[74]

One can hardly overestimate the significance of this pronouncement. The organ of the CC CPSU was actually advising Israel to arrive at a peace agreement with the Arab *states* through withdrawal from territories occupied during the June 1967 war ("withdrawal in accordance to the Security Council resolution"), before it would have to deal with the Palestinians, who, in contrast to the "Arab states," did have territorial claims to Israel proper. *Pravda* seemed to be expressing apprehension about the growth of the Palestinian resistance, which could escalate the situation beyond control. Thus, the article clearly dissociated *Pravda* from Arab maximalism in general and Palestinian militancy in particular. Moreover, Kozhevnikov and Blishchenko seemed to epitomize *Pravda*'s 1967-1968 line and bring into sharp relief its consistent efforts to dampen Arab militancy.

The line advocated by the *Pravda* group was, as we have seen, consistently opposed by the *Izvestiia* and *Krasnaia zvezda* groups. These two organs' unqualified support for Arab maximalism was illustrated once more when on December 18, 1968, they gave publicity to Zayyat's (Egyptian government spokesman) statement to the effect that any proposal for a political settlement had to address itself to two problems "vital for the Arab nation," namely, "the liquidation of the consequences of the Israeli aggression of 1967 *and the consequences of the establishment of the state of Israel in 1948.*"[75]

This statement was followed by another harsh outburst, in which *Izvestiia*'s "International Commentary" stated that

> Israel wants to dictate peace on its own terms. Having swallowed pieces of Arab territory, Tel Aviv wishes to digest them, relying on the US and other imperialist countries for support. Yet, Israel *will not live long enough to see* this kind of peace. Only the *full* liquidation of the consequences of the Israeli aggression and the restoration of justice can ease the tension.[76]

The consistently divergent line pursued by *Izvestiia* and *Krasnaia zvezda* in the period following the official endorsement of Security Council Resolution 242 and, in particular, their December pronouncements may have some interesting implications for the problem of decision making in the USSR. As indicated above, the decision to adopt the Security Council resolution as the official Soviet policy imposed some limits on press discussion, specifically, it precluded overt disavowal of the idea of a political settlement. As we have seen, however, *Izvestiia* and *Krasnaia zvezda* found sufficient opportunities to voice their dissenting opinion and express unequivocal support for Arab maximalism—in an apparent effort to pressure the decision-makers to change the official line.

Yet available evidence indicates that the policy advocated by the *Izvestiia* and *Krasnaia zvezda* groups was not heeded by the decision-makers. Official statements made public during this period followed *Pravda*'s mildness rather than

Izvestiia's stringency. Moreover, on December 21, 1968, the Soviet foreign minister, Andrei Gromyko, arrived in Cairo, reportedly with the aim of gaining Nasser's support for a Soviet peace initiative. *Izvestiia*'s and *Krasnaia zvezda*'s December pronouncements may well indicate the position toward the visit these groups took in closed forums. However, in spite of their vocal opposition, which was presumably coupled with direct approaches through formal channels, the decision to embark on a peace initiative was carried through. According to Western reports, on December 30, 1968, the USSR presented the United States with a plan for Great Power contacts on the Middle East.[77]

It is noteworthy, however, that the *Izvestiia* and *Krasnaia zvezda* groups appeared undaunted by the defeat of the line they had persistently advocated for over a year. They continued to oppose vocally the very idea of a political settlement for the entire month following the presentation of the Soviet proposals. More interestingly still, *Pravda* during the same period promoted the peace initiative in a cautious, virtually esoteric manner, as if attempting to minimize the gap between it and its opposition.

The following should help to illustrate this point.

Pravda's first reference to the situation in the Middle East in 1969 appeared on January 3. The commentary, signed by *Pravda*'s senior commentator, Primakov, addressed itself mainly to the Israeli raid on the Beirut international airport. However, this seemingly ordinary article, which reiterated Soviet support for the Security Council resolution of November 1967, contained at least two hints of a Soviet initiative. The first was the title of the commentary—"Active Steps Are Necessary." More revealing still was Primakov's reference to "the great responsibility of the United Nations Security Council, particularly its *permanent members*" to solve the Middle East crisis, which "is fraught with danger."

On the same day, *Izvestiia* published an article bearing exactly the same title as *Pravda*'s commentary. However, the article, signed by *Izvestiia*'s Middle East correspondent, Kudriavtsev, did not include any detectable reference to the Security Council's permanent members or, for that matter, to anybody else's responsibility to solve the Middle East crisis.

Two days later, on January 5, *Pravda* wrote that "the Western powers are ready to talk about the need to reach a political settlement, knowing that war will not be to their benefit. Yet they refuse to undertake action to promote a settlement." This pronouncement may be seen as another hint about the USSR's efforts to initiate Great Power contacts on the Middle East problem.

On January 11, *Pravda* went to great pains to refute "rumors circulated in the West" alleging that the Soviet Union was acting "behind the Arabs' back with the aim of elaborating a plan to solve the Middle East crisis." This may be a "negative" indication that Moscow did in fact contact the West.

Neither *Izvestiia* nor *Krasnaia zvezda* published any references to the Soviet peace initiative.

On January 19, 1969, the Cairo *al-Ahram* published what it claimed was the Soviet proposal for a Middle East settlement, as submitted to the US, British, and French governments. On January 25, *Pravda* printed a commentary by E. Vasil'ev, one that set out proposals for a stage-by-stage Israeli withdrawal. The plan set forth in the article, bearing the authority of an official statement, was identical to what *al-Ahram* had published six days earlier as the Soviet proposal for settlement. The plan, defined as a "concrete way for the realization of the Security Council resolution," made the following proposals:

1. A simultaneous declaration by the Israeli and Arab governments of readiness to terminate the state of war and to conclude a peace settlement following an Israeli withdrawal from occupied Arab territories. "In this context, Israel will declare its readiness to start withdrawing its forces as of a fixed date."
2. The withdrawal will be supervised by UN observers.
3. On the first day of the withdrawal, Israel and the Arab states will deposit with the UN corresponding documents on the termination of war and on respect and

recognition of the sovereignty, territorial integrity, and political independence of every state in the region and its right to exist within secure and recognized borders.

4. Agreement will be achieved, possibly through Jarring, concerning the secure and recognized borders, the freedom of navigation, a just solution to the refugee problem, the guarantees to territorial integrity and political independence of each state. This agreement will constitute a "package deal" concerning all the aspects of settlement.

5. The Israeli withdrawal will be executed by stages according to the following timetable. During the first month, the Israeli forces will withdraw to certain intermediate lines in the Sinai, the West Bank, and the Qunaytira region. On the same day that the Israelis reach the first line of withdrawal in the Sinai, the UAR will introduce forces into the Canal zone and start clearing operations. During the second month, the Israeli forces will withdraw to the June 5, 1967, lines. In the liberated territories, full administration by the appropriate Arab state will be restored. During this stage, UN forces will occupy positions in the Gaza Strip and in Sharm al-Shaykh, thus restoring the *status quo ante bellum*.[78]

6. The UN Security Council will adopt a resolution concerning the deployment of UN forces and reendorse the principle of freedom of navigation through the Tiran and Aqaba straits.

7. After the completion of Israeli withdrawal to interstate demarcation lines, the documents previously deposited with the UN will be enacted.

8. The UN Security Council will adopt a resolution providing guarantees for the Arab-Israeli boundaries, with the possibility of Great Power guarantees not excluded.

Pravda's commentary went on to stress the "great responsibility" of the Security Council's permanent members to "help [the parties] to reach a settlement based on the full implementation of the November 1967 Security Council resolution." As if to prod the "interested parties" to accept the initiative, Vasil'ev added a note of urgency: the Middle East crisis is "fraught with danger, thus complicating the entire international situation. Eruption of a new war in the Middle East will constitute a threat to world peace." Moreover, asserted the commentator, the "development of the situation has reached a point from which events can evolve in two directions only: either toward a political settlement or . . . [toward] a new phase of dangerous escalation."

Pravda was the only central Soviet organ to publish the peace plan. *Izvestiia* and *Krasnaia zvezda* maintained silence. Subsequently, at the beginning of February, all three reported in short TASS dispatches the acceptance of the *"French* proposal to conduct Big Four talks, in order to facilitate the Jarring mission."[79]

This chain of events lends itself to the following explanation. *Pravda*'s initial caution in promoting the peace initiative may be seen as an attempt to prevent any further alienation on the part of the opposition. Its effort to de-emphasize the scope of the internal dispute may well have been coupled with behind-the-scenes attempts to gain the support of the *Izvestiia* and *Krasnaia zvezda* groups. The decision to bring the debate into the open may indicate the failure of attempts to win the opposition's support for the proposed policy. Moreover, one may speculate, the CPSU's decision to give publicity to the peace initiative may reflect an effort to summon the support of other incumbent groups.

At this point, it is impossible to determine whether the opposition was finally persuaded by the arguments of the CPSU group or whether the decision was adopted (imposed) despite the opposition's resistance.

In any event, sometime in late January 1969 the USSR decided actively to engage in bilateral and multilateral talks with the United States, Britain, and France. This decision precluded overt opposition to the peace initiative and to the peace efforts, thus limiting *Izvestiia*'s and *Krasnaia zvezda*'s room to maneuver even more. However, as in the situation prevailing in November-December 1968, the emer-

gence of common parameters of analysis threw the basic differences among the three press organs into even sharper
relief.

For the sake of clarity, an attempt will be made to delineate the common parameters of analysis before proceeding
with an investigation of the evolving divergences. Needless to
say, such a division is entirely arbitrary.

The Imperfect Convergence

Common Parameters of Analysis

Perhaps the most obvious element in the convergence of
the lines pursued by *Pravda, Izvestiia,* and *Krasnaia zvezda*
was the joint presentation of the November 22, 1967, Security Council resolution as "the one and only basis of peace in
the Middle East."[80] Moreover, it was consistently pointed out
that the Soviet position "is based on the Security Council
resolution" and that the Soviet Union was doing everything
in its power to promote and secure the implementation of
the resolution.[81] At the same time, Soviet global policy was
presented as striving for détente and normalization in conflict
areas.[82]

Though the differences among the Soviet press organs
will be analyzed below, it may be interesting to indicate here
that *Pravda* and *Izvestiia* seemed to differ on the interpretation of what they both considered the most important provision of the Security Council resolution, namely, the
demand for an Israeli withdrawal. *Izvestiia* was very consistent in demanding the withdrawal of Israeli troops from *all*
the occupied Arab territories, but *Pravda* generally spoke
about withdrawal from the occupied territories. *Krasnaia
zvezda* seemed to waver between the two, at times presenting
the demand for a total withdrawal of the Israeli forces from
all the occupied territories, at times requiring Israeli withdrawal from the occupied Arab lands.

Having presented the Soviet position as one favoring a
swift political settlement based on the November 1967
Security Council resolution, *Pravda* and *Izvestiia* proceeded
to portray the Arab position as one of "realism" and striving

for peace.[83] Quantitatively, there was a 3:1 ratio between *Pravda*'s and *Izvestiia*'s respective references to Arab "peacefulness." *Krasnaia zvezda,* as in 1968, refrained from playing up Arab "flexibility" and "moderation."

This Arab position was frequently contrasted to Israel's "intransigence" and "aggressiveness":

> While the Arab countries, first and foremost the UAR, demonstrate their goodwill toward resolving the crisis through political means, Israel continues to sabotage attempts to achieve a peaceful solution and bases its policy on military provocations against the Arab countries. . . . The realistic approach and correct position of the UAR increase its authority in the international arena, but Israel's criminal policy and intransigence push the Tel Aviv leaders deeper and deeper into the abyss of political isolation.[84]

Krasnaia zvezda repeatedly stressed and condemned Israeli "intransigence," yet it failed to contrast it to Arab flexibility.[85]

This partial convergence among *Pravda, Izvestiia,* and, to a lesser extent, *Krasnaia zvezda* may be the result of a decision adopted sometime in January 1969 (or perhaps a month earlier) to engage actively in efforts aimed at achieving a political settlement. This decision, and the fact that since the early spring of 1969 the Soviet Union had engaged in multilateral and bilateral contacts with the United States, Britain, and France, apparently precluded disagreement about the general desirability of a political settlement. Following this decision, all Soviet press organs were presumably mobilized to provide a propaganda background to the Soviet peace initiative. In accordance with the principle of democratic centralism, overt discussion of this point was henceforth restricted. Differences, if any, were to be expressed only through meaningful silences.

The convergence of the Soviet press organs' lines was by no means one-sided, i.e., as if *Izvestiia* and, to a lesser extent, *Krasnaia zvezda* were drifting toward a stationary *Pravda* line. For one, *Pravda* abandoned its attempts to persuade Israel that a peaceful settlement would suit Israel's best interests.

Instead, from the beginning of 1969, *Pravda* joined *Izvestiia* and *Krasnaia zvezda* in voicing thinly veiled threats to the effect that "Israel will have to collect the bitter fruits of its shortsighted policy."[86] In another article, *Pravda*'s commentator Medvedko flatly pointed out that "Israel is creating a dangerous precedent of noncompliance with international law, the help of which it may need in the future."[87]

Pravda's more stringent stance toward Israel may be explained by the fact that now, with the USSR actually involved in "peace activity," Israel's "obstructionism" was perceived as a direct challenge to the Soviet Union.

More important, *Pravda* adopted in 1969 *Izvestiia*'s general analysis of the Arab-Israeli conflict. Recurrent statements by *Pravda*'s senior commentators and CPSU officials set forth the concept that the Arab-Israeli conflict was "the result of an acute clash between the forces of imperialism and [those] of progress and national liberation."[88] In this context, *Pravda* stressed that "the assault of imperialist and Zionist forces" could be effectively rebuffed only through "maximal mobilization of all antiimperialist forces . . . and alliance between the Arab national liberation movement and the socialist community, as well as other revolutionary, democratic, and peace-loving forces in the international arena."[89] It thus stated in ideological terms what *Izvestiia* and *Krasnaia zvezda* had been asserting all along, namely, that the Soviet-Arab alliance was vitally important to the USSR. In addition, *Pravda*'s appeal for unity was lent urgency by the fact that the USSR officially committed itself to the idea of a political settlement. In these conditions, Soviet-Arab unity of position and unity of action were all the more necessary.

Starting in the early spring of 1969, the Soviet press organs engaged in a year-long campaign aimed at bringing home the idea that the situation in the Middle East was on the verge of explosion and fraught with the danger of a major conflagration. (In view of the spiraling escalation of hostilities, particularly along the Suez front, this description was not far from the truth.) By enhancing the impression that an all-out war was imminent, the Soviet Union perhaps wished to prod the Western powers, first and foremost the United States, into drastic action to bring peace to the Middle East. By the same token, the Soviet image as a factor of restraint and the guardian of peace in the area was promoted.

At the same time, the Soviet media emphasized the "qualitative change" in the Middle East balance of power, as evident in the "increasingly effective rebuff given to the Israeli aggressors by the Arab armies and air force."[90] Moreover, it was reiterated that "the times when Israeli outrages passed unpunished are definitely over."[91] "Major, far-reaching changes have occurred in the region, the underestimation of which may cost Israel dearly."[92]

In presenting the Middle East balance of power as having shifted in the Arabs' favor, the Soviet Union may have been pursuing several goals:

1. to indicate that the Arabs (and thereby the USSR) enter negotiations from a position of strength;
2. to enhance the Soviet position as the Arabs' faithful ally and underline the effectiveness of Soviet military aid programs;
3. to reinforce the pressure brought to bear on the United States and Israel, threatening that should an all-out war break out, Israel and "its supporters" would find themselves in an inferior position.

Having outlined the general analysis common to *Pravda, Izvestiia,* and *Krasnaia zvezda,* we may proceed with an analysis of the divergences within this framework.

Points of Divergence

As surmised above, the decision to engage in peace efforts put an end to public discussion of the general desirability of a political settlement. However, a quantitative analysis reveals a 4:2:1 ratio among *Pravda, Izvestiia,* and *Krasnaia zvezda,* respectively, in the number of references to the various aspects of and prospects for a political solution of the Arab-Israeli conflict. This discrepancy may indicate continued disagreement over the relative importance to be attributed to the peace efforts.

Since *Krasnaia zvezda* was apparently the least interested in the peace campaign, a closer examination of its position may help to shed some light on this "disagreement within agreement."

On February 28, 1969, *Krasnaia zvezda* published a commentary signed by Colonel Ponomarev and R. Vasil'ev, which stated that

> The UAR made great efforts to achieve a political settlement. However, Tel Aviv's stubborn position renders the *increase of the UAR's military might absolutely necessary*. . . . Zayyat has pointed out that *it will be a grave mistake to place all hopes and attention on political settlement* and to forget our military needs.

Krasnaia zvezda did not venture any overt opposition to the principle of a political solution. It did, however, warn against pinning excessive hopes on the peace efforts. It voiced thinly veiled apprehension that Soviet involvement in the peace efforts might lead to a decrease in the military aid programs to the Arab states. In indicating that this would be a "grave mistake" *Krasnaia zvezda* might have been championing not only the Arab interest but also the parochial interest of the Soviet military, since curtailment of military aid to the Middle East might have brought a general decrease in resources allocation to the Soviet armed forces. Moreover, in citing an Egyptian official, *Krasnaia zvezda* might have been voicing an indirect warning that ignoring Egypt's needs might imperil the Soviet-Arab alliance and thereby the Soviet position in the Middle East.

As if to reinforce its point that it would be politically injudicious and inexpedient to pin all hopes on a political settlement, *Krasnaia zvezda* continued to repeat that the chances of reaching such a settlement "are very meager," since "the very idea of a political settlement, which connotes an unconditional withdrawal from the Arab lands, is an anathema to the Israeli leaders."[93] Moreover, asserted *Krasnaia zvezda*, Israel's whole position toward the crisis was based on its desire to enlarge its territory; expansionism is an integral part of Israel's political and ideological credo and the basic reason for its "fierce opposition to Great Power talks, to Soviet-American contacts, and to the Security Council resolution in general, all of which foresee an Israeli withdrawal from the occupied Arab lands."[94]

Throughout 1969 *Krasnaia zvezda* referred frequently and in detail to the "great increase" in the Arab states' military capabilities and to their "resolve to rebuff new aggression."[95] It expressed assurance that "a new war will not end with an Israeli victory."[96] However, though agreeing with the assessment (presented also by *Pravda* and *Izvestiia*) that a new balance of power prevailed in the Middle East, *Krasnaia zvezda* was very apprehensive about its stability.

Time and again attention was called to the "steady growth" of Israel's military potential:

> The Israeli extremists do not limit themselves to talking about the possibility of a new war. . . . According to all the data, they are making every effort to increase their military potential. Israel's defense budget is steadily growing, devoted in part to the purchases of modern weapons, and in part to accelerated arms production, with the aim of achieving self-sufficiency in the near future. . . . Concomitantly with accumulation of technology and armaments, great attention is paid to the steady increase of the Israeli Army's level of combat readiness.[97]

Some of these articles included detailed lists of the types and quantities of Israeli tanks, aircraft, and missiles.[98] Three articles in 1969 claimed that Israel was "working on the development of a nuclear bomb."[99] Moreover, *Krasnaia zvezda* singled out two specific types of weapons, the introduction of which might change the balance of power in Israel's favor, namely, the US-made Phantom fighter-bomber and the British Chieftain tank, "which will render the Israeli armored divisions invincible in desert battles."[100]

There was a ratio of 2.1 to 1 between articles emphasizing the growth of Israel's military potential and articles speaking in terms of a balance of power favoring the Arabs. These two lines seemingly contradicted each other. Yet they were in fact variations on one and the same theme, namely, the Soviet military's continuous campaign to ensure military aid to the Arab states and, by the same token, to increase resources allocation to the Soviet armed forces. Lauding Arab military might, achieved with the "help of faithful friends," *Krasnaia zvezda* also attempted to prevent complacency and "resting on laurels," as well as to bring home the opinion that *any* balance of power is relative and subject to change.[101]

For almost six months the military appeared to be the only group to venture overt opposition to the Soviet involvement in and preoccupation with the peace campaign. The fact that the *Izvestiia* group continued to harbor misgivings about the expediency of the peace efforts can be inferred only from a comparative quantitative analysis of this organ's references to the various aspects of efforts to achieve a political settlement. In other words, in the period between February and June 1969, *Izvestiia* preferred to camouflage its opposition, expressing dissent in almost a surreptitious manner.

Izvestiia's reluctance to indulge in vocal opposition may be explained by several factors. First, Soviet involvement in bilateral and multilateral contacts with the West, aiming at the achievement of a political solution in the Middle East, could have imposed more strict limitations on an official organ (such as *Izvestiia*) than on an organ meant primarily for internal consumption (such as *Krasnaia zvezda*). In other words, the ascendancy of the moderate line and the consequent engagement in a policy of détente could have compelled those responsible for *Izvestiia*'s line to resort to less explicit means of voicing dissent.

On the other hand, the *Izvestiia* group could have chosen to temper its line in response, presumably, to the change in the global constellation. In the early spring of 1969, the protracted tension between the USSR and the People's Republic of China grew into a series of armed clashes, with both sides suffering casualties. From *Izvestiia*'s viewpoint, the situation along the lengthy Soviet-Chinese border could have made a rapprochement with the United States politically expedient even if it were only temporary.

Krasnaia zvezda's continued adherence to a militant line vis-à-vis the United States in both the Middle East and global contexts may have reflected the military's opinion that the trouble on the Chinese border did not justify détente or a reversal of the aggressive policy in the Middle East and the Mediterranean.

However, by the summer of 1969 the lingering debate surfaced again, involving all three organs and the groups they represented in heated debate and vigorous political activity.

Since the internal Soviet debate was taking place against the background of, and was presumably precipitated by, the developments on the Arab-Israeli front, perhaps a brief assessment of these developments would be helpful.

In March 1969, Egypt initiated heavy artillery duels along the Suez front in an apparent effort to prod the great powers into quick and drastic action to bring about a political solution. The military exchanges were accompanied by saber-rattling on the part of the Egyptian media in a concerted effort to create the impression that an all-out war was about to erupt at any moment.[102]

On April 23, 1969, Egypt officially repudiated the UN cease-fire of 1967 and declared it no longer binding in view of the Israeli fortifications along the Suez Canal. The Soviet media ignored this declaration, apparently considering it a slap in the face—after all, it came in the midst of bilateral contacts with US representatives and after a personal note from Brezhnev, reportedly urging restraint, had been presented to Nasser.[103]

On May 1, following another Israeli raid on targets in upper Egypt (Naj' Hamadi and Adfa), Nasser delivered perhaps his most belligerent speech since June 1967: "We are planning to attack. . . . Our forces are prepared to move into the Sinai."[104] Moscow generally ignored this outburst of militancy, and only *Pravda* found it appropriate to reply. An unusually strongly worded article published on June 6, 1969 (the anniversary of the Six-Day War), made it clear that the Soviet Union did not want another conflagration in the Middle East and restated the Soviet insistence on a political solution. The article, signed by V. Rumiantsev, an official of the CC Middle East Department, condemned the "opponents of Egypt's progressive development" who "whip up nationalist and revanchist moods in the nation and in the army in an attempt to push the UAR onto an adventurist course." (This may be an oblique reference to young Egyptian army officers, who, according to Lebanese press reports, were increasingly dissatisfied with Nasser's refusal to sanction a new military round with Israel and resentful of the Soviet influence they blamed for this refusal.)[105]

In an obvious attempt to arrest the trend toward a split between the Arab militants and the Soviet Union, *Pravda* underlined the vital need for a close alliance between the "UAR's progressive regime and the socialist community." Peking was brought in as the villain, alongside the "reactionary imperialists," for trying to give the Arab struggle a "character deprived of social significance" (i.e., a purely nationalist character) and diverting it from the "revolutionary struggle of our time" (i.e., from the Soviet-led communist camp).

Rumiantsev went on to assert (though it seemed a hope rather than a conviction) that public opinion in Egypt increasingly favored moderation and that "an understanding was growing that strengthening of the internal front on a progressive social basis, improving the morale and combat preparedness of the armed forces, and adopting a sober and realistic attitude to the solution of the conflict by political means will in the long run open the way to restoration of the country's territorial integrity." "Any other approach," warned Rumiantsev, such as "that encouraged by imperialist and reactionary propaganda, recently joined by voices from Peking," propaganda that called for "a recarving of the map of the Middle East," was aimed at pushing Egypt onto an "adventurist course," as a result of which "the present progressive regime will not be able to continue."

Pravda's explicit criticism of and dissociation from Arab belligerency was not seconded by any other organ. Moreover, only a few days before the appearance of Rumiantsev's article, *Izvestiia* published a lengthy commentary reassuring the Arabs of continued Soviet support for their "just cause."

The article, signed by *Izvestiia*'s New York correspondent, M. Sturva, refuted "vicious lies" spread by "Zionist circles and Washington hawks," lies alleging "erosion of the Soviet position" and claiming that "the Soviet Union no longer insists on a full withdrawal." "This is a sheer lie," stated *Izvestiia*, explaining that

> The Soviet Union considers the Security Council resolution of November 22, 1967, which was accepted by the Arab states, [*sic*, only Egypt and Jordan accepted] as the only basis for settlement. The resolution foresees, as is well known, withdrawal of Israeli troops from all Arab territories occupied in 1967. This refers to the Sinai penninsula, the Gaza strip, the West Bank of the Jordan river, the Arab part of Jerusalem and the Golan Heights in Syria.[106]

On June 4, 1969, *Izvestiia* gave prominence to the fact that *al-Ahram* reprinted Sturva's article, terming it "a resolute answer to Western propaganda's vicious campaign." On the next day, *Izvestiia* informed its readers that another Cairo paper, this time *al-Masawwar,* published "a summary" of *Izvestiia*'s May 31 article under the headline "The Soviet Union Continues to Insist on Israeli Withdrawal from All the Occupied Territories."[107] On the same day, *Izvestiia*'s senior commentator Koriavin repeated assurances as to "unchanged Soviet support of the Arab position, particularly of the demand for a total withdrawal of Israeli occupying forces," and again repudiated "hostile propaganda efforts aimed at undermining Soviet-Arab friendship."[108]

This discrepancy between *Pravda* and *Izvestiia* was apparently a continuation of their still unresolved dispute over the position to be adopted toward Arab maximalism and the Arab cause in general. *Pravda* seemed to be genuinely annoyed by the Egyptian bellicosity, considering it a deviation from the line urged by the CPSU and perhaps even as a betrayal of this line. *Izvestiia*, which all along manifested apprehension that appeals for moderation might anger and alienate the Arabs and thus prove detrimental to Soviet interests, engaged in an effort to reassure the Arabs of continuous Soviet support. It is interesting to point out that

Izvestiia continued its dissent in spite of *Pravda*'s extraordinarily unequivocal statement, by a ranking CPSU official,
condemning Arab extremism.

Ensuing events seem to indicate that the opposition's
arguments were not heeded by the decision-makers.

On June 10, 1969, with the World Communist Conference in progress in Moscow, Soviet Foreign Minister Gromyko arrived in Cairo. The aim of the visit was presumably to
discuss with Nasser a proposed statement by the Big Four
delegates before the UN adjourned for the summer vacation
and to receive exact indications of how far Egypt was prepared to go in seeking a political settlement.

The Soviet press announced Gromyko's visit on June 10,
i.e., the very day of his arrival in Cairo. Thus, like the visit of
December 1968, it was given no advance publicity. This, together with the fact that Gromyko left Moscow in the midst
of the World Communist Conference, gave the visit an air of
urgency.

Though no details concerning the Gromyko-Nasser talks
were published, Western correspondents saw the length and
intensity of the deliberations as indicative of difficulties. The
Egyptians were said to have been disappointed by the plan,
and their response reportedly required Gromyko to consult
repeatedly with Moscow by telephone.[109]

The joint communiqué published at the end of Gromyko's visit clearly indicated that a wide gap still existed between the Soviet and the Egyptian positions. Moreover, it appeared to harbinger an Egyptian rejection of the official
Soviet line as advocated by *Pravda.*

Issued on June 14, 1969, the communiqué repeated
both parties' insistence on a full implementation of the
November 1967 Security Council resolution and on Israeli
withdrawal from all the land occupied in 1967. Although
withdrawal was not made a preliminary condition to a settlement and although the Palestinian issue was passed over in
silence in an apparent concession to the USSR, the communiqué failed to spell out the UAR's agreement to the step-by-
step settlement proposed by the Soviet Union and the United
States.[110]

Moreover, as may be inferred from the language of the communiqué, Egypt continued to insist on Israeli withdrawal from all the territories occupied in the June war. Egypt's refusal to agree to territorial adjustments, at least not in advance of a full Israeli withdrawal, "meant, in fact, the rejection of the American idea of a package agreement under which all elements would go into effect simultaneously."[111] By implication, this was also a rejection of the Soviet proposal of January 1969, which, at least implicitly, left the door open for negotiations concerning the future demarcation lines.

Thus it seems that the most Moscow could have gained was time. Subsequent Eyptian pronouncements made it quite clear that the UAR thought its armed forces strong enough to liberate the occupied territories through military means should political efforts fail.[112] On July 17, 1969, Nasser stated that "what has been taken by force could only be regained by force." This statement was preceded by what this author considers to be the first official announcement of the "War of Attrition," namely, Nasser's speech delivered on July 23, 1969, at the opening of the ASU National Assembly's third session.[113] On the same day, Muhammed Fawzi said, "We have begun the war of liberation. . . . We have moved from active defense [a stage announced in September 1968] to liberation."[114]

Pravda gave vent to its disaffection by refraining from giving any publicity to these outbursts of militancy, which was a far cry and an obvious retreat from the "mutual conviction that the Middle East crisis could and should be solved by political means."[115] This conviction, *Pravda* asserted, was achieved during Gromyko's visit.

Izvestiia and *Krasnaia zvezda,* which apparently did not harbor any illusions about the actual results of the Gromyko visit, could not but see Egypt's militancy as a boost to their position. Both gave publicity to and commented extensively on Nasser's bellicose pronouncements, stressing that "the Arab nations are ready to fight until the end for the liquidation of the consequences of the Israeli aggression. . . . The hotheads in Tel Aviv and their imperialist supporters should ponder over the significance of [Nasser's] words."[116] In a later commentary, *Krasnaia zvezda* asserted that "President Nasser knew what he was talking about when he declared on July 23 that Egypt is ready to rebuff any attack. . . . The Soviet support of the Arabs' just cause is the guarantee of the withdrawal of the Israeli occupiers."[117]

Moreover, the *Izvestiia* and *Krasnaia zvezda* groups used Egypt's increased militancy and the implicit defeat of the CPSU's line as an "excuse" to cease all references to the very idea of political settlement. Increasingly aligning themselves with the Arab position, they repeatedly asserted that no settlement was possible "without satisfying the lawful Arab demand to withdraw the Israeli troops from all the territories occupied by them," a demand to which, in their opinion, Israel would never agree willingly.[118]

The extent of *Izvestiia*'s and *Krasnaia zvezda*'s alignment with Arab bellicosity may be further illustrated by the following citation from *Krasnaia zvezda*'s editorial of September 4, 1969:

> The increased defensive potential of the Arab states enables them to continue the struggle for freedom, for the return of all the occupied territories, and for the defense of the legal rights of the Palestinian nation. The Arab nations draw inspiration from the aid and support given them by all the forces of progress, particularly by their avant-garde, the world communist movement.

Thus, Egypt's refusal to agree to any concessions on the Arab-Israeli issue provided the background for the reemergence of a joint, vocal opposition on the part of the *Izvestiia* and *Krasnaia zvezda* groups. However, as may be inferred from subsequent events, the CPSU group was not as yet ready to relent in its position.

On June 25, 1969, Ali Sabri arrived in Moscow. Officially, the visit took place within the framework of interparty relations between the CPSU and the Arab Socialist Union.

On July 15, the Soviet media reported Sabri's meeting with the CPSU secretary general, Brezhnev. No explanation was provided for Sabri's unusually long stay in the Soviet

Union or for the fact that he met with Brezhnev only on the eve of his departure. (Obviously, Sabri could have held some secret meetings with Brezhnev and other CPSU officials before the one meeting that was made public.)

According to the Soviet press report on the Brezhnev-Sabri meeting, the two officials conducted "fruitful" talks on a "variety of issues of mutual interest." In a specific reference to the Arab-Israeli issue, the report states that "the talks underlined the resolve of both the CPSU and the Arab Socialist Union to strive for the full implementation of the November 1967 Security Council resolution, which foresees Israeli withdrawal from occupied Arab lands."[119]

Thus, the formula elaborated by Sabri and Brezhnev was a significant deviation from the one included in the communiqué summarizing Gromyko's June talks with Nasser. The Gromyko-Nasser communiqué spoke about Israeli withdrawal from *all* the occupied territories. The Brezhnev-Sabri announcement spoke only about withdrawal from territories.

It is possible that Nasser instructed his deputy to arrive at a compromise and elaborate a new, more moderate, formula. However, in view of the unrestrained bellicosity of Nasser's pronouncements during the same period, this explanation seems doubtful. Is it possible that Sabri acted independently in his talks with Brezhnev? Did he defy Nasser's instructions?

The hypothesis that Sabri did in fact act independently seems to be corroborated by the fact that Sabri was put under house arrest immediately upon return to Cairo.[120] In early September, he was ousted from his posts as vice-president and chairman of the ASU Organizational Committee.[121] Available reports were unclear as to what prompted Sabri's dismissal, but they did indicate that it was connected with his June visit to Moscow. The Beirut *al-Jarida* reported on September 17 that Sabri "and some of his followers" were arrested because of their alleged involvement in a Soviet-inspired plot to overthrow Nasser. "The Kremlin," the report continued, "has been dissatisfied with Nasser because of a dispute over the Egyptian president's demand for more arms and the Middle East question as a whole."[122]

It is virtually impossible to determine whether Sabri's

ouster was connected with any actual attempt to overthrow Nasser (with or without Soviet endorsement). It is plausible, however, that an act of defiance, if his agreement with Brezhnev really was one, could have been sufficient reason for Sabri's arrest and ouster. To carry this speculation one step further, one may argue that Brezhnev, aware of the waning support for his idea of a political settlement from both his Politburo colleagues and Nasser, engaged in a "private deal" with Ali Sabri. Sabri, whose political ambitions were no less pronounced than his militancy on the Arab-Israeli issue, might have agreed to support Brezhnev on the question of a political settlement as a *quid pro quo* for Soviet support for his future bid for power.

It is impossible to substantiate this interpretation of events. Yet *Pravda* appeared curiously embarrassed by Sabri's ouster and by the ensuing rumors about a Soviet-inspired coup d'etat. *Izvestiia* and *Krasnaia zvezda* reported Sabri's dismissal in an identical, short TASS dispatch (on September 23 and 22, respectively) without any further commentary, but *Pravda* published on September 26, 1969, a lengthy and somewhat obscure *démenti*. The article, said to be based on its "own information," stated that

> Recently, an anti-Arab and anti-Soviet campaign was started in the Western press with the aim of disrupting the steady development of Soviet-Arab relations. The Western propaganda was inspired by the recent changes in the Egyptian Army, as well as in the Arab Socialist Union, events that were reported by the Soviet press. It is clear that the changes were promoted by the UAR government's striving for a correct placement of cadres in correspondence with the tasks facing the UAR.... Western news media claimed that highly significant events were occurring in Egypt. One newspaper reported that Ali Sabri attempted to stage a coup d'etat and that the Soviet Union was involved in this venture. Such reports aim only ... to cast a shadow on Soviet-Egyptian relations at a time when the Soviet Union provides the Arab states with all-around help and support.[123]

Pravda did not deny that Sabri attempted to seize power.

Nor did it deny the allegation that the USSR was involved in the abortive coup d'etat. The out-of-context invocation of Soviet help has a peculiar ring, to say the least.

The next reference to these events was in *al-Ahram* on November 26, 1969. The Cairo daily quoted Anwar el-Sadat as saying that "certan enemies and troublemakers" had informed the Soviet Union of Egypt's readiness to "accept a certain position." Though Sadat failed to reveal the identity of the "enemies and troublemakers," the implication was all too clear. His revelations may go far to support the hypothesis that Ali Sabri might have attempted to strike a private deal with Brezhnev, thus sacrificing Egypt's position on the Arab-Israeli issue.

The Ascendency of the Hard-Liners

The apparent failure of what might have been a last-ditch effort to secure support for the peace efforts, combined, as it were, with an evident stalemate in the Big Four talks and recrudescence of military activity on the Israeli-Egyptian front, precipitated a gradual shift in *Pravda*'s line.

This shift first became detectable by mid-September 1969, with *Pravda* siding with *Izvestiia* and *Krasnaia zvezda* in an overt censure of US policy in the Middle East. It may be interesting to point out that *Pravda*'s first attack on the United States was published in close proximity to the renewal of great power talks in New York.

Thus, in a commentary on September 14, 1969, *Pravda* described the American decision to supply the Israeli air force with Phantom fighter-bombers as "another example of the aggressive line pursued by the imperialists. . . . By supplying arms to Israel, Washington assumes full responsibility for acts that endanger peace."[124] On September 28, *Pravda*'s commentator Yermakov connected US policy in Vietnam and the situation in the Middle East: "The Israeli aggressors imitate the American tactics in Vietnam, attempting to achieve a military victory at any cost and pursuing aggression while talking about peace."

This new harsh line was further crystallized on October 2, 1969. *Pravda*'s commentary entitled "To Force Israel to

Comply with the UN Demands" was signed by an "Observer," a title customarily appended to a significant editorial. "Observer" explicitly accused the United States of hypocrisy: "The United States talks about the need for a political settlement and conducts contacts with the Soviet Union while at the same time supplying Israel with offensive, ultramodern weapons." "A legitimate question arises: did anyone want to utilize some diplomatic sideshows to cover up his support of Israel and its aggressive actions."[125]

Subsequent commentaries also carried the accusation that the United States was playing falsely, using the peace talks as a smoke screen.[126]

A similar charge was included in Zamiatin's (head of the Foreign Ministry's Press Department) statement at a press conference, a statement published by the media on November 1, 1969. On December 21, in an article by G. Ratiani, *Pravda* termed Israel an "American proxy," asserting that "there is a division of labor between the US and Israel." Moreover, it warned that

> If the United States and Israel do not stop frustrating peace efforts, *they* will find themselves in peril. It is a serious mistake to assume that the old tactics of conducting a war by proxy *will save the US from dangerous consequences.* The socialist states are on the side of the Arab countries.

This statement was one of the most unequivocal warnings *Pravda* has ever directed at the United States in connection with the Middle East. As such, it epitomized the qualitative change in the CPSU's position. By mid-November, *Pravda* moved even closer to the opposition and voiced unqualified support for the Arab national postulates.

A combination of factors was apparently responsible for the shift toward a more stringent approach. For one, it seems that the Soviet leaders became increasingly aware of the fact that Nasser would not or could not agree to any territorial adjustments. *Izvestiia* and *Krasnaia zvezda* sensed that the Arabs were growing impatient with the protracted peace talks as early as July 1969 (presumably the most explicit "hint" was provided by Nasser in his July 23 speech), but *Pravda* seemed much slower in adjusting its line.

On November 6, Nasser delivered a speech to the National Assembly and left no doubts about the Egyptian position. "Attempts to reach a political solution have been until now a wasted effort. The definite conclusion we must draw is that there is no longer any way except to open our path to what we want by force, over a sea of blood and under a horizon of fire."[127] This speech, accompanied as it was by frequent accusations by the Arab media that the Soviet Union betrayed the Arab cause,[128] might well have been the final stimulus that prompted the change in *Pravda*'s position. It was no longer possible to remain oblivious to the evident hardening of the Arab position without seriously damaging Soviet prestige and position in the Arab world.[129] Unable to persuade Egypt to adopt a more flexible and "realistic" approach, *Pravda* could not but join the drift toward extremism. This might have appeared particularly crucial in view of the forthcoming Arab Summit in Rabat, at which Egypt's relative moderation was bound to be outweighed by Syrian, Libyan, and Algerian militancy.

On another level, the gradual convergence in the lines pursued by the Soviet press organs might have come from an increasing awareness that the United States was not exerting sufficient pressure on Israel. The American decision to supply Israel with Phantom fighter-bombers and to allow American citizens to serve in the Israeli defense forces was probably perceived as a double cross and sheer deception. It put the USSR in an awkward position vis-à-vis the Arab states and perhaps no less significantly, reinforced the argument of those Soviet leaders who had warned all along against trusting the "imperialists."

The easing of Chinese pressure on the Soviet borders might have also contributed to the change of line, rendering the USSR less eager to cooperate with the United States and less interested in détente. In other words, deescalation with China and the strengthening of the USSR's position in the communist camp as a result of the World Communist Conference could have denied a powerful argument to those

Soviet leaders who advocated a rapprochement with the United States, thus strengthening the opponents of détente.

The new line found its reflection not only in a harsh position vis-à-vis the United States but also in stepped-up efforts to enhance the Soviet-Arab alliance.

On November 27, 1969, the Declaration of Warsaw Pact Members on the Middle East was published. It pledged continued support for the Arabs in their "struggle against Israel *and its protectors*" and reiterated the notion that a "stable and just peace is impossible without Israeli withdrawal from the occupied Arab lands." The declaration called for "a just solution of the problem concerning the lawful rights and interests of the Arab nation of Palestine, which is waging a heroic struggle for national liberation." The reference to the "lawful rights of the Palestinian *nation*" (an issue omitted from previous communist statements) and the fact that the Warsaw Pact declaration failed to refer to the Arabs' or their own striving for peace in the Middle East were a clear demonstration of the new hard line.

Commenting on the Warsaw Pact declaration, *Izvestiia* wrote: "The warning included in the . . . declaration put an end to the Western propaganda campaign that claimed that the Soviet Union does not insist on Israeli withdrawal from all the occupied Arab territories and agrees to some territorial adjustments."[130] On December 4, *Izvestiia* reported that the UAR National Assembly termed the Warsaw Pact members' declaration "an inspiration for the continuation of our struggle."[131]

Izvestiia's and *Krasnaia zvezda*'s evident satisfaction may be explained by the fact that the Warsaw Pact declaration and the new policy it epitomized signified the victory of the approach they had been advocating all along.

The change in the Soviet attitude was not lost on the United States. On November 26, Joseph Sisco told a Senate committee that the Soviet attitude in the bilateral talks "raises doubts about its wilingness to play an actively constructive role on behalf of peace in the Middle East."[132] On November 28, a US spokesman announced that the Big Four talks would resume on December 2. According to UPI, the decision to resume the multilateral talks followed the apparent failure of bilateral contacts. [133]

The new Soviet line was further manifested during Sadat's Moscow visit. Sadat arrived in Moscow on December 9, 1969, accompanied by Foreign Minister Riyad and War Minister Fawzi. Officially, the delegation was defined as "party-governmental." However, the only party representative, Sadat, was immediately termed by the Soviet media as Nasser's "personal envoy." [134]

Speaking at a Kremlin luncheon given in Sadat's honor, Prime Minister Kosygin pledged that the USSR would adopt "active measures aimed at strengthening the defensive potential of the UAR and that of other Arab states." Moreover, he stated,

> Now that the Israeli aggression continues, the Soviet people consider the struggle waged by the Palestinian organizations for the liquidation of the traces of the Israeli aggression a just, antiimperialist struggle for national liberation.

This was the first time a Soviet official endorsed the Palestinian *organizations'* struggle. Although the correlations between the Soviet leaders' public pronouncements and the lines pursued by their press organs will be analyzed at a later point, it may be interesting to emphasize here that it was the chairman of the Soviet Council of Ministers who delivered perhaps the toughest speech since 1967, a speech that fell in line with the stand hitherto promoted by *Izvestiia*.

The explicit pledge to supply Egypt with additional arms and the endorsement of the Palestinian organizations, though balanced with a reference to the Security Council resolution and to the Soviet intent to continue "the struggle for a political settlement," further revealed the hardening of the Soviet position and confirmed the tougher line adopted in the November 27 declaration of Warsaw Pact Members.

Neither Kosygin's speech nor the joint communiqué published on December 12 referred to the so-called Rogers Plan, which Egypt had officially rejected and to which the USSR had yet to reply.

On December 14, 1969, *Pravda* carried a commentary signed by Vladimir Mikhena (a commentator whose name had never before appeared beneath articles dealing with the Middle East). It criticized the United States' "one-sided stand against the Arabs" and added that nothing the "Washington propagandists" did could conceal the US support for Israel's "aggressive actions." Furthermore, Mikhena claimed, "a justified apprehension" was being voiced in the Arab states that "the American propagandists' effort" was aimed at disguising Washington's attempts "to sow strife and discord in the Arab world."

This language is rather curious. First, *Pravda*'s definition of the Arab categorical rejection of the Rogers Plan as "apprehension" was an understatement, if not a misrepresentation, of reality. Moreover, *Pravda* seemed to have gone to great pains to avoid referring directly to the Rogers Plan, using instead the euphemism "Washington's propaganda efforts." Could these indicate that the CPSU organ was not ready as yet to renounce the idea of a negotiated settlement?

In contrast, *Izvestiia* and *Krasnaia zvezda* were very explicit in their criticism of the Rogers Plan.[135] For example, *Izvestiia*'s commentary of December 20 repudiated the plan point by point:

> The formula of Rhodes-style negotiations is nothing more than a masked acceptance of the Israeli demand for direct negotiations. . . . The suggestion of Israeli withdrawal from the Sinai, with retention of [Israeli] control over Sharm al-Shaykh and the Gaza Strip contradicts the spirit and the letter of the Security Council resolution of November 22, 1967. . . . Rogers attempts to substitute [the requirement for] unconditional withdrawal with a "compensation" suiting Israeli territorial and strategic interests. . . . In sum, the American Secretary of State does everything possible in order to twist the situation in Israel's favor and to ruin Arab unity.

In a later commentary, *Izvestiia* added a new point, namely, that "the Rogers Plan is aimed at securing the interests of the oil monopolies and originates from the Pentagon's strategic plans rather than from a desire to achieve peace in the Middle East."[136]

Krasnaia zvezda was even more detailed in its comment and as unequivocal as *Izvestiia* in repudiation of the Rogers Plan. A lengthy article signed by G. Savin (presumably a senior commentator who contributed infrequently and only on crucial topics) accused Rogers of "turning upside down the whole question of settlement based on the Security Council Resolution of November 1967":

> According to him [the American Secretary of State], the Arab countries should first convince Israel of their sincerity, and only thereafter will it be possible to deal with the question of withdrawal. Strange logic—the victim of aggression has to prove his peacefulness to the aggressor. . . . Moreover, according to Rogers, Jerusalem should be a united city. Thus, he ignores the very existence of the well-known resolution of the UN General Assembly on the restoration of prewar status to this city. . . . The American representative's plan does not mention even one word about the problems concerning the Syrian and Jordanian occupied regions, or the problem of the Palestinian refugees. . . . Such statements cannot but be considered by Tel Aviv as new encouragement of and support for aggression and annexation. . . . The US plan heightened Arab indignation with the American policy toward the Middle East.[137]

Thus while *Izvestiia* and *Krasnaia zvezda,* consistent with their general line, rejected the Rogers Plan outright, *Pravda* appeared still to adhere to the possibility of achieving a negotiated settlement. However, this last minute effort to save the peace initiative was thwarted by the hard-liners. On December 25, 1969, the Soviet Union reportedly handed its official reply to the Rogers Plan, rejecting eight out of the ten major American proposals.[138]

The foregoing analysis seems to indicate the existence of a more or less steady alliance between the *Izvestiia* and *Krasnaia zvezda* groups. Throughout 1967-1969, these two groups opposed, with varying intensity, the *Pravda* line of achieving a political settlement of the Arab-Israeli dispute. As we have seen, up to November 1969 the arguments voiced by *Izvestiia* and *Krasnaia zvezda* went unheeded, and official

Soviet policy evolved along the lines proposed by *Pravda*. Subsequently, however, under the impact of regional and global developments and because of increasing pressure from the opposition groups, the official policy was modified to reflect the platform of the opposition.

All this evidence allows several conclusions to be drawn and substantiates some of the hypotheses underlying this study.

First and most obvious, the Soviet attitude toward problems connected with the Arab-Israeli dispute was not monolithic. There were differences in attitudes and approaches and even suggestions of alternative political lines, and they were implicitly—and at times explicitly—argued in the Soviet press. Perhaps the most important finding of this study is the relatively broad freedom of debate on such matters as the Soviet involvement in the Arab-Israeli dispute. Even the adoption of a policy decision, while imposing certain limits on the debate, failed to squelch it altogether.

The case studies examined above indicate that in 1967-1969, the official Soviet policy of a political settlement of the Arab-Israeli conflict was elaborated and pursued despite the existence of vocal opposition from at least two policy groups. This may be explained as follows. It is conceivable that the *Pravda* group is more than a *primus inter pares*. It may have the power and authority to impose policy decisions over the opposition of other incumbent groups. Moreover, this authority is probably accepted and acknowledged by all the groups involved.

However, the supremacy of the CPSU is seemingly not absolute or inviolable. This may be inferred first and foremost from the very existence of a debate as well as from the fact that dissent continues even after a policy decision is adopted. Clearly, if the Party's authority were absolute, debate and opposition would be all but useless and would probably be prohibited altogether.

The Party may have to surrender its "mandate" and modify the policy under two conditions: (1) if the policy initiated by the Party proves inexpedient; (2) if the opposition groups succeed in either isolating (outvoting) Party representatives in the decision-making forums or persuading them of the judiciousness of the opposition's arguments and the folly of their own.

The evidence tends to corroborate this explanation, which may be conveniently summed up and proposed as a model of Soviet decision making—the "qualified primacy" model.

On another level, the alliance between the *Izvestiia* and *Krasnaia zvezda* groups appears to substantiate the hypothesis that in the Soviet political context, groups tend to coalesce on issues. We have seen these two groups voicing misgivings about the expediency of casting the USSR in the role of a staunch supporter of a political settlement and channeling the Arab politics accordingly. Both groups based their argument on the premise that the preservation of the Soviet-Arab friendship is vital in terms of the Soviet interest.

With the aim of further analyzing the origins and bases of the alliance between the groups represented in *Izvestiia* and *Krasnaia zvezda,* we shall examine the attitudes of all three organs toward the United States and its role in the Arab-Israeli conflict.

A Military-Industrial Complex in the USSR?

*Case Study 1: Divergent Attitudes toward the
United States and Its Role in the Arab-Israeli Conflict*

As indicated in the first chapter, the Six-Day War produced a wave of resentment toward and condemnation of the United States and its alliance with Israel. All Soviet press organs presented a uniform line on this issue throughout 1967. During 1968, however, a clear divergence developed, again separating *Pravda* from *Izvestiia* and *Krasnaia zvezda.*

Pravda considered Israeli "intransigence" as the main cause of tension in the Middle East, accusing the US "only" of "encouraging" and "supporting" the Israeli aggression through political and military aid.[139] In contrast, *Izvestiia*'s and *Krasnaia zvezda*'s line appeared much more oriented toward the United States. For example, instead of speaking of "encouragement" or "inspiration," *Izvestiia* flatly stated

that "the US threw the Israeli forces into battle."[140] Therefore, "the US is an equal partner to the blame for continued
tension in the Middle East."[141] Israel was invariably seen as
an American (or imperialist) proxy, which, waging a war
against the Arab national liberation movement, exempted its
"masters" from direct military intervention in the Middle
East, an intervention needed to change a situation that "has
become increasingly inconvenient for the US and its
allies."[142]

As will be recalled, in 1967 the Soviet organs were united
in the view that the Six-Day War had changed the balance of
power in the Middle East in favor of the "forces of socialism
and progress." Although this basic assumption seemed to be
present in 1968 as well, only *Izvestiia* and *Krasnaia zvezda*
frequently referred to "imperialist attempts to redress the
situation and restore the strategic and economic positions
they have lost."[143]

This discrepancy might have had important implications
for the policy that, in the respective opinion of each organ,
should be adopted by the USSR. *Pravda*'s manifest obliv-
iousness to the existence of any threat to the Soviet position
in the Middle East might have led to advocacy of a "static,"
conservative policy. *Izvestiia*'s and *Krasnaia zvezda*'s opinion
that Soviet gains were constantly threatened by "imperialistic
encroachments" might have resulted in urging a more aggressive policy of response toward the US and more unequivocal
support of the Arabs as a means of safeguarding a balance of
power favorable to the USSR.

As if to lend urgency to its point, *Izvestiia* emphasized
that "imperialist encroachments" threatened not only the
Soviet position in the Middle East, but also the security of the
Soviet state itself: "In throwing the Israeli forces into battle
the US attempts to change the balance of power in the
Middle East and turn it into a springboard of aggression
against the Soviet Union and the socialist countries."[144]

This direct threat to the USSR, the socialist community,
and the world national liberation movement was, in *Izvestiia*'s
opinion, the main reason for the increasing support for the
"just Arab cause" by "all progressive humanity."[145] This was

tantamount to saying that by supporting the Arabs the Soviet Union was directly defending its own security and state interests.

The foregoing analysis, if correct, may shed some new light on *Izvestiia*'s and *Krasnaia zvezda*'s consistent alignment with the Arab stand. Perceiving the Soviet-Arab alliance as vital to the Soviet national interest, these organs may have considered attempts to dampen Arab militancy harmful to this alliance and thereby not in the Soviet strategic interest. *Pravda*, considering the Soviet position in the Arab world secured, allowed itself to advocate a policy of moderation; it was apparently not alarmed by the possibility of an angry Arab response. Moreover, by stressing the United States' direct role in the conflict and pointing out the global repercussions of the American-Israeli alliance,[146] *Izvestiia* and *Krasnaia zvezda* depicted the Arab-Israeli conflict as an integral part of the global confrontation between the "forces of imperialism and reaction" and those of "socialism and progress."[147] This approach corresponded with and reinforced their opinion that the chances for a political settlement of the Middle East conflict were very slight: the irreconcilability of the Arab and Israeli positions reflected and was in turn reflected in, the broader, universal irreconcilability between the socialist and imperialist camps.

Pravda, on the other hand, attempted to play up the prospects of a political solution and preferred to portray the Arab-Israeli conflict as a local (or localized) dispute between the governments of Israel and the Arab states. Any other approach would necessarily weaken *Pravda*'s effort to minimize the seriousness of the conflict. Furthermore, assuming that *Pravda*'s advocacy of a political settlement was sincere, it is possible that *Pravda*'s moderate and self-restrained line toward the United States reflected awareness that a political solution could be achieved only with American cooperation.

These differences may also have had an impact on and reflected Soviet internal policies, specifically the issue of resource allocation. *Krasnaia zvezda*'s editorials and the public statements of the Soviet army commanders (in *Krasnaia zvezda*) frequently presented the "constant tension in the

Middle East, which constitutes an integral part of imperialist assault throughout the world," as the rationale for "the necessity to increase the vigilance and strength of the Soviet armed forces and improve their combat readiness."[148]

In all these pronouncements, the Soviet army was singled out as the "defender of the socialist motherland, of the revolutionary achievements of all nations, and of the cause of socialism and communism," and was portrayed as "the Army of Liberation, in which the toilers see the shield of peace and social progress."[149]

Thus, *Krasnaia zvezda*'s pronounced lack of interest in a political settlement and its consistent emphasis on the crisis situation prevailing in the Middle East (and throughout the world) seemed to be an integral part of the Soviet military's campaign to secure increased resource allocation to the armed forces.

Krasnaia zvezda's repeated references to Israel's arms acquisitions and ever growing military-industrial potential, including claims that Israel "is on the verge of nuclear capability," might have reinforced the military's argument.[150] *Izvestiia* faithfully seconded *Krasnaia zvezda*'s reports about the steady growth of Israel's military potential.[151]

The alignment between *Krasnaia zvezda* and *Izvestiia* thus appeared to transcend agreement on a foreign policy issue. Unity between the press organ of the Soviet Ministry of Defense and that of the Soviet Council of Ministers on what may be considered an issue of broad political, economic, and strategic ramifications may perhaps indicate the existence of a military-industrial complex in the Soviet political context.

As a further illustration of the cooperation between *Izvestiia* and *Krasnaia zvezda* on an issue involving both a political and economic decision, we shall examine their attitudes to the problem of Soviet naval deployment. It should be stressed that the following section is by no means a complete analysis of the Soviet goals and position in the Mediterranean; nor does it provide detailed data on the scope and cost of the Soviet deployment in this area. Our main concern is to substantiate, as far as possible, the hypothesis that there is a military-industrial complex in the USSR and to assess its role in decision making. Consequently, the problem of Soviet naval development is used only as another case study.

Case Study 2: The Press Debate on the
Development and Deployment of Soviet Naval Power

As it stressed the need for an overall strengthening of the Soviet military might, *Krasnaia zvezda* seemed to ascribe special importance to the development of the Red navy.

During the latter part of 1967 and throughout 1968, it published numerous articles on and made numerous references to naval development and deployment. The gist of these commentaries was that "the Soviet navy has become a navy of the oceans. Its strength and entrance into the global ocean has put an end to imperialist naval domination."[152]

In an article in *Krasnaia zvezda* on July 28, 1968, Admiral Kasatonov, the first deputy commander of the Soviet navy, singled out the Red navy as "the guardian of Soviet state interests."[153] A later editorial of September 29 called for increased vigilance in the navy in view of "mounting tensions throughout the globe, as evident in Vietnam, the Middle East, and Europe." As it turned out, these references were only the harbingers of the "great campaign."

On November 2, 1968, *Krasnaia zvezda* published a commentary by R. Vasil'ev. Examining at length the deployment of the NATO "military and military-naval might in the Mediterranean," and the intention to reinforce the Sixth Fleet with a "multinational armada made up of [NATO] military-naval forces deployed in the Atlantic Ocean," Vasil'ev introduced a new, extremely interesting notion:

> Attempts by NATO strategists to justify their scuffle in the Mediterranean with references to the Soviet presence there are, to put it mildly, very strange. So Soviet warships in the Mediterranean, which are located in fact close to their own borders, create a menace there. And the American Sixth Fleet, infamous for its numerous provocations against the forces of peace and progress in the Mediterranean [region], allegedly does not threaten anybody. However, the Mediterranean nations have a completely different point of view. . . . The threat presented to the Mediterranean by the NATO aggressors becomes in-

creasingly apparent and cannot but evoke justifiable alarm on the part of all peace-loving nations.

This line was further developed in an article by Vice Admiral N. Smirnov in *Krasnaia zvezda* on November 12, 1968. The gist of the article, entitled "Soviet Ships in the Mediterranean," was to contrast the aggressive goals of the American and NATO presence in the Mediterranean and the peace-guarding mission of the Soviet Navy. More significant, however, were two other points elaborated by Vice Admiral Smirnov:

1. The American and NATO presence in the Mediterranean is a direct threat to the Soviet Union and other socialist countries, which are the targets of the Sixth Fleet's nuclear and conventional weapons.
2. "In these conditions, the security interests of the USSR dictate a steady increase in our defenses. As is well known, our state is a Black Sea power and, consequently, a Mediterranean power. We cannot remain indifferent to the military adventures being organized in close proximity to the USSR's borders. Soviet warships in the Mediterranean . . . are in the front line of the motherland's defense."

Two days later, on November 11, *Izvestiia*'s editorial repeated Smirnov's statement almost verbatim, stressing even more than *Krasnaia zvezda* the immediate threat to the Soviet security: "The Soviet south and southeast are the primary and immediate targets of the Sixth Fleet's nuclear missiles." *Krasnaia zvezda*'s and *Izvestiia*'s November campaign was echoed in the military journals, for example, *Morskoi Sbornik* and *Soviet Military Review. Pravda,* however, maintained silence.

Before long, the line propagated jointly by the military organs and by *Izvestiia* was adopted as the official Soviet position. On November 24 the Soviet media published a TASS announcement, an official response to the NATO session in Brussels:

> The Soviet Union, as a Black Sea power and, consequently, as a Mediterranean power, is exercising its *indisputable right* to be present in this region. Soviet warships are deployed in the Mediterranean not in order to create a threat to any nation or state. Their task is to promote peace and stability in [this] region.[154]

Clearly, this announcement was primarily an *ex post facto* justification of an existing situation. However, significance may be attributed to the fact that the military journals' and *Izvestiia*'s joint campaign promoted the issuing of a statement that may be considered the "Bill of Rights" of Soviet naval presence in the Mediterranean. One can only assume that *Krasnaia zvezda*'s and *Izvestiia*'s public statements were coupled with pressure delivered in closed forums in a concerted effort to impress the importance of naval development and deployment upon the decision makers. *Izvestiia*'s joining the campaign of the military journals may perhaps substantiate the hypothesis ventured above, that is, that there is a military-industrial complex in Soviet politics.

It is virtually impossible to determine the impact, if any, of the November "Bill of Rights" and the preceding campaign on actual plans for the development and deployment of the Red navy.[155] This obvious limitation notwithstanding, the foregoing analysis, illustrating how a press campaign conducted jointly by two organs resulted in a policy statement consistent with the line they had advocated, provides an interesting insight into the Soviet policy-making process.

Furthermore, the proceedings and results of the debate concerning the Soviet position vis-à-vis the United States in the Mediterranean appear to corroborate the "qualified primacy" model of Soviet foreign policy making: under certain conditions the ruling group is persuaded (or forced) to accept the arguments of the opposition and adjust official policy accordingly.

5. Doctrine versus Pragmatism: Attitudes toward the Progressive Arab Regimes

The search for rewarding methods of exploiting the opportunities offered by the rise of the Third World has occupied the Soviet leaders at least since the Nineteenth CPSU Congress of 1952. Since the newly independent regimes, while emotionally anti-Western, have also generally been noncommunist, the problem has presented doctrinal complexities to Moscow.[1]

Although a practical policy toward the Third World evolved in 1955, it was not until 1960-1961 that theory was wedded to the new reality. The formula of "national democracy," put forth by the 1960 Moscow Declaration of Eighty-one Communist Parties and defined more fully in the 1961 Draft Program of the CPSU, appeared to meet the demands of the situation: noncommunist regimes were embraced whenever they fought Western political and economic influence, maintained military neutrality (together with close friendship for the USSR), implemented radical social and economic reforms, and gave the local Communist parties the right to exist and organize. The 1960-1961 compromise permitted practical aid to noncommunist regimes but forbade their ideological endorsement at the expense of local Communist parties.

The "national democratic" state was not viewed as a state of one class, but rather as a state in which an entire segment of the populace was given the task of eliminating the reactionary elements that still existed. This section—the progressive forces—was composed of a united front of workers, peasants, the democratic intelligentsia, and a segment of the national bourgeoisie. In a "national democratic" state, it was not necessary for the proletariat to assume the leading role, for any "progressive" class could initiate the necessary reforms. Actually, the whole doctrine appears to be an attempt to pave the way for the gradual development of the prerequisites for a transition to socialism in countries in which the proletariat was extremely weak.[2]

In December 1963, following a period of inconsistency and debate,[3] Khrushchev turned his back on the 1961 Party Program and explicitly endorsed socialism of the national type. He offered, in fact, to recognize the revolutionary standing of "national socialist" leaders, provided they met certain conditions—above all, friendship toward the Soviet Union.[4] Viewed in retrospect, this pronouncement seems to have been an important turning point in the controversy. After that date, the upper hand appeared to rest with those who favored embracing regimes of the type defined and who wished to maintain, for pragmatic reasons, friendly relations with their ruling elites, even if this meant the deliberate renunciation of independent Communist parties in a number of countries.[5]

Yet, the debate between what may be called "party orientation" (an attitude that regards the independence of Third World Communist parties as important in terms of Soviet policy and visualizes dialectical relations between the communists and the incumbent regimes) and the "nonparty" approach (an attitude that minimizes the role and significance of a distinct communist organization and conceives Soviet interests and communist action mainly in terms of harmonious relations with the ruling elites) did not end in 1963.[6]

The "nonparty orientation" did not suffer any setbacks as a result of Khrushchev's ouster. On the contrary, the official attitude of Khrushchev's successors was an even more far-reaching departure from the party-oriented attitude. Since Brezhnev's ascendancy, priority has been given to the CPSU's relations with the ruling parties of the Third World "progressive regimes" over relations with national Communist parties.[7]

This attitude received its ideological sanctification in Brezhnev's report to the CPSU's Twenty-third Congress in 1966. In broad terms, the report tended to distinguish between four categories within the "developing" world:

1. Neocolonialist states, which may have achieved political independence but were dominated by avowedly pro-Western regimes (Saudi Arabia was mentioned)
2. States that were following the "road of progressive social development" and moving along the "noncapitalist" path of development
3. Countries that were building socialism
4. States or political forces engaged in a "national liberation struggle"

As for the third category, no countries were mentioned by name, probably reflecting some disappointments in the recent past. At the time of the Twenty-second Congress, the corresponding category of present or potential "national democracies" included, in addition to Cuba, Indonesia, Ghana, Guinea, and Mali.[8] The whole discussion of how states might evolve from "national democracy" to socialism received minimal attention at the 1966 Congress. Instead, the second category was enlarged to include countries that were not pro-Western in orientation and that were engaged in "progressive" social change.

In his report, Brezhnev indicated an attitude of broad tolerance toward the states in the second category, i.e., those following the "noncapitalist" path of development:

> Major changes have been carried out in such countries as the United Arab Republic, Algeria, Mali, Guinea, Congo-Brazzaville, and Burma. . . . It goes without saying that the form and scale of these processes vary from country to country. The revolutionary creative work of the people who have proclaimed the construction of socialism as their objective introduces distinctive features into the forms of development along the road of social progress.[9]

The common framework of anti-Western and antiimperialist policies created a unity of purpose between the Soviet Union and the "progressive" regimes in the Arab world i.e., the UAR, Syria, Iraq, and Algeria.

The "progressive" Arab regimes were described as united by their common aims: "All of them are struggling to strengthen their national . . . economic and social independence."[10] Prominent in all were "the determination of the revolutionary democrats who have assumed power [in each of them] to effect fundamental social reforms on the non-capitalist path of development, [their] reliance on the working sections of the population for support, and [their] bid to strengthen the state sector of the economy."[11] Soviet pronouncements stressed that it was in the Soviet Union and other socialist states that the "progressive" Arab regimes would find their "natural and proven allies in their struggle against imperialism, colonialism, and neocolonialism. . . ."[12] It was further emphasized that the constantly expanding and "disinterested aid" granted by the USSR to these countries was given unconditionally and did not entail Soviet interference in their internal affairs.[13]

The United Arab Republic

The UAR as the Cornerstone of Soviet Middle East Policy

In the immediate aftermath of the Six-Day War, the USSR appeared resolved to persist in and consolidate its presence in the Arab world in general and in the UAR in particular. Aware that its position and prestige had been seriously damaged by the results of the June war, Moscow engaged in a vast campaign aimed at recouping its losses and firmly establishing the Soviet Union as the sole champion of the Arab cause. Within this framework, relations with the UAR were elevated to a central position. Apparently, a strong UAR and a strong Nasser were seen as the prerequisite of a continued Soviet presence in the Arab East.

Starting immediately after the events of June 9-10, 1967 (i.e., Nasser's resignation and return to power)—events hailed by the Soviet press as the victory of the "socialist trend" in the UAR—and continuing throughout the period under discussion, Soviet media stressed the stability and viability of the Nasser regime. It was pointed out that "the progressive regimes of the UAR, Syria, and Algeria, against whom the spear of aggression was directed, were able not only to withstand the difficulties, but also to continue carrying out far-reaching socioeconomic transformation coupled with antiimperialist policy."[14]

The fact that the UAR's "progressive" regime had been preserved despite the Israeli aggression and the ensuing difficulties was acclaimed testimony to the viability of the revolutionary democracies not only in the Middle East but in the Third World in general. The UAR was presented as living proof that "the ease with which the reactionary coup d'etat was carried out in Ghana is not . . . a natural development for all countries that have taken the noncapitalist path of development but only where anticapitalist measures have not struck root and do not enjoy the support of the masses."[15]

Krasnaia zvezda's commentary went even further:

> Cairo has begun to play a significant role in the process of national liberation of nations. It occupies a place of honor among the Arab states and, on a broader plane, in the whole Third World. Moreover, the socioeconomic transformation carried out in the UAR has made it one of the countries paving new, still unknown to history, roads to liberation and a better future.[16]

Krasnaia zvezda's reference is particularly interesting insofar as it significantly expanded the Khrushchevian concept of different roads to socialism and allowed much greater latitude than had been originally meant. Although *Krasnaia zvezda* failed to provide any further elaboration on this issue, its remark may well have been the key to its approach toward the Arab "progressive" regimes. In stressing the uniqueness of the Egyptian "experiment," *Krasnaia zvezda* allowed little room for the application of the Soviet experience (in plain terms, for Soviet interference with the UAR's internal affairs).

Throughout the period under investigation, the Soviet press organs repeatedly warned that Egypt's position as "the key country in the Middle East" made it an immediate target of "imperialist assaults." "The progressive regime in the UAR is considered by the forces of imperialism as the main obstacle impeding the strengthening of imperialist and neocolonialist positions in the Middle East," wrote *Izvestiia*.[17] And *Pravda* added: "The increased potential of the Egyptian revolution causes serious anxiety in imperialistic circles, who fear the further weakening of their position in the Middle East."[18] In these conditions, all three organs agreed, "any attempts to weaken the support [rendered by] international socialism to the Arab countries would be a direct subversion of the national liberation front in the Middle East."[19] Conversely, any attempt on Egypt's part to stray from the "progressive" path would play into the hands of the imperialist aggressors and seriously imperil the very existence of the state.[20]

These three strands of the Soviet propaganda web seem to serve one and the same purpose—to back and reinforce the efforts to recoup and strengthen the Soviet position in the Arab East. Emphasizing the significance and potential of the Egyptian revolution on both the regional and global levels, the Soviet press organs provided an ideological justification for the immense Soviet investment in Egypt. Stressing the economic and political stability of the Nasser regime, they implicitly asserted that this investment was safe and politically sound. Pointing to the constant imperialist threat to the UAR's "progressive" achievements, they reinforced the notion that the Soviet-Arab alliance was vitally necessary. Assertions that Egypt's very existence depended on the continuation of the "progressive" reforms may have reflected hope that with time Egypt would come closer to what Moscow considered "scientific" socialism (i.e., socialism based on the Soviet model).

Clearly, advancement of the "revolutionary process" in the UAR and the strengthening of the world national liberation movement were of intrinsic value to the "motherland of socialism." However, in their apparent effort to justify the Soviet investment in and commitment to the UAR, the Soviet press organs transcended the ideological dimension and indicated overtly that the development of friendly relations with Egypt served the Soviet national interest:

> Soviet-UAR relations put an end to imperialist monopoly over influence in this important region. Soviet aid in strengthening the defense capabilities of the UAR and wide cooperation in many other areas facilitate the upsetting of imperialist intrigues against the Arab national liberation movement. The Egyptians sincerely want to pay back the Soviet people for all they have done for them. And if the USSR's prestige in the Eastern Mediterranean is now higher than ever before, the UAR and other Arab countries have been and are instrumental in this process.[21]

The UAR's Internal Scene as a Forum of Debate

The UAR's rise to a position of centrality was further reflected in the broad coverage of its internal events in the Soviet press. Throughout 1968-1969 there was roughly a 2:1 ratio between articles and news items dealing with Egypt and those dealing with all the other Arab states.

During 1968, Soviet comment centered upon three main internal events: the February demonstrations, the March 30 Program and the reorganization of the Arab Socialist Union (ASU), and the November demonstrations.

The February 1968 demonstrations: a hostile provocation? In January 1968, Egypt witnessed the trials of the generals held responsible for the June defeat and the trials of Marshal Amer's accomplices in the abortive coup d'etat of June 1967. Both exposed the public to numerous instances of laxity, corruption, and incompetence. In February, grassroots antimilitary sentiment reached a high point with the outbreak of student-worker riots protesting the light sentences given to the generals.[22]

There was an interesting diversity in Soviet reporting of the riots. *Pravda* was the first and only organ to report the demonstrations of February 27; this it did in a short TASS item, without any commentary. The item spoke only about Egyptian "students" protesting the light sentences given to those responsible for the defeat.[23] On the next day, *Pravda* updated the initial information, stating that "workers em-

ployed in the armaments plants in Hilwan led the demonstrations and were later joined by students."[24] *Izvestiia* carried a
similar report, adding only that "in Hilwan a huge industrial
complex is being built with Soviet assistance."[25] Both papers
indicated that "in many instances the police intervened,
causing unnecessary bloodshed."[26] Though both papers attempted to remain objective, their sympathy with the
demonstrating workers was readily apparent.

Krasnaia zvezda did not follow *Pravda*'s and *Izvestiia*'s
lead. In fact, it did not mention the February demonstrations
until March 5, when, together with *Pravda* and *Izvestiia*, it
published excerpts from Nasser's March 2 speech at a
workers' rally in Hilwan. According to the Soviet report,
Nasser defined the clashes between the demonstrators and
the police as the result of "misunderstandings, differences of
opinion, and lack of sufficient information." All three organs
emphasized that Nasser "paid tribute to the masses, stressing
that the workers, together with the peasants, constitute the
main force of the revolution."[27]

While the March 5 report was *Krasnaia zvezda*'s only
reference to the riots, *Pravda* and *Izvestiia* continued to
comment on this issue, revealing an increasing diversity of
opinion.

According to *Pravda*'s commentary of March 8, "the
Muslim brothers and their American supporters utilized the
riots for their own purposes, [namely] the weakening of the
internal front and besmirching the socialist choice." *Pravda*
expressed confidence that "this aim was not achieved and
will never be achieved. . . . Deviation from the socialist path
is inconceivable."

Izvestiia's commentary preferred to dwell upon the initial
motivations of the demonstrators, who "were moved by a
sincere concern for the successful and swift elimination of
the consequences of the Israeli aggression." And, it added, "it
is not their fault—it is rather a pity—that subversive elements
attempted to use this [sincere indignation] for their own purposes."[28]

The discrepancy between *Pravda*'s and *Izvestiia*'s interpretations of the February events may be seen as a further

reflection of their divergent attitudes toward the issue of a political settlement. *Izvestiia,* which all along appeared apprehensive lest Soviet failure to identify with the Arabs' national goal and lest pressure to present the Arab position as one of support for the idea of political solution set the Arabs against Moscow, may well have been using the February riots to reinforce its argument. On the other hand, *Pravda,* apparently more confident in Soviet ability to influence Arab politics, tended to ignore the fact that one of the main demands voiced by the Hilwan demonstrators was the complete liberation of every inch of Arab territory.[29]

Pravda's commentary included another interesting point. The final paragraph of the article stated:

> We are referring to a region immediately adjacent to our southern borders. The national progressive regimes [of this region] symbolize the striving of all Arab nations for national liberation, social progress, and friendship with the Soviet Union.

This may have been the first time a Soviet press organ mentioned the "direct proximity" of the Middle East, i.e., its vital importance in terms of the Soviet strategic interest, in the context of *internal events.* Thus, *Pravda* proclaimed as early as March 1968 the direct Soviet interest in a commitment to the preservation of a "progressive" regime in the UAR.

Quo vadis Egypt? Divergent interpretations of the March 30 Program and the reorganization of the ASU. Almost immediately after the restoration of order, the Egyptian president undertook steps designed to meet certain of the demonstrators' demands. A new trial was ordered to mete out heavier sentences for the generals held responsible for the defeat, and negotiations were started between student leaders and deputies of the National Assembly.[30] Subsequently, Nasser announced the release of students arrested in the riots, who, in their turn, "declared confidence in Nasser and support of his socialist line."[31] On March 20, 1968, came the second installment of short-range reforms—the formation of a new cabinet, headed by Nasser and consisting of thirty-five members. More than any of its predecessors since 1953, the March 1968 cabinet represented the infusion of new blood: fourteen new ministers were sworn in, all of them civilians. The higher civilian presence corresponded to the antimilitary feeling among Egyptians. Significantly, at least half of the new cabinet ministers were drawn from university faculties; almost all of these were highly respected and popular professors with strong pro-student and reformist orientation.[32]

Soviet comment on these events was at best laconic. On March 22, 1968, *Pravda, Izvestiia,* and *Krasnaia zvezda* reported the reorganization of the Egyptian cabinet. Short TASS items consistently noted that Zakariya Muhyi al-Din had resigned from all his posts (which certainly caused little sorrow in Moscow). At the same time, all three press organs tended to minimize the significance of the change, stressing instead that "all key positions remained unchanged." On April 2, *Pravda, Izvestiia,* and *Krasnaia zvezda* cited in the same aloof manner Nasser's statement that "the reorganization of the government aimed at the inclusion of young and talented elements." Neither commentary nor any elaboration was provided. It took almost a month and the introduction of the March 30 Program to elicit some positive response.

On April 28, *Pravda*'s commentator Primakov wrote that "the reorganization [of the UAR government] strengthened the position of those who defend the line aimed at development of the state sector [of the economy] and activization of the national masses and weakened the position of antirevolutionary administrators." *Krasnaia zvezda* followed with a similar comment on May 5. *Izvestiia* maintained silence.

On the Muslim New Year's Day, March 30, 1968, Nasser announced the third installment of reforms. The March 30 Program provided for the rebuilding of the Arab Socialist Union (ASU) through a system of successive, multilevel elections—a fundamental departure from the previous appointive procedures. Nasser stressed the necessity of "bringing new blood" into the ASU and into "all levels of the government and economic bureaucracy." In addition, he proposed ten guidelines for drafting a permanent constitution, stipulating inter alia that "all socialist gains must be preserved and strengthened." Such gains were said to include the proportional representation given to workers and peasants in all elected popular councils; the participation of workers in management and their sharing of profits; and the right to free education and health and social insurance. Explicit guarantees of basic freedoms and the supremacy of law were to be given, and an independent judiciary was to maintain them.[33]

Pravda and *Izvestiia* announced the inauguration of the program on March 31, stating that it "provides for the reorganization and strengthening of the ASU, elections at all levels, unification of the national forces, liquidation of the consequences of the Israeli aggression, defense, and strengthening of the socialist achievements." *Krasnaia zvezda* carried a similar version of Nasser's "programatic speech of March 30" two days later, on April 2. Subsequent commentary revealed some interesting realignment and divergent attitudes toward the program.

First, *Pravda* joined *Izvestiia* and *Krasnaia zvezda* in stressing that the program ought to be seen in the context of Israeli aggression. Moreover, "one of the main aims [of the program] is the mobilization of all the nation's resources for the task of liquidating the results of the Israeli aggression."[34] *Pravda*'s alignment with the line endorsing, at least verbally, Arab militancy has several possible explanations. It is possible that the lesson of the February demonstrations was not lost on those responsible for *Pravda*'s line. Another possibility (which does not necessarily exclude the former) is that *Pravda* preferred not to introduce a note of disapproval, particularly since the connection between internal ASU reorganization (in and of itself a positive development from the Soviet point of view) and the military solution of the Arab-Israeli conflict was mainly academic. Thus, *Pravda*'s temporary alignment with *Izvestiia* and *Krasnaia zvezda* in support of Arab militant rhetoric had probably more to do with the context than with the issue itself.

This alignment notwithstanding, *Pravda* and *Izvestiia* appeared to be at odds over another, perhaps more substantial, issue relating to the March 30 Program. While *Izvestiia* tended to interpret the program as an attempt to cleanse (*ozdorovit'*), reorganize, and especially *democratize* the UAR's economy and body politic, *Pravda* was preoccupied with the ideological dimension. Perhaps a comparison of the respective commentaries will help to clarify the point.

On May 5, 1968, *Izvestiia* published a commentary signed by its Middle East commentator, Demchenko.

> The March 30 Program envisages a change in the principles of ruling the country (*izmenenie printsipov upravleniia stranoi*). ... An important place is given to the reorganization of the governmental and administrative organs, *based on multilevel democracy*. ... The program provides for all-around development of industry and agriculture, will guarantee full employment, deepen cooperation between the nation and its armed forces. ... It aims to create a situation conducive to the mobilization of all the nation's forces for the liquidation of the consequences of the Israeli aggression and *subsequent* development in the direction of socialism.[35]

Perhaps the most interesting point here is *Izvestiia*'s opinion that the liberation of the occupied territories was a precondition of Egypt's transition to socialism. This view was diametrically opposed to *Pravda*'s approach, which saw the accomplishment of the transition to socialism as a prerequisite of a successful struggle against Israel. Since this seems to reflect a basic schism between the two organs, we shall deal with it in more detail later. Meanwhile, let us continue the comparative analysis of *Izvestiia*'s and *Pravda*'s reactions to the March 30 Program.

In contrast with *Izvestiia*, *Pravda* refrained from playing up the "democratic" aspects of the program, asserting instead that "the basic aims of the .. program [are] the preservation of socialist achievements and provision for political and socialist liberties." Unfortunately, it failed to explain what the term "socialist liberties" might mean.[36] Furthermore, in contrast with *Izvestiia*'s factual reporting, *Pravda* manifested a somewhat factitious exuberance, hailing the March 30 Program as all but a Bolshevik action platform:

The program changes the very principles of ruling the country. The center will shift from administrative organs to the Arab Socialist Union. The ASU Congress will become the highest organ. . . . The Congress will elect a Central Committee, which will execute leadership through its political, military, economic, and social commissions. For the first time the principle of *democratic centralism* becomes the basis of the ASU's organization. This reorganization is vital in view of the new, *extremely crucial* role of the Arab Socialist Union. . . . The second main characteristic of the program is the replacement of administrators by individuals with appropriate qualifications, and, most important, *devoted to the cause of the revolution.*[37]

In a later commentary, printed after the program was approved by a nationwide referendum, *Pravda*'s Bolshevik frame of reference is even more apparent:

The Arab Socialist Union was defined [in the program] as the socialist avant-garde leading the nation, expressing its will, and controlling the implementation of the socialist goals. [The program provides for] organization according to the principles of democratic centralism, multilevel elections, criticism and self-criticism, and collectivism of leadership.[38]

At first glance, the dispute between *Pravda* and *Izvestiia* seems mainly academic. Clearly, the March 30 Program was not intended to and could not democratize the Egyptian political system or, for that matter, turn the UAR into a socialist country. Thus, both organs were guilty, to a certain degree, of reading too much into the text and indulging in wishful thinking. However, our main concern here is not to juxtapose facts and subreption but to compare divergent interpretations of a given reality and discern the reasons underlying the divergence.

The gap between *Izvestiia*'s and *Pravda*'s interpretations of the March 30 Program may be attributed to the fact that they catered to different audiences—the first to the "experts," the second to the "reds." Yet, this explanation appears insufficient, primarily because ideological phraseology is typical of all Soviet communications. In this particular case, for example, *Krasnaia zvezda*'s interpretation of the March 30 Program was identical in both content and terminology to that of *Pravda*.[39]

Thus, the divergence between *Izvestiia* on one hand and *Pravda* and *Krasnaia zvezda* on the other hand seems to transcend semantics and to reflect a deeper schism, namely, conflicting postulates over the "very principles of governing a country." Efficiency versus "devotion to the revolution"; "promised democratic reforms" versus the leading role of the party; democracy versus "democratic centralism"; liberty versus "socialist liberties"—these were the main points of divergence among *Izvestiia, Pravda,* and *Krasnaia zvezda*.[40]

The depth of the schism in *Pravda*'s, *Izvestiia*'s, and *Krasnaia zvezda*'s interpretations of the March 30 Program is all out of proportion to its objective significance. Hence it is quite possible that the Egyptian reform was used as a forum to debate views and opinions that could not be safely voiced in another context. To take this line of thought one step further, the centrality and broad applicability of the issues discussed may imply reference to events occurring within the Soviet bloc, specifically, the Prague spring.

On another level, *Krasnaia zvezda*'s alignment with *Pravda* further illustrates the premise, suggested above, that Soviet policy groups tend to coalesce around issues, with allies on, say, a strategic issue adopting diametrically opposed stands when an internal issue is concerned. Thus, on the basis of available evidence, the Soviet political process seems to be characterized by temporary, shifting alliances, forged mainly to influence a decision on a specific issue.

The November 1968 demonstrations: divergences continue. In late November 1968, another wave of student unrest swept Egypt. "Peaceful marches by college students protesting the cancellation of automatic admission to universities soon turned into violent clashes with the police."[41]

Interestingly enough, the divergent Soviet interpretations of the November events were similar in many aspects to those that polarized Soviet comment earlier. *Izvestiia* was the only organ to note that the rioting students protested "a new education law."[42] Both *Pravda* and *Krasnaia zvezda* left their readers in the dark about the immediate causes of the demonstrations. Instead, they dwelled at length on the "fact" that the riots were "the work of the enemy [who] attempts to undermine the unity of the internal front."[43] *Krasnaia zvezda* was even more specific: "The aggressors, who failed to achieve their goal [to topple the progressive regime in the UAR] through direct aggression, now attempt to wreck the internal front through means of psychological warfare."[44]

Izvestiia was apparently reluctant to accept the standard explanation that the riots were organized by agents-provocateurs. In an oblique and cautious manner, it stated its opinion that the general mood of disaffection and frustration prevailing in Egypt ought to be considered the main factor behind the November events: "Although the demonstrations lacked a mass character and were not supported by the workers, they expressed, nevertheless, the Egyptian nation's anxiety and forced it to examine more carefully some aspects of the internal situation."[45]

The divergence continued when *Krasnaia zvezda* and *Pravda* cited, on December 6 and 5, respectively, "demands voiced by the Egyptian press" calling for "severe punishment" of those who "stood against the freedom of their country and its internal stability." *Izvestiia* refrained from publishing this appeal.[46]

The dissimilarity between *Izvestiia*'s attitude toward the November events and that of *Pravda* and *Krasnaia zvezda* paralleled the lines that had divided these organs in February 1968. *Pravda* persisted in its dogmatic view that any unrest in a "progressive" country is by definition "the work of the enemy," thus ignoring the deeper social, economic, and psychological factors that triggered the events. The evident hardening of *Pravda*'s position toward the November riots may perhaps be attributed less to the fact that these demonstrations were not supported by the workers and more to the bitter lessons of student unrest in countries such as Czechoslovakia, Poland, and France. Another interesting point is *Izvestiia*'s "liberal" approach toward internal events, a sharp contrast with its "hawkish" stand on foreign policy issues.

Conversely, *Pravda*'s position suggests that not all "doves" are necessarily "liberals." In fact, only *Krasnaia zvezda* was ideologically coherent and consistent on both foreign and domestic issues. This consistency was perhaps the underlying factor in what appeared to be a shift of coalitions, i.e., *Krasnaia zvezda*'s alignment with *Pravda* on a domestic issue and with *Izvestiia* on a foreign policy issue.

The Grand Debate of 1969:
What Are the Objectives of Involvement?

The year 1969 witnessed a quantitative change in Soviet reporting of Egypt's internal affairs. Nearly all political events—whether the ASU National Assembly's session, a session of the UAR cabinet, the adoption of a new budget, or the submission of a report on the work of the ASU local committees—were duly reported by the Soviet media. Speeches by Egyptian leaders were cited and re-cited at length alongside citations of Egyptian press pronouncements. This inordinate preoccupation with the UAR's political life no doubt reflected the fact that Egypt had become the cornerstone of Soviet involvement in the Arab East.

Here, however, a significant cleavage emerged among the respective positions of the three press organs. *Izvestiia* and *Krasnaia zvezda* joined *Pravda* in reporting (in TASS items) the internal events taking place in the UAR. Yet *Pravda* accompanied its TASS reports with some ten "independent" commentaries on the political and ideological structure of the Egyptian regime, while *Izvestiia* and *Krasnaia zvezda* made do with one "independent" article. This ratio of 10:1 appears particularly odd as far as *Izvestiia* is concerned, since it had its own correspondent in Cairo.[47] Before engaging in any attempt to examine this discrepancy, a survey of the relevant articles may be in order.

During the first eighteen months following the Six-Day War, the UAR's position on the spectrum of ideological developments was virtually taken for granted. The Egyptian regime was invariably portrayed as revolutionary, progressive, and undergoing a socialist transformation. Not until 1969 were serious attempts made to clarify the operative terms and examine their applicability to the actual situation in Egypt.

One of the first attempts at a more discriminating approach was made by Primakov in his *Pravda* commentary of May 5, 1969:

> In many resolutions of the Arab Socialist Union one meets the expressions "socialist society," "socialist measures." This obviously does not mean that socialism has been built in the UAR. . . . However, the [very] employment of such terminology is important from the vantage point of the basic *tendencies* of the country's development. In the existing conditions . . . this [terminology] reflects the changing political and *class* balance of power in the UAR.[48]

While justifying the applicability of socialist terminology to the conditions currently prevailing in the UAR, *Pravda* nevertheless took to task the basic premises of the UAR's ideology, namely, Arab socialism:

> The theory rejecting development of revolutionary processes and subjecting everything to the establishment of a nonclass or superclass "national unity" only plays into the hands of counterrevolutionary elements. Furthermore, since the aggressors' aim was to topple the progressive regime, those who advise against the movement forward play into the hands of the enemy.[49]

Thus, Arab socialism was portrayed as detrimental to the cause of the revolution and dysfunctional in terms of Egypt's national goals. Stressing that it was impossible "to lead the country on the road of progress without social upheavals and class struggle," *Pravda* commentators urged Nasser to "utilize the rich experience of other states and adopt decisions that would safeguard the revolutionary achievements."[50] This was all but an overt attempt to induce Egypt to adopt the Soviet model of "scientific socialism."[51]

Pravda's scrutiny of the basic ideological premises of the Nasser regime was accompanied by overt criticism of the Arab Socialist Union.

In 1969 the exuberant optimism with which *Pravda* described the future role of the Arab Socialist Union was gone. Apparently disappointed with the pace of implementation of the March 30 Program, *Pravda* pointed out time and again that "the ASU has yet to become a political party, fulfilling the role of the leader of the national masses."[52] In a later article, *Pravda*'s senior commentator, E. Primakov, went into greater detail:

> The Arab Socialist Union has not become a political party. The road to its construction is blocked by subjective and objective difficulties, such as the position of the leading military nucleus, [Nasser and his entourage?], . . . the traditional fear that the establishment of a party . . . will lead to intensification of "class clashes," and many other factors. Many of the ASU's organizations are choked by reactionary elements. At the same time, [however], the striving toward the establishment of a party within the ASU has increased.[53]

In the same article, Primakov criticized what he considered "passivity in organizational and political work" on the part of the Arab Socialist Union. Such passivity, he indicated, "is being used by counterrevolutionary elements who strive to undo what the revolution has already achieved."

As they lamented the fact that the ASU did not meet Soviet expectations and did not become an "avant-garde organization," *Pravda*'s commentators stressed that the ASU's assumption of a "leading role" was "essential for the continuation of the UAR's progressive development."[54]

Egypt's continuous development on the path of progress was in turn linked to the achievement of what it considered its main national goal, namely, the liberation of the occupied territories:

> Undoubtedly, the consolidation of the internal situation and the mobilization of resources for the liquidation of the consequences of the Israeli aggression depend first and foremost on the regime's social basis, on the deepening of the progressive

transformation, and on the strengthening and activization of the Arab Socialist Union as the leading force of Egyptian society.[55]

Pravda presented the "deepening of Egypt's socialist transformation" as the prerequisite for a successful struggle against Israel. It thereby indicated its own scale of values and order of preference concerning the future course of Middle East events. The liberation of the territories lost to Israel was virtually denied any intrinsic value. Instead, the Arab national goal was presented as a by-product of the more crucial process of internal realignment. In Marxist terms, *Pravda* saw the socialist transformation as the base that determined the superstructure, in this case, the elimination of the consequences of the Israeli aggression.[56]

Pravda's attitude may have had a direct bearing on both the quality and quantity of the aid, military and otherwise, that in its opinion should be granted to Egypt. Moreover, it might have been implying that it considered the continuation of the progressive reforms as a prerequisite for the continued supply of Soviet aid needed for the struggle against Israel. In other words, it might have been proposing to grant Soviet aid in direct proportion to the pace and depth of the socialist transformation of the UAR regime.

The foregoing analysis throws into sharp relief *Pravda's* basic perception of Soviet relations with a client country. In its opinion, these relations ought to be based on a certain reciprocity. In the case of Egypt, *Pravda* appeared to view the ultimate socialization (or, more precisely, Sovietization) of the UAR's political structure as the trade-off for continued aid and support. This position obviously clashed with official Soviet statements, which asserted that Soviet aid was disinterested and had no political strings attached.

Interestingly enough, *Pravda's* dogmatic approach and stringent demands were limited to ideology and political structure. As far as Egypt's economy was concerned, it manifested pragmatic flexibility and tolerance.

Analyzing steps "recently adopted by the UAR, aiming at the revitalization of the private sector [of the economy] and establishment of economic ties with capitalist countries,"

Pravda stated that "problems of economic tactics have always received primary importance in all revolutions, particularly in countries with an inadequately developed industry."[57]

Pravda's exoneration of Egypt's economic "tactics" lends itself to the following explanation. Despite their own propaganda stressing Egypt's economic stability, those responsible for *Pravda*'s line were aware of the fact that Egypt's economy was at the brink of catastrophe. Unable or unwilling to increase Soviet financing, they could not but endorse Egypt's going "one step backward."[58] As long as the development of the governmental sector (where the lion's share of Soviet investment was) continued to "receive primary attention," no harm was seen in receiving "tactical" help from the West.[59]

Pravda's endorsement of an Egyptian "New Economic Policy" might also shed some new light on its "ideological offensive." Its approach may have represented an attempt to apply the Soviet experience of combining economic relaxation with stepped-up ideological and political pressure. This trend, set in motion by Lenin at the Tenth Party Congress in 1921, is still characteristic of Soviet politics. The continued offensive against "counter-revolutionary elements," increased vigilance, and, most important, safeguarding and strengthening the leading role of the party are the only context in which economic liberalization can be carried out without endangering the "progressive" nature of a regime.

In contrast with *Pravda*'s preoccupation with the pace and depth of the UAR's progressive transformation, *Izvestiia* refrained throughout 1969 from subjecting the UAR to scrutiny or criticism. It published only one article dealing exclusively with Egypt's internal affairs. The article, by its senior commentator Koriavin, was printed on July 23, 1969, on the occasion of the seventeenth anniversary of the Egyptian revolution. The article included a brief and very general survey of Egypt's "revolutionary achievements" since 1953, such as "achievement of political independence and national sovereignty, abolishment of feudal rule, and agrarian reform and industrialization." The only reference to the UAR's ideological position was a noncommital statement to the effect that "these achievements allowed Egypt to make the choice in favor of a progressive development." This enigmatic and equivocal statement was in sharp contrast with *Pravda*'s position.

The divergence between *Pravda* and *Izvestiia* appeared to center on immediate strategy rather than on long-term goals. One can safely assume that the continued progressive transformation and the UAR's eventual transition to socialism would be considered a desirable development by any Soviet political group. However, agreement on this issue does not make the schism between *Pravda* and *Izvestiia* less acute. Rather, it throws the basic points of their dispute into even sharper relief. What was more crucial for immediate Soviet interest—development of socialism in the UAR, or the strengthening of the strategic Soviet-Egyptian alliance? To what extent, if at all, should the pace of the UAR's "socialist transformation" have been an issue between Egypt and the USSR? Was the Soviet position in Egypt strong enough to allow it to criticize the very principles of that country's ideo-political structure and interfere in its internal affairs outright?

Izvestiia's approach was doubtlessly more realistic and pragmatic than *Pravda*'s. Aware of the fact that the Soviet position in the Arab East in general and in Egypt in particular was not established and did not rest on ideological affinity, *Izvestiia* was presumably apprehensive lest attempts to alter the basis of these relations weaken the alliance and thus prove detrimental to the Soviet interest. In other words, in *Izvestiia*'s opinion, the Soviet Union should have been satisfied with the immediate strategic benefits it derived from the preservation and strengthening of its position in Egypt. Demands of ideo-political payoffs and attempts to influence internal processes may well have been tantamount to cutting the very branch upon which one is sitting. Furthermore, *Izvestiia* apparently considered the Soviet aid program one of the most important vehicles of Soviet influence in the Arab world. In its opinion, therefore, as long as this goal was served, aid should have been granted without any strings, ideological or otherwise, attached.

Izvestiia's stand on the internal issue seemed similar to its attitude toward the idea of a political settlement of the Arab-Israeli conflict. In both cases, it manifested apprehension that the Soviet position vis-à-vis the Arab states was not strong enough to warrant attempts at channeling Arab politics along Soviet lines. In both cases, moreover, it regarded the preservation of the Soviet-Arab alliance as the paramount criterion, as the only standard that should determine Soviet attitude toward and policy in the Arab East.

In retrospect, *Izvestiia*'s 1969 position seems to be the forerunner of the approach all three Soviet organs adopted in 1970, namely, noninterference in the internal affairs of the Arab progressive regimes as long as their basic "antiimperialist" (i.e., pro-Soviet) policy was continued.

Krasnaia zvezda followed *Izvestiia*'s policy of abstention, publishing in 1969 only one article analyzing Egypt's internal structure. However, it did take a position on the issue of Egypt's development, stating that "the conflict with Israel should not impede the process of the UAR's socialist transformation, but rather deepen it."[60] This statement may be considered a middle position—between *Pravda*'s opinion that the socialist transformation was the prerequisite for the liberation of the occupied territories and *Izvestiia*'s appeal for the liquidation of the traces of the Israeli aggression and only then development in the direction of socialism. However, the ambiguity of *Krasnaia zvezda*'s language, ambiguity that is even more apparent in the Russian original, gives rise to two different interpretations. First, *Krasnaia zvezda* may have been reinforcing *Izvestiia*'s line and attempting at the same time to persuade *Pravda* that the achievement of the Arab national goal (i.e., the liberation of the occupied territories) would not necessarily come at the expense of sociopolitical goals (i.e., Egypt's transition to socialism). Moreover, the achievement of the latter might well be precipitated by the former. On the other hand, *Krasnaia zvezda*'s statement may be interpreted as "advice" to Egypt to pursue both goals at the same time. In this interpretation, the word "should" is taken literally—the pursuit of the national goal should not be allowed to impede the achievement of the socialist goal.

Krasnaia zvezda assumed the same ambivalent position

when speaking about the Arab Socialist Union and its political role: "A wide and deep process is currently under way to establish a real mass organization that ... would make it possible, in *due course,* to lay the fundaments for a political party—the avant-garde of all progressive forces."[61] This statement certainly fell short of *Pravda*'s evident impatience with the slow pace of the ASU's politicization and its criticism of the ASU's passivity. On the other hand, by attaching importance to the ASU and expressing optimism about its prospects, *Krasnaia zvezda* went beyond *Izvestiia*'s disregard of the whole issue.

Krasnaia zvezda's attitude may be explained as follows. It appeared to share *Izvestiia*'s view that immediate Soviet interest precluded indulging in criticism of Egypt's political makeup. This conclusion seems to be supported both by *Krasnaia zvezda*'s abstention from the ideological campaign and by its refusal to voice any criticism in the only article it did publish. On the other hand, it is quite possible that there were groups within the military establishment that tended to attribute greater intrinsic value and immediate importance to the "socialization" of Egypt than did the *Izvestiia* group. Thus, *Krasnaia zvezda*'s suggestion that these two goals could and should be pursued simultaneously may be seen as an attempt to bridge the gap between *Pravda*'s and *Izvestiia*'s positions and between differences within the military establishment itself. The dual course suggested by *Krasnaia zvezda* would, if attainable, presumably serve Soviet interests best.

The Reorganization of the UAR's Armed Forces as a Further Reflection of Basic Schisms

The gap dividing *Pravda*'s and *Izvestiia*'s perceptions of UAR-USSR relations is further reflected in their divergent evaluations of the UAR armed forces. In 1969 the debate between these two organs centered on the reorganization of the Egyptian armed forces, a process that, as explained above, was carried out upon Soviet request and with the help of Soviet advisers.

Pravda's articles on this reorganization appear, at least at first sight, to follow the pattern that characterized Soviet

attitudes in the period immediately after the Arab defeat: a
focusing on the socio-political shortcomings of the UAR
armed forces.

In *Pravda*'s opinion, the most important aspect of the reorganization of the Egyptian army and, by implication, the
main goal of the Soviet aid in this undertaking were "the
liquidation of the military bourgeoisie through a far-reaching
purge."[62] The removal of a "few hundred generals and senior
officers" and their replacement by those "dedicated to the
people and the revolutionary cause, undoubtedly changed the
situation in and status of the Egyptian armed forces."[63] The
purge, according to *Pravda* commentators, was necessary
primarily because the defeat in the Sinai was a "direct result
of the overt recreancy of the military bourgeoisie. These
businessmen in uniform betrayed not only the revolution but
their military duty as well. Instead of defending their motherland's territorial integrity and liberty, they defended their
own privileges."[64]

Consequently, in *Pravda*'s opinion, the main achievement
of the reorganization drive was to extricate the Egyptian
revolution from its difficulties: "By liquidating the bourgeoisie in uniform, who refused to accept the socialist choice . . .
and strove to force the regime to renounce it, the Egyptian
revolution freed itself from a heavy burden."[65] It is noteworthy that *Pravda* commentators ignored the possible
impact of the reorganization upon the combat performance
of the Egyptian Armed Forces. Though they mentioned
measures obliging "army and navy officers to spend more
time with their men and center their attention upon the fulfillment of their military duties," their primary concern was
with the socio-political results of the reorganization.[66]

Pravda's line gives rise to several conclusions. Evidently,
it considered the Egyptian military a powerful political and
social institution, capable of shaping, or at least significantly
influencing, the whole political structure of the regime. Moreover, the Egyptian officer corps was depicted as an intrinsically reactionary element, as a factor hindering the socialist
transformation, and ipso facto, as a factor hostile to Soviet
influence.[67] Hence, *Pravda*'s recurrent insistence on the need

to carry out a complete and far-reaching purge of the officer corps—with the aim of weakening the political power of the Egyptian military. Thus, it appears that the main goals of the reorganization of the Egyptian army, as perceived by *Pravda*, were to relegate the officers to their barracks and to deprive them of their socioeconomic privileges and traditional political role, thus facilitating the "socialist transformation" of the UAR regime.

This analysis, if correct, may shed some new light on the reasons for *Pravda*'s drive to accelerate the process of establishing the Arab Socialist Union as the "leading" force in the UAR. A viable political party, were the ASU to become one, could fill the vacuum created by the attenuation of the military's political power.

Izvestiia's attitude toward the reorganization of the Egyptian armed forces and the Soviet role in and expectations from this process was no different from its general line of supporting Arab national postulates and noninterference in internal affairs. It centered its attention on the "improved combat readiness of the UAR armed forces" and the "qualitative change in the Middle East balance of power," resulting, in its opinion, from "the reconstruction of Egypt's defense structure."[68] It left unexplored the problem of the Egyptian military's political role and ignored the sociopolitical impact of the reorganization of the UAR's armed forces.[69] This position may well have been a further reflection of the basic schism dividing *Pravda*'s and *Izvestiia*'s approaches, with the latter considering the strategic balance of power, rather than ideological endeavors, the focal point of Soviet policy toward the Middle East. Furthermore, *Pravda* and *Izvestiia* were apparently at odds over the basic purpose of Soviet military aid to Egypt. *Izvestiia* saw the Soviet aid program as a means to promote Soviet influence and strategic positions in the Arab East (through the strengthening of the Soviet-Arab alliance), but *Pravda* seemed ready to acquiesce and endorse these programs only insofar as they furthered the process of socialist transformation in the recipient country.

Krasnaia zvezda's position on the issue of Soviet-Egyptian military relations will be analyzed in another section. Here

we shall limit ourselves to the proposition that it was concerned mainly with the combat preparedness and ideological
prowess of the Egyptian soldiers and, like *Izvestiia*, attributed
primary importance to the enhancing of Soviet influence in
the UAR. Consequently, *Pravda* was the only Soviet central
press organ to focus attention on the impact of Soviet
military aid programs on the recipient country's political
structure and future course of development.

The Syrian Arab Republic

The Soviet media's preoccupation with Egypt, which reflected the latter's emergence as the cornerstone of Soviet
involvement in the Arab East, came to a certain extent at
Syria's expense. A quantitative analysis of the articles and
news items published in 1968-1969 by the three Soviet press
organs reveals an overall ratio of 1.3 to 2 between items dealing with Syria and those dealing with the UAR. However, a
content analysis of these reports indicates that Soviet interest
in Syria did not decline in the postwar period. An extensive
network of political, economic, and military ties was maintained and steadily developed. Numerous delegations traveled
between Moscow and Damascus, virtually paralleling in their
level and frequency those exchanged with Egypt.[70] The
Soviet economic investment in Syria, though obviously
smaller than that in Egypt, was steadily growing, particularly
when the construction of the Euphrates High Dam and development of petrochemical projects began. At the same time,
there was an evident qualitative and quantitative increase in
Soviet military aid programs, though again on a smaller
scale.

In surveying Soviet press reports on Syria in the period
1968-1969, one can hardly avoid the impression that the
Syrian Arab Republic enjoyed the status of a special
favorite. It was treated as an *enfant terrible,* whose excesses
were accepted with a tolerant smile.

Tolerance of Syria's
Position on the Arab-Israeli Issue

The Soviet media's connivance at Syria's attitude toward

the idea of a political settlement is perhaps the most striking example of the Soviet "special attitude." As may be recalled, Syria did not recognize the November 22, 1967, Security Council resolution on the Middle East and refused to cooperate with Dr. Jarring. In 1967 this policy met with an indignant Soviet rebuttal. In 1968-1969, however, the Soviet Union refrained from any direct criticism of Syria's position on the Arab-Isreali issue. Instead, Soviet press organs constantly pointed to "Syria's resolve to fight for the liberation of the occupied territories" and described Syria's stand as "understandable."[71]

Izvestiia's and *Krasnaia zvezda*'s support of Syria's militant rhetoric was consistent with their general line of unqualified support for the Arab national postulates, but *Pravda*'s position was somewhat inconsistent. It was, throughout this period, the chief proponent of a political settlement and took great pains to present the UAR's position along these lines. By giving voice to Syrian belligerence, *Pravda* only emphasized the yawning gap between its own policy and that of Syria.

Evidently, there was a consensus in Moscow to allow Syria what was denied to Egypt, namely, "its own point of view on party affairs, on the situation in the Arab world, and on the ways and means of liquidating the consequences of the Israeli aggression."[72]

The emergence of such a consensus (i.e., *Pravda*'s adherence to *Izvestiia*'s and *Krasnaia zvezda*'s consistent line) has two explanations: On the one hand, the Soviet tactics might have been dictated by the internal political situation prevailing in Syria, i.e., by the fact that the most militant faction was also the most pro-Soviet. Another explanation, which does not necessarily exclude the former, is that the readiness to tolerate Syria's belligerence reflected awareness of the preeminence of Egypt's, rather than Syria's, position on the Arab-Israeli issue. Once Egypt defined its position in support of a political settlement, Syria might well have followed Egypt's lead. Yet even if Syria were to persist in its refusal to negotiate with Israel, the Soviet loss would be negligible. A partial settlement on the Egyptian front, one that provided for the reopening of the Suez Canal, was much more important for Soviet interests than a settlement on the Golan Heights.

In at least one aspect, however, *Pravda*'s alignment with *Izvestiia* and *Krasnaia zvezda* was not complete. *Izvestiia* and *Krasnaia zvezda* gave prominence to the military aspect of Soviet-Syrian relations, but *Pravda* tended to play it down. Though giving publicity to official military exchanges (such as Marshal Grechko's March 1968 visit), *Pravda* refrained from printing any comments on the Syrian armed forces. The other two papers, on the other hand, indulged in lengthy expositions glorifying the Syrian army, its heroism, and its performance.

Thus, *Izvestiia*'s commentary of April 17, 1968,[73] described Syrian military men as "professional soldiers, fearless fighters dedicated to their combat tasks, imbued with high morale, resolved to defend the achievements of the revolution and give a decisive rebuff to the enemy's encroachments on the liberty and sovereignty of their motherland." In a similar vein, Colonel Sgibnev, who accompanied Marshal Grechko on his visit, wrote in *Krasnaia zvezda* on April 16, 1968:

> The Syrian army is a real modern army, equipped with up-to-date armaments [later in the article Sgibnev points out, with evident satisfaction, that this equipment is very well maintained]. The training is based on the achievements of leading military doctrine. . . . The soldiers train with great enthusiasm and show a high level of combat preparedness. The commanders manifest brilliant talent.

The high esteem for and exuberant satisfaction with the Syrian army was in sharp contrast with the reserve the same author had for the Egyptian armed forces.[74] Unfair as such a comparison may appear (the Syrian army's performance was hardly tested in actual combat in the postwar period), it nevertheless suggests that the Soviet military was more satisfied with the Syrian trainees than with the Egyptian. No less interesting is the fact that *Izvestiia* apparently shared the military's opinion.

Concerted Caution:
Attitudes toward the Syrian Ba'th

Pravda, Izvestiia, and *Krasnaia zvezda* apparently agreed that Syria should be allowed to have "its own point of view" not only on the Arab-Israeli issue but on internal affairs as well. Consequently, they refrained from subjecting the Syrian regime to scrutiny or criticism. Even *Pravda* did not embark upon any campaigns designed to accelerate the pace of Syria's "progressive" development. Instead, it adopted *Izvestiia*'s neutral, almost objective, manner of reporting.

In line with this approach, Soviet press commentaries refrained from endowing socialist epithets on the Syrian regime. Syria was referred to as a country that "had chosen the noncapitalist path of development" and was listed among the "progressive" regimes.[75] However, the term *undergoing socialist transformation,* frequently applied to Syria in 1966, was now reserved for Egypt alone. In this case, *Krasnaia zvezda* was the one to deviate from this line; it stated in an "independent" commentary that "the Syrian nation has embarked, with the help of the USSR, on the road leading to new socialist life."[76]

In contrast to the restraint evident in all three organs' independent commentaries, socialist phraseology was liberally employed when citing pronouncements by Syrian leaders. Thus, for example, on August 2, 1968, the three organs quoted the deputy secretary general of the Syrian Ba'th, Salah Jadid, to the effect that "the Syrian nation had chosen the socialist path of development."[77] Perhaps the best illustration of this policy was the Soviet-Syrian correspondence of April 23, 1968. A Soviet telegram greeting "the Syrian nation and government" on the independence day stated that "the Soviet nation follows with interest the efforts of the Syrian nation to carry out progressive socioeconomic transformation" (telegram signed by Kosygin). The Syrian response, signed by Prime Minister Zu'ayyin, was: "The Syrian nation is ready for any effort, any sacrifice, [needed for] the accomplishment of the socialist transformation."

The Soviet attitude toward the Syrian regime in general and the abstention from applying socialist epithets in particular (epithets earlier applied to the same regime and continually used in the case of Egypt) may perhaps have stemmed from the volatility of the internal situation in the Syrian Arab Republic.

During 1967 two conflicting schools of political thought crystallized within the Syrian Ba'th along the traditional lines of "radical" and "nationalist" orientations. The radicals were bent on assigning top priority to the policy of socialist transformation and its achievement in the fastest possible way. For this purpose, they were striving to reorganize the regime on the Soviet model, increase economic and political dependence on the USSR, and "pay" for it by allowing the Syrian communists a larger share in governmental affairs and aligning the country more closely with the communist bloc. They rejected any cooperation with "reactionary" Arab regimes and gave paramountcy to the principle of "popular liberation war." The nationalists, on the other hand, wanted to accord top priority to "armed struggle" against Israel. They demanded the adjustment of socialist ideology to the requirements of the defense effort as well as more reliance on Arab strength than on the socialist bloc. Domestically, they were prepared to collaborate with what they called "national progressive" forces, i.e., elements further to the right.

The radical wing was particularly dominant within the party's central apparatus, claiming also the support of some officers. The nationalist wing enjoyed the backing of many army officers as well as a considerable following among the party rank and file. It soon became apparent that these groupings were not equally cohesive, let alone powerful. While the more rigid military organization and hierarchy made the nationalist wing more monolithic, the radical civilians were split into several factions centered around key personalities and motivated by personal and sometimes confessional rivalries.[78]

The ups and downs of this protracted factional struggle may perhaps have been the reason for Soviet press caution. Criticizing or supporting one of the competing factions could, given the volatility of the situation, have involved substantial political risks. It is impossible to ascertain to what extent the official noncommitted approach was maintained in practice.[79] The Soviet press did manifest a uniform objectivity toward both factions.

There was yet another factor in the Syrian equation—the Syrian Communist party. The question of cooperation with the communists was one of the key issues in the intra-Ba'th struggle. The Communist party, for its part, maneuvered between the rival factions, stressing the points of agreement between itself and the ruling group, yet insisting on cooperating only with the "left wing" and stepping up pressures for greater participation in the government.[80] Though it is extremely difficult to assess the extent to which the Syrian Communist party acted independently or upon orders from Moscow, it is clear that the very existence of such a powerful party (headed by a highly respected former Comintern activist) made the situation even more complicated. The slightest mistake could have proved detrimental to the Syrian communists or the Soviet position in that country or both. The situation appeared to dictate caution to both the Syrian communists and their Soviet comrades.

The March 1969 Crisis Changes Soviet Attitudes

Moscow maintained its official neutrality throughout 1968. The October 1968 ouster of Prime Minister Zu'ayyin and Foreign Minister Makhus, both prominent leaders of the pro-Soviet radical wing, failed to elicit any public response from Moscow. The Soviet press reported on October 30, 1968, that a new government had been formed in Syria but that "key positions remained unchanged." The fact that Zu'ayyin and Makhus were not included in the new cabinet was passed over in silence.

By the end of 1968, the uneasy truce between the radical and nationalist factions (headed by Salah Jadid and Defense Minister Hafiz al-Asad, respectively) started to crumble, reaching crisis proportions by the early spring of 1969. According to Lebanese press reports, Syria was on the verge of a civil war, with both wings, civilian and military, actually preparing for it.[81]

The seriousness of the March crisis and the danger of a

civil war changed the Soviet official attitude. Interestingly enough, *Krasnaia zvezda* initiated the change.

As early as March 6, 1969, *Krasnaia zvezda* published a lengthy commentary that called attention to the "increasing activity of internal and external reaction in the Syrian Arab Republic." Moreover, it warned, "the internal reaction joined hands with imperialist circles, *striving to interrupt the process of socialist* transformation . . . to weaken Syria's position in its struggle against the Israeli occupiers, to *undermine its* international position and its *relations with the forces of liberation and with the socialist countries.*"[82]

The implications of *Krasnaia zvezda*'s statement were clear. The situation in Syria could no longer be regarded as an internal affair, since the ascendancy of reactionary forces (i.e., Asad's faction) threatened the very basis of the Soviet-Syrian alliance and thereby the Soviet position in Syria. Implying that Soviet strategic interests were at stake, *Krasnaia zvezda* may well have been calling for action aimed at tipping the scales in favor of the faction that could be trusted to maintain friendship with the USSR.[83]

If the March 6 statement was indeed an appeal for action, it remained a lonely cry. No other Soviet press organ voiced support for *Krasnaia zvezda*'s opinion. Yet the Lebanese newspaper *al-Hayat* reported on March 8 that a meeting of Soviet bloc ambassadors was held in Damascus to discuss joint efforts to save the Jadid faction. The same source indicated that Moscow had threatened to discontinue arms shipments to Syria.[84] This report, if accurate, may support the conclusion that the Soviet military's advice was at least partially heeded by the Soviet decision makers, perhaps even over the opposition of other groups. This conclusion is based on the assumption that *Krasnaia zvezda* did in fact reflect the military's opinions as voiced in closed forums. *Izvestiia*'s and *Pravda*'s silence may be interpreted either as opposition to the military's stand or as an indication that these two groups were not invited to voice their opinion publicly on this particular issue.

Whatever the reasons for *Pravda*'s and *Izvestiia*'s silence may have been, it was not maintained for long. *Izvestiia* voiced its opinion on March 20. It went to great pains to refute "panicky reports" that claimed that Syria was on the "verge of internal upheaval." Though *Izvestiia* did not identify the propagators of these "panicky reports," there is little doubt that it had in mind *Krasnaia zvezda*'s report and presumably intelligence briefings submitted in closed forums.

Using the credibility a firsthand report gives, *Izvestiia*'s commentator Demchenko wrote:

> I have witnessed several coups in Arab countries. However, the appearance of Damascus these days is not even reminiscent of the picture typical to such events. There are no tanks on the streets. . . . Military outposts have not been fortified. The city center is bursting with life. . . . All the ministries are working as usual. Both central newspapers appear daily, and there are no limitations on internal travel. . . . The attention of the country does not center on preparations for any coups but rather on the deteriorating situation on the front with Israel.

Thus, Demchenko, presumably repeating the opinion the *Izvestiia* group voiced in closed forums, apparently indicated that there was no basis for Soviet concern or, consequently, for Soviet action. More significantly still, since Syria's "main concern was the confrontation with Israel" (i.e., it needed continuous Soviet military assistance), it was doubtful whether *any* faction would venture a rift with the USSR.

Izvestiia hastened to add that the discussion within the Ba'th did not center on, and therefore could not affect, Syria's progressive orientation. "The path chosen is beyond any question, beyond any doubt." Therefore, in *Izvestiia*'s opinion, the problem could and should have been solved by the Ba'th itself, specifically by its forthcoming extraordinary conference. "Experience shows that the party is capable of solving acute crises. A compromise could be worked out in this case as well," concluded *Izvestiia*'s commentator.

By asserting that the crisis in Syria was an internal affair of secondary importance, one that did not threaten either the Soviet strategic position in Syria or Syria's basic political orientation, *Izvestiia* adopted a position diametrically opposed to that of the military. It should be stressed, however, that although they differed over the *evaluation* of a given situation, both organs viewed the problem through the same prism, namely, the Soviet strategic interest. In other words, the dispute between the military and the *Izvestiia* group did not focus on the *principle* of Soviet interference in Syria's internal affairs, but rather on the *applicability* of this principle to the situation prevailing in Syria in March 1969.

When *Pravda* broke its silence and joined the discussion on March 26, it presented an uneven combination of the two conflicting approaches. *Pravda* appealed, in the name of the Syrian Communist Party, for a "swift solution of the crisis," "national unity," and "safeguarding the antiimperialist line."[85] In addition, it cited appeals by "mass organizations" calling for the continuation of "the progressive line, strengthening of the economy and defenses, and liquidation of the results of the Israeli aggression." Through this "subtle" remark, *Pravda* made it clear that the continuation of the "antiimperialist line" was a prerequisite for further Soviet military and economic aid. One cannot but assume that this point was conveyed to Syria through other channels as well. *Izvestiia,* apparently agreeing with *Pravda*'s position (or, more accurately, with *Pravda*'s compromise) published a virtually identical statement. *Krasnaia zvezda* kept its silence, presumably expressing thereby its disaffection with the compromise and its adherence to its earlier advocacy of decisive action.[86]

The intra-Ba'th crisis was finally brought before an extraordinary session of the party. The Congress concluded on March 30, 1969, without resolving the basic impasse. The existing balance of power within the Ba'th was maintained, Defense Minister Asad continued to enjoy a free hand in all matters pertaining to defense, and Jadid kept control over the party apparatus.[87]

It is extremely difficult to assess actual Soviet behavior in the face of the March crisis and the extent to which this behavior corresponded to or reflected the internal dispute evident in the Soviet press. According to a UPI report of April 12, 1969, only because of Soviet "intervention" had a compromise been achieved and the civilian wing remained in power. According to this report, the Soviet ambassador had handed Asad an ultimatum threatening a break of relations, a halt in arms deliveries, and a demand for immediate repayment of all loans unless he made "some act of loyalty" to Moscow.[88] This report, if correct, would suggest that the USSR actually acted upon the military's advice and exerted tremendous pressure on Asad. However, the accuracy of the UPI report is questionable. It seems unlikely in retrospect that the USSR would go to such extremes just to achieve a shaky compromise between Asad and Jadid. In other words, the UPI report appears doubtful in light of the actual outcome of the alleged Soviet pressure.

More crucially, a course of action such as the one described in the report was bound to involve substantial risk. To submit an ultimatum meant to put at stake the entire network of relations with Syria and perhaps even imperil the Soviet position in other Arab countries. Given the unpredictability and volatility of the situation, the Soviet Union could hardly have afforded such a gamble.

On the basis of available evidence, it appears that the military's suggestion was only partially heeded by the Soviet decision makers. That is to say, the Soviet position was brought home to the conflicting factions through some subtle threats (as in *Pravda*'s March 26 statement) rather than through heavy-handed pressure.

The hypothesis that the USSR acted more along the lines of *Pravda*'s statement than along the lines advocated by the military is further reinforced by the three press organs' reactions to the Ba'th's extraordinary conference and its results. *Krasnaia zvezda* simply ignored the whole event, thus presumably indicating continued adherence to its opinion that timely action could have secured a more favorable development of the situation. *Pravda* and *Izvestiia,* on the other hand, voiced unqualified satisfaction with the compromise achieved. Thus, on April 7, 1969, *Pravda* noted that the final resolution adopted by the Congress called for the "consolidation of all political and economic efforts for the struggle against the usurpers."[89] According to *Pravda*'s report, "the

Congress endorsed the strengthening of relations with the socialist countries, first and foremost with the USSR." *Izvestiia* followed suit, publishing an identical report on April 8. 'Krasnaia zvezda* remained silent.

On April 12, in an article by its Damascus correspondent, Medvedko, *Pravda* aligned itself *ex post facto* with *Izvestiia*'s opinion (voiced in the midst of the crisis) that the crisis was "much ado about nothing." It also asserted that the results of the Congress and "the reconciliation within the [Ba'th] evidenced political maturity and were greeted with satisfaction by Syria's friends."[90]

The argumentative character of *Pravda*'s and *Izvestiia*'s pronouncements might indicate that the military was persisting in its criticism of the policy adopted, even though *Krasnaia zvezda*'s reaction was "only" continued silence. In fact, *Pravda* and *Izvestiia* went to great pains to rebut the main points of *Krasnaia zvezda*'s argument:

> The Conference *reendorsed the basic principles of foreign, inter-Arab, and internal policy safeguarding* successful movement on the *progressive* path of *development.* The Conference ordered the new party leadership to continue and develop cooperation with other Syrian progressive forces. . . . Stressing the necessity to mobilize all forces and all resources for the struggle for the liquidation of the results of the Israeli aggression, the Conference underlined the need to *continue with the social and economic transformation,* which will guarantee the success of this struggle. On the international plane, particular attention was paid to the endorsement of a course aimed at *strengthening all-around cooperation and friendly relations with the socialist countries, first and foremost with the Soviet Union.* The results of the conference would be instrumental in the stabilization and *strengthening of the progressive regime* in Syria and would increase its contribution to the antiimperialist struggle.[91]

On April 23, 1969, *Pravda* published a statement attributed to President Nur al-Din al-Atasi that refuted any allegations about Soviet interference in Syria's internal affairs. To Atasi's statement *Pravda* added the explanation that "the growing authority of the Soviet Union . . . was a thorn in the side of Syria's enemies, who did not hesitate to falsify the truth and spread rumors alleging Soviet interference in Syrian internal affairs."[92]

For all intents and purposes, the crisis was over. So apparently was *Krasnaia zvezda*'s disaffection with the course of events in Syria. When President Atasi arrived in Moscow at the beginning of July, *Krasnaia zvezda* greeted him with the same exuberant enthusiasm as *Pravda* and *Izvestiia.*

Brezhnev, Kosygin, Podgornyi, Ponomarev, and others were on hand to greet the Syrian delegation at the Moscow airport. For the next nine days, the visit was the focus of Soviet press attention. Daily reports, often accompanied by photos, reviewed the delegation's talks, meetings, and sightseeing trips. Numerous articles stressing the vital importance of Syrian-Soviet friendship were published. On July 11, with the delegation still in Moscow, the Soviet media reported the signing of a contract providing for "further development of economic and technical cooperation between the Syrian Arab Republic and the USSR." Evidently, the reconciliation had some very tangible underpinning.

The joint communiqué published on July 13 was an exercise in diplomacy and tact. All controversial issues were carefully glossed over. Both parties jointly condemned Israeli "aggression, which creates a dangerous situation in the Middle East." Furthermore, it was stated, the USSR and the SAR "consider it necessary to strive for the safeguarding of the lawful rights and interests of the Arab nations, including the Arab nation of Palestine." Needless to say, the idea of a political settlement was not even mentioned.[93]

As far as internal Ba'th affairs were concerned, Atasi apparently received official Soviet endorsement of the new balance of power. The new leadership was acclaimed as "carrying out a socialist transformation," thereby elevating the Atasi regime to a position of ideological parity with the UAR.

The spirit of reconciliation and mutual goodwill prevailed throughout the rest of 1969 and, in fact, throughout the remaining part of the period under discussion.

It appears that the March 1969 crisis had some sobering effect on both sides, promoting a realization that good relations were in their mutual interest. The Asad faction must have realized that the achievement of its declared goal was, to a large extent, linked to and dependent on continued Soviet aid and support. The Soviet leaders, on the other hand, had to abandon the hope that Syria would become the first Soviet satellite in the Middle East. The March crisis made it clear that the radicals' known or alleged connection with the Syrian Communist Party and the USSR could easily turn into a weapon in the hands of their opponents. Moreover, the Syrian communists' meddling in the Ba'th's internal politics ultimately worked against their own interests as well as against those of the Soviet Union, which was naturally considered responsible for communist activity. Therefore, presumably under Soviet pressure, the Syrian communists held back so as not to polarize the Ba'th and, from April 1969 on, stopped being a destabilizing factor in the internal power struggle.[94]

The subsequent development of Soviet-Syrian relations, which were not marred even by such events as the anticommunist campaign of May 1970 or Asad's take-over in November of that same year, suggests the ascendancy of a new line in Soviet policy, namely, noninterference in the internal affairs of a "progressive" regime as long as that regime maintained its basic antiimperialist line in the international arena. This line, advocated throughout by *Izvestiia,* became by spring 1970 the point of convergence of *Pravda*'s, *Izvestiia*'s, and *Krasnaia zvezda*'s approaches; the trade union organ remained the only proponent of the earlier policy.

However, before proceeding with an analysis of developments in 1970, Soviet attitudes toward yet another "progressive" regime call upon our attention.

Iraq

Attitudes toward Iraq:
Touchstone of Basic Schisms

Soviet attitudes toward Iraq as expressed in the Soviet

press in the period 1968-1969 constitute one of the most interesting case studies of divergent approaches toward the "progressive" Arab regimes. The relatively moderate Soviet military and economic investment in Iraq and, *ipso facto,* the relative lack of commitment to and involvement in that country made it an ideal forum for discussion. Since divergent opinions were expressed much more freely about Iraq than about other "progressive" regimes, attitudes toward that country may well be the touchstone of the general lines pursued by the three organs under investigation.

For *Pravda,* Iraq was mainly an object of criticism and censure. Most, if not all, of the shortcomings it found in Iraq could easily be found in Syria or in Egypt. By the same token, its criticism of Iraq was applicable, at least by implication, to all "progressive" Arab regimes.

Pravda depicted Iraq as an "unstable country, troubled by frequent coups," lacking any "democratic governing organs [since] its parliament is not functioning and local officials are nominated instead of being elected." The development of the Iraqi "revolution is handicapped by the size and level of influence of the bureaucrats and reserve officers [who are] closely connected with the big bourgeoisie." Moreover, lamented *Pravda* commentators, "in Iraq, as in Egypt, the army is the backbone of the regime, with the officers enjoying far-reaching privileges and a high standard of living."[95]

Pravda's reluctance to offer any advice about what Iraq should do to correct the shortcomings reinforces our initial impression that the CPSU organ was less interested in Iraq per se than in what the Iraqi regime stood for. In other words, Iraq was employed as a symbol or euphemism for all the "progressive" Arab regimes. As has been indicated above, the *Pravda* group did harbor certain expectations about the direction and nature of the social evolution of the "progressive" regimes. Consequently, disillusionment must have been all the more. Thus, it is possible that in denouncing Iraq, the *Pravda* group was giving vent to its general frustration with the pace of the "socialist transformation" in the Arab world.

Krasnaia zvezda took a different approach. Of a total of

twenty-two items it published in 1968 about Iraq, all but three were on military affairs.[96] *Krasnaia zvezda*'s preoccupation with military affairs may be further illustrated by the fact that Marshal Grechko's March 1968 visit to Iraq was reported seven times in *Krasnaia zvezda,* twice in *Izvestiia,* and only once in *Pravda.* The same ratio prevailed when the Soviet organs reported the September 1968 visit of an Iraqi military delegation or the anchoring of a Soviet naval squadron in the port of Basra.[97]

Krasnaia zvezda's all-military thrust probably reflected the Soviet military's perception of Iraq as a base and springboard for naval presence and expansion in the Persian Gulf and Indian Ocean. On another level, by ignoring Iraq's internal affairs *Krasnaia zvezda* might have been arguing that the ideo-political attributes of a regime were of secondary interest to the USSR, especially if that regime could offer high strategic payoffs.

Although it failed to show even the slightest interest in Iraq's politics, *Krasnaia zvezda* nevertheless scrutinized the Iraqi armed forces, particularly the officer corps. "Iraqi senior officers hold physical effort in contempt," wrote Colonel Sgibnev in *Krasnaia zvezda* on April 14, 1968. "They refuse to participate in training, leaving their units to junior and noncommissioned officers. They are not interested in the personal problems and wellbeing of their men."

Though the criticism was balanced with assurances that "the shortcomings are recognized" and that "first steps toward improvement have already been undertaken," the general tone of disaffection was readily apparent. So was the implicit applicability of *Krasnaia zvezda*'s criticism to the Syrian and Egyptian armed forces. Thus, *Krasnaia zvezda* employed a technique similar to that used by *Pravda,* namely, criticizing Iraq with Syria and Egypt in mind. This technique may perhaps be best described as an application of the old Arab proverb "na qidir 'ala hamatuh qum la mihatuh," which in free translation means "one hits one's wife instead of one's mother-in-law."

Izvestiia did not participate in these "sublimation" exercises. Its manifest lack of interest in Iraq's internal politics (or, for that matter, officer-soldier relations within the Iraqi armed forces) was consistent with its general line of noninterference in the internal affairs of the "progressive" Arab regimes. Since the *Izvestiia* group harbored no illusions about the real nature of these regimes and therefore had scant hopes about their socialist prospects, it hardly needed a safety valve to vent its frustration. It consistently maintained that the Arab regimes should be embraced for what they were, for what they could offer in strategic payoffs. In terms of the Soviet interest, as perceived by the *Izvestiia* group, the Arabs' internal affairs and "progressive" endeavors were of secondary importance.

Izvestiia's commentaries on Iraq clearly indicated that in this case the USSR could and should expect economic as well as military-strategic returns. Nearly all of its references to Iraq focused on the Iraqi economy, particularly its oil.[98]

The extent and nature of Soviet interest in Middle Eastern oil is a point of controversy among experts. Without engaging in lengthy deliberation, I would venture support for those who assert that there is a Soviet long-term political and economic interest in Arab oil. First and foremost, the Soviet Union or, for that matter, any power cannot possibly remain indifferent to oil if it is at all concerned with the politics of the region. Since the Middle East is an arena of superpower rivalry, oil, the region's main resource, can hardly be excluded from the equation.

On the economic level, "presently observable schedules of production and internal consumption in the European communist area indicate that the net export position of the group will be under no threat in the next few years, but by 1980 an overall CEMA deficit is likely."[99] At the same time, the Soviet Union may have an economic interest in importing oil and gas on a tangible scale. Moreover, assuming that Soviet payment imbalances with the industrialized countries have not evaporated by the end of the decade, oil and gas will continue to offer an attractive vehicle for augmenting Soviet hard currency earnings, particularly in view of the apparent trend toward rising world market prices. "It seems a reasonable bet that by the end of the decade the CEMA countries as a group will be shopping for something of the order of 100 million tons of crude oil equivalent."[100]

If the Soviet Union emerges as a significant oil importer, rising prices (if Moscow comes forward as a simple buyer from a state-owned company) and escalating royalty rates (if the import is the end result of a development contract) could adversely affect short-run Soviet economic interests. As a buyer of oil extracted by others, the USSR is unlikely to offer a straight hard currency deal. Its trade in oil, as in other goods, will probably continue to depend heavily on bilateral agreements in which technical assistance and producers' goods—or arms—are offered in exchange for the desired import.[101]

Professor Becker's analysis may shed some light on both *Izvestiia*'s emphasis on Iraq's oil wealth and its refusal to condemn Iraq's internal policy. If a long-term need for imported oil was indeed perceived by the Soviet economic planners, they could have argued that ostracizing Iraq would prove detrimental to the USSR's own interest. Moreover, even in the short run and on a purely economic level, trade between the Soviet Union and Iraq (producers' goods for oil) could have appeared more attractive to the *Izvestiia* group than trade between the USSR and, say, the UAR (producers' goods for cotton). This point is further reinforced by an *Izvestiia* commentary entitled "Mutual Benefit," which states that "Regardless of the obvious outrage of Western oil magnates, the world oil market is becoming an arena of co-operation between the socialist and the Arab countries, co-operation based on principles of mutual benefit and *genuine economic equality*."[102]

This article clearly implied that, in *Izvestiia*'s opinion, Iraq could offer much more than a profitable economic deal. "Commenting on [an agreement signed between the Soviet Union and Iraq in June 1969 providing for Soviet assistance in oil production], the American news agency Associated Press ... termed this event a 'first achievement of a policy aimed at strengthening Soviet influence in the Persian Gulf.' " Though *Izvestiia* hastened to add that AP "twisted the facts," the démenti was far from forceful, particularly in view of

Izvestiia's remark that "the Yankees' outrage is understandable." Obviously, a Soviet press organ cannot speak of spreading Soviet influence (i.e., an imperialist practice) without employing Aesopian language. The obliqueness of the remark notwithstanding, *Izvestiia*'s point was entirely clear: Iraq should be embraced for the economic and strategic benefits it could offer Moscow. Consequently, a policy alienating Iraq was dysfunctional and detrimental to the Soviet interest. Moreover, in *Izvestiia*'s opinion, the same yardstick should be applied to Soviet relations with all the "progressive" Arab regimes. Interest—political, economic, strategic, or any combination thereof—should be the paramount criterion determining Soviet policy in the Middle East (and presumably elsewhere).

Comparative analysis of *Pravda*'s and *Izvestiia*'s divergent attitudes toward Iraq graphically illustrates how far apart their positions were. The evidence presented above clearly indicates that *Pravda*'s dogmatism was constantly challenged by *Izvestiia*'s pragmatism. *Izvestiia* considered strategic and political benefits enough to warrant extensive Soviet aid, but *Pravda* consistently argued that ideological "conversion," (i.e., the "progressive" regimes' continuous drift toward the Soviet model of socialism) could not and should not be excluded from the equation. In practice, the discrepancy between the positions of *Pravda* and *Izvestiia* presumably found its reflection in debates over the course of action to be adopted in response to internal events in the "progressive" Arab regimes. On the evidence available, the *Izvestiia* group probably argued a laissez faire approach as long as a regime adhered to a basic pro-Soviet line. The *Pravda* group, on the other hand, presumably advocated exerting a more vigorous influence on Arab politics, both on the internal and the international levels.

The divergent lines pursued by these groups came to their final clash in the summer of 1968.

The July 1968 Coup d'Etat: A Turning Point in Soviet Relations with the "Progressive" Arab Regimes

In July 1968 General Ahmad Hasan al-Bakr ousted Abd-

al-Rahman Aref and assumed power in Baghdad. The coup
d'etat and its aftermath proved to be a watershed for the
three Soviet press organs and a turning point in *Pravda*'s attitude.

Initially, *Pravda, Izvestiia,* and *Krasnaia zvezda* carried
identical reports of the take-over, which "came to secure national unity, legality, and democratic liberties."[103] All three
duly quoted the new regime's promises "to continue
[former] oil policies, honor international obligations, and
strengthen friendship with the Soviet Union."[104] Apparently,
these promises were considered satisfactory by *Izvestiia* and
Krasnaia zvezda. As of July 24, the Iraqi coup d'etat was
simply taken off their agenda.

Pravda, on the other hand, engaged in a unique public
dialogue with the new regime. Almost every day, it published
Iraqi declarations of friendship and pledges of loyalty; yet it
did so without one word of comment and under such noncommittal headlines as "Declaration of the Iraqi Government."[105] It was a one-sided courtship, with the Iraqi leaders
attempting to solicit Soviet endorsement and pledges to continue with the aid programs, and with *Pravda* ready to give
publicity to the Iraqi "flattery" yet denying support or
endorsement.

Pravda soon clarified the rationale behind its behavior. In
an article on August 12, it made it quite clear that it was not
ready to bestow endorsement simply because the Bakr regime
had replaced the Aref junta, which, "because of its corruption and a yawning gap between slogans and deeds, did not
enjoy anybody's sympathy."[106] Having made clear that it
should not be counted among the mourners of the deposed
regime, *Pravda* indicated that endorsement would be contingent upon a certain reciprocity, namely, the extension of pro-
Soviet policy to the internal arena. "In Iraq, as in many other
countries of the Third World, there is a wide gap between
antiimperialist foreign policy, including close relations with
the socialist countries, and internal policies, including the im-
prisonment of thousands of political activists."[107] Such a gap
would no longer be tolerated, warned *Pravda*, stressing at the
same time the vital importance of continued Soviet aid and

support for the future development of Iraq.

Pravda also presented what appeared to be a detailed list of demands, the fulfillment of which would attest to the new regime's sincere intention to close the gap between foreign and domestic policy. The main demands were "the unconditional fulfillment of the amnesty decree" and the establishment of "a united front of all national-progressive organizations, including the communists."[108]

Evidently, the Iraqi response (if any) to this thinly veiled ultimatum was deemed unsatisfactory. On August 23 another Iraqi declaration of friendship was printed without any comment. Three days later, *Pravda* submitted its second "ultimatum," which was signed authoritatively "own information" (this term generally identifies an important editorial statement):

> The international progressive public [euphemism for the USSR] received with interest the declaration of the new government concerning amnesty.... However, several incidents evoke indignation. Many communists, particularly leaders, were not released from prison. Others were forced to pay their way by signing declarations denouncing communist activity. Such actions weaken the significance of the positive steps undertaken by the new regime and prevent normalization. The release of political prisoners will be the acid test of the new regime's policy.[109]

Pravda's position is unique in both form and content. As has been indicated, at least since 1964 official Soviet policy gave priority to relations with the ruling parties of the "progressive" Arab regimes over, and at the expense of, relations with independent Communist parties. Overtly championing the cause of the Iraqi Communist party and presenting further relations with the ruling elite as contingent upon its attitude toward the communists, *Pravda* abandoned the nonparty approach (which, belittling the role and significance of a distinct communist organization, conceptualizes Soviet interest and communist behavior in terms of good relations with ruling elites) and adopted the party-oriented approach (which, regarding the independence of Arab communist parties as important for Soviet policy, envisages dialectical relations between the communists and the incumbent regimes).

Pravda probably considered the change of regime a suitable time to present ultimatums on behalf of the communists. The inherent weakness of the Bakr regime, Iraq's strained relations with other Arab countries, and especially Iraq's dependence on continued Soviet aid and support made the new regime highly susceptible to Soviet pressure.

Neither *Izvestiia* nor *Krasnaia zvezda* participated in this public debate with Iraq. *Pravda*'s solitary defense of the Iraqi Communist party may be explained by the possible existence of a division of labor among the Soviet press organs, with *Pravda* naturally being entrusted with representing and championing the interests of fraternal Communist parties. However, *Izvestiia*'s and *Krasnaia zvezda*'s abstention probably attested to their opposition to *Pravda*'s approach and their continuous adherence to the nonparty orientation. Consistent with their general line, the *Izvestiia* and *Krasnaia zvezda* groups might have argued that *Pravda*'s position was no more than a risky gamble, dysfunctional in terms of the Soviet political, economic, and strategic interests in Iraq.

In any event, *Pravda*'s last ultimatum (August 26, 1968) proved effective. On September 9, *Pravda* could announce on its front page (under a banner headline) that "unconditional amnesty" had been granted to all political prisoners in Iraq. Two days later, in a lengthy article by its senior commentator Primakov, *Pravda* praised the Bakr regime for its "positive steps aimed at *internal*, antiimperialist consolidation." At the same time, the new regime's "efforts to solve the Kurdish problem" were endorsed.[110]

It appears, however, that the shift in *Pravda*'s position and its much delayed readiness to endorse Bakr were promoted not only, or not mainly, by the improvement in Ba'th–Communist party relations. By the end of August, the Bakr government took a step that was probably more important to Moscow than the toleration of communist activity in Iraq,[111] namely, it voiced unequivocal support for the Soviet invasion of Czechoslovakia. The Iraqi statement, the most strongly worded of several Arab pronouncements in this regard, was given great prominence in *Pravda*.[112] Considering the Western communists' criticism of Soviet action against Czechoslovakia, the Iraqi pronouncement must have been extremely pleasing to the CPSU. Furthermore, the position of the Iraqi government and, for that matter, the position of the Egyptian and Syrian governments as well, presented the whole issue of alliance in a new light. The "progressive" Arab regimes, though admittedly noncommunist and even anticommunist in their internal policies, nevertheless sided with the USSR and supported its policy when support was most needed. The position of the Arab governments might have led those within the *Pravda* group to conclude that in critical situations clients might prove to be more reliable than purely ideologically motivated followers. Henceforth, *Pravda* adhered consistently to the nonparty orientation, giving priority to relations with the ruling elites of the Arab regimes over relations with independent communist parties. Never again in the period under review did it explicitly condemn an Arab "progressive" regime for persecuting communists or leftists.

Moreover, these events precipitated a gradual shift in the CPSU's general attitude to the internal makeup and policies of the Arab "progressive" regimes—as first became apparent in the case of Iraq.

Throughout the remaining part of 1968 and 1969, *Pravda* consistently abstained from denouncing Bakr's internal policies, even though the previous critical approach was still being taken toward Syria and especially Egypt.[113] Subsequently, probably under the impact of the dual process of increasing military commitment and gradual disillusionment with the socialist prospects of the "progressive" Arab regimes, *Pravda*'s line virtually converged with the lines of *Izvestiia* and *Krasnaia zvezda*. By spring 1970, all three were united in the opinion that the internal policies and composition of the "progressive" Arab regimes were not of major interest to the USSR as long as they adhered to their basic "antiimperialist" policy in the international arena, i.e., as long as they maintained close ties with the USSR. Moreover, it was the opinion of the press organs of the CPSU, the Soviet Council of Ministers, and the Ministry of Defense, that pursuit of an antiimperialist line was sufficient to entitle these regimes to ever increasing Soviet aid and support.

Part 3
Convergence and Polarization within the Soviet Leadership

6. From Involvement to Commitment: Debate and Decision

Moscow's Dilemma

The first month of 1970 witnessed a dangerous escalation on the Israeli-Egyptian front. Employing their air force as a "flying artillery," the Israelis struck repeatedly at targets in the Nile Delta and as little as five miles from the center of Cairo. Egyptian-manned MIG-21 C/D interceptor aircraft and SA-2 Guideline surface-to-air missiles proved all but totally ineffective against these attacks: the Israelis flew around and through the former and beneath the latter. In the process, some 150 of the UAR's small corps of trained pilots were shot down. At the same time, Israeli aircraft consistently and successfully attacked the SA-2 sites themselves, opening up gaps in the system and preventing its restoration.[1] The local effects on the standing and credibility of President Nasser's regime were considerable, and the Soviet Union, the manifest inadequacy of whose equipment and training was demonstrated daily, was exposed to contempt.

On January 22, 1970, President Nasser secretly arrived in Moscow, apparently to impress upon the Soviet leaders the seriousness of the situation and to demand the introduction of "modern weapons that will offset Israeli air superiority."[2] (Details of the January visit remained secret. No Soviet source ever referred to it. The UAR public did not learn about the visit until July 1970, when Nasser revealed that on January 22 of that year he had arrived secretly in Moscow "in order to review the situation." Nasser added that "after four days of talks, the Soviet leaders declared that they would throw all their weight behind us in assisting us to defend our homeland. They told me that the required support would reach us in no more than thirty days. The Soviet leaders honored their promise."[3])

Moscow was faced with a difficult decision. On one hand, the military and political situation appeared critical indeed. On the other hand, Nasser was asking for weapons that had never been deployed outside the Warsaw Pact borders. Moreover, in view of the lack of adequate know-how in the Egyptian army, the supply of such weapons was bound to involve Soviet personnel directly in an ongoing conflict.

The initial decision to rearm the UAR in the wake of the Six-Day War and the Soviet commitment to help the UAR recover its territory had acted as a boomerang. In early 1970, Moscow was again faced with the dilemma of a risky direct military intervention on Egypt's side or abstention at the cost of losing prestige, credibility, and, possibly, strategic positions. This time, however, Soviet maneuverability was seriously circumscribed. Aloofness was no longer a viable alternative.

Faced with such a quandary, Moscow initially tried to opt for some halfway house. It introduced newer types of arms: MIG-21 J interceptors, with greater speed, longer range, and better armament than the MIG-21 C or D; ZSU-23/4 four-level 23mm antiaircraft guns; SA-2 missiles with shorter reaction time than earlier models; and, above all, mobile SA-3 Goa surface-to-air missiles with a far better low-altitude capability than the SA-2. According to an estimate published by *Strategic Survey,* as of March 31, 1970, some 4000 Soviet operators were present in Egypt and manning twenty-two SA-3 sites. (SA sites normally contain four launchers each.)[4]

The stepped-up arms deliveries were accompanied by vigorous political activity. A few days after Nasser's departure from Moscow, Prime Minister Kosygin was reported to have sent a message to President Nixon, requesting the United States to restrain Israel: "We would like to tell you in all frankness that if Israel continues its adventurism . . . the Soviet Union will be forced to see to it that the Arab states have means at their disposal with the help of which due rebuff to the arrogant aggressor could be given."[5] Kosygin's message may be compared to the Soviet premier's use of the hot line in June 1967, which in both cases showed Soviet reluctance to commit itself directly to battle.

However, the initial measures proved insufficient. The Israeli raids continued, though by mid-March the Israeli air force limited its activity mainly to the Canal zone.[6] In his March 20 television speech Defense Minister Moshe Dayan defined the stepped-up Soviet arms supplies as "the first stage of the Sovietization of the Egyptian war machine." And he added: "The Russians are building a system on the ground that will permit an increasing Sovietization of Egyptian warfare and facilitate the piloting of Soviet planes by Soviet crews. I do not expect this to occur, but steps have been taken to make this possible."

Dayan's evaluation proved shortsighted. Within thirty-eight days, Israeli sources reported that Soviet pilots were flying operational missions for Egypt.[7]

The decision to commit Soviet personnel directly to combat was preceded by a heated public discussion that swept the Soviet press, one that presumably reflected debate within the Soviet leadership between those in favor of deepening Soviet involvement through direct participation in Egypt's defense and those who feared that an escalation of the Soviet involvement could lead to direct American participation in the conflict and increase the danger of superpower confrontation. Analysis of this discussion may provide interesting insights into the Soviet decision-making process.

Debate and Decision

Krasnaia zvezda was the first to air its opinion publicly. On March 14, it wrote:

> In order to be worthy of the lofty title of internationalist, one cannot make do with words and wishes. *Practical* steps are necessary, along with *active* participation in the struggle of other nations for freedom and independence.[8]

A day later, another article indignantly pointed out that the UAR's air space was unprotected and that Egyptian citizens were exposed to barbarous air raids.[9] The commentator quoted Nasser's claim that the Israeli air force was three times as strong as the Egyptian. This was so because Israel had three pilots for every aircraft, which enabled each plane to carry out nine sorties a day. "The *insufficient* number of Egyptian pilots does not permit more than three sorties a day for each plane." Moreover, in accordance with Nasser's instructions, one group of pilots was constantly undergoing training; another group was continually kept on the alert; and the rest were under orders to avoid dogfights with enemy planes (apparently in order not to lose more pilots). "Such a policy will bear fruit after some time; but meanwhile Israel enjoys supremacy [and is] increasing it by recruiting Western mercenaries as pilots," the commentator concluded.

The detailed description of the plight of the Egyptian air force, together with the emphasis on the fact that a shortage of pilots was Egypt's main stumbling block, spoke for itself. And if Israel was recruiting foreign mercenaries, was it not "the internationalist duty" of Soviet pilots to take part in Egypt's defense?

On March 18, *Krasnaia zvezda*'s weekly political commentary stated that "the Arabs are not alone in their struggle. Their friends will not deny them the aid necessary to secure their vital interests."[10]

Krasnaia zvezda's commentators recurrently stressed that Israel was "damaging the military potential of the UAR . . . especially its missile network."[11] This admission was inconsistent with Soviet allegations that claimed that Israel was bombing civilian targets.[12] But it may well have been an implicit demand on the part of the Ministry of Defense that Soviet military installations be defended against destruction. (The Soviet military must have been particularly anxious to protect the recently supplied ultramodern missiles manned by Soviet operators.)

On March 21, *Krasnaia zvezda*'s solitary challenge to official Soviet policy was answered by *Pravda;* Vice-President Sadat's speech was the forum of this esoteric debate. *Pravda* and *Krasnaia zvezda* were the only two press organs to publish Sadat's speech, with each opting to cite different parts of it. *Krasnaia zvezda* cited extensively Sadat's description of the American-Israeli plot to overthrow the Egyptian regime: the USA gave this assignment to Israel with a deadline of June 6, 1970, the date on which American evacuation of Wheelus Field (American airbase in Libya) was to have been completed.

Pravda, however, referred only briefly to the "imperialist intention to overthrow the UAR regime" and dealt neither with the impact of the Israeli air raids on the morale of the Egyptian population nor with the direct connection (stressed in the passage quoted by *Krasnaia zvezda*) between the air raids and the stability of the Nasser regime. *Pravda* defined the air raids as no more than "another stage in the escalation of the Israeli aggression." Equally enlightening is the fact that while *Krasnaia zvezda* quoted Sadat on "the noble stand of the Soviet Union and the many-sided aid it grants Egypt in the struggle against imperialism and aggression," *Pravda* simply left this passage out.

Krasnaia zvezda warned against a real and *immediate* danger to the Egyptian regime and, by implication, to the Soviet position in that country. If Egypt was to become an American substitute for bases in Libya, it was a Soviet interest that was imperilled. Moreover, it stressed that Egypt was fighting against "imperialism and aggression," i.e., that the UAR was confronting not only Israel but the whole imperialist camp. The UAR was thereby acting as a Soviet proxy, and, as such, it was fully entitled to receive whatever Soviet aid it might need. *Pravda,* on the other hand, though ready to agree that there was an American-Israeli plot to topple the UAR regime, did not see any immediate danger, for an imperialist plot against a progressive regime is a permanent phenomenon, inherent in the very nature of imperialism. In *Pravda*'s opinion, therefore, "it is up to the Egyptian armed forces to defend their motherland."[13]

On the same day, *Izvestiia*, though it did not use Sadat's speech as a forum of discussion, nevertheless contributed its own opinion. Referring to Dayan's threat to escalate the air raids and bomb "densely populated cities," *Izvestiia*'s political observer, Tyssovskii, warned: "Tel Aviv should remember that any attempts to carry out Dayan's threats will meet with the most severe punishment."[14]

Krasnaia zvezda's handling of Sadat's speech only hinted at the military's opinion that Soviet interests were being threatened by the course of the "War of Attrition," but another article, published three days later, made this point explicitly: "The Middle East has become an arena in which the forces of socialism and progress confront the forces of imperialism and reaction." It added that "the Middle East borders immediately on the southern boundaries of the socialist commonwealth."[15] Although many articles similar in spirit were published during the period under investigation, the timing of this one (the first in 1970) was apparently of particular significance. With the internal discussion presumably under way, such a commentary may have been an attempt to exert pressure on the decision-makers in order to secure increased commitment to the region in which a direct confrontation with the chief enemy threatening the Soviet periphery was taking place.

During the last week of March, *Izvestiia* gave recurrent indications of support for the military's position, publishing references to the seriousness of the situation almost every day. According to *Izvestiia*'s reports (published under eye-catching headlines), there were "clear indications" that Israel intended to step up its air raids in an attempt to terrorize the Egyptian population and topple the Nasser regime.[16] Similar reports were published in *Krasnaia zvezda*.

On March 31, *Krasnaia zvezda* and *Izvestiia* published a speech Sadat delivered at a mass meeting in Cairo. As he stated, "Any attempt to cast doubt on the noble Soviet position vis-à-vis the UAR serves the interests of our enemies." Sadat's words might have been a warning to Moscow to the effect that there were people in Egypt, perhaps within the leadership itself, who actually doubted the "noble Soviet position," claiming that it had not done enough to defend Egypt. *Pravda* and *Trud* ignored the speech. *Izvestiia*'s and *Krasnaia zvezda*'s emphasis on the speech may indicate that they understood Sadat's words as a warning and took it seriously, feeling that he may well have been right. Furthermore, it is possible that by publishing Sadat's speech, these two organs echoed the argument presented in closed forums by the *Izvestiia* and *Krasnaia zvezda* groups. This hypothesis is further supported by their consistent emphasis on the vitality of the Soviet-Arab alliance and their assertions that any rift would prove detrimental to the Soviet interest.

It is interesting to note that *Izvestiia* cited Sadat's speech side by side with a rather bizarre article recounting the escapades of the Israeli secret services. The article, signed by two unknown journalists, V. Liadov and L. Sidorov, linked Israeli commando activity in Egypt's heartland with espionage conducted by American-Jewish tourists in the USSR. According to Liadov and Sidorov, these actions stemmed from the same source, namely, "the world Zionist headquarters," and were financed by and worked for international imperialism and reaction. This may have been the first time a Soviet organ perceived a direct link between the internal security of the USSR and that of an Arab regime, with both being threatened by clandestine Israeli operations. One day later, on April 1, *Izvestiia* reported that the article was "reprinted in Cairo newspapers." (This episode is rather curious: the speed with which *Izvestiia*'s commentary was reprinted in Egypt suggests that the Cairo editors received a copy of the article, perhaps even in Arabic, at least on the same day the relevant issue of the Russian paper went to print. Moreover, it seems that in order to be able to report on April 1 the appearance of the article in Cairo papers, *Izvestiia* editors must have had advanced knowledge of this fact.)

The first days of April witnessed the continuation of what had become a quadripartite debate. *Pravda* and, more markedly, *Trud* ignored the events taking place along the Suez front (this up to April 9, 1970, when the Israeli bombing of al-Bakr led to a new protest campaign), but *Krasnaia zvezda* and *Izvestiia* gave prominence to reports about successful operations carried out by the Egyptian army, stressing the heavy casualties it had suffered. This may have been an attempt to persuade those in the Soviet leadership who were still hesitant that, although the Egyptian army was fighting bravely, it could not stand alone against the enemy's superiority.

The gap between the Party leadership and the trade union on the one hand and the Ministry of Defense and Council of Ministers on the other hand may also be seen in the conciliatory tone of the speech delivered by Secretary General Brezhnev in Khar'kov on April 15, 1970. In this speech, delivered in the midst of the protest campaign condemning Israeli "atrocities" (i.e., the raid on al-Bakr), Brezhnev made no reference whatsoever to the Israeli deep-penetration air raids nor to any danger threatening the Arab progressive regimes. Instead, he spoke of the need for a political settlement "that will bring peace and security to all the nations of the region" and pointed to the growing stabilization of the progressive Arab regimes.

The conciliatory tone of the speech was in sharp contrast not only to the line taken by *Krasnaia zvezda* and *Izvestiia* but also to *Pravda*'s and Brezhnev's 1970 position.

The following day, *Krasnaia zvezda* responded, stating that "the Mediterranean has been prepared [by NATO] as a springboard against the socialist states and the progressive regimes of the Arab East." Here again it painted the situation entirely in black: The Soviet Union, its periphery, and its vital interests were being threatened. The Ministry of Defense was apparently again exerting pressure in an attempt to tip the scales of decision making.

At some point between April 16 and April 24, 1970, Brezhnev was presumably convinced by the arguments of the military and the coalition that formed around it. In his meeting with Ali Sabri, which took place on April 24 (and was reported on April 25), he declared that "the CPSU and the entire Soviet nation will actively support the just struggle of the Egyptian nation for the full liquidation of the consequences of the Israeli aggression."

On the same day, April 25, *Krasnaia zvezda* and *Izvestiia* carried a front-page report of Sabri's meeting with Marshal Grechko and N. P. Dagaev ("colonel-general in the Soviet air force"). Apparently, the long-avoided decision to involve

Soviet airmen in combat missions in the Middle East had been taken. On April 29, Israel revealed that Soviet pilots were flying operational missions for Egypt.[17] One day later, the United States confirmed Israeli reports.[18] On May 15, the *New York Times,* relying on US and other Western intelligence sources, reported that "about 100 Soviet pilots have been sent to Egypt in recent weeks to man three to four squadrons of jet interceptors." Throughout May, *Pravda, Izvestiia,* and *Krasnaia zvezda* made explicit hints about the measures taken to defend Egypt's skies.[19] On May 23, the Egyptian Minister of War, Muhammad Fawzi, expressed his gratitude to the Soviet Union for its "active contribution to the strengthening of the defense capacity of the UAR." On May 30, President Nasser, in a speech in Khartoum, thanked the Soviet Union for aid "without which Egypt might have found itself in a very serious situation. Thanks to active Soviet aid, the Egyptian forces have been able to repulse the deep-penetrating Israeli air-raids."[20]

What has been described here may well validate the basic premise of this study, namely, that the Soviet press organs do in fact serve as channels of input through which incumbent policy groups impress their opinion upon the decision-makers. One may add that the debate in the Soviet press presumably reflected only to a certain extent the actual heat of the debate that undoubtedly took place in closed forums.

The deployment of substantial numbers of Soviet military personnel in Egypt was unprecedented in the history of Soviet relations with noncommunist countries. Indeed, with the possible exception of Cuba, it was without parallel outside the Warsaw Pact countries.

The risks involved in a decision to commit Soviet soldiers to the defense of a nonsocialist country engaged in an armed conflict with a Western ally cannot be overestimated. Yet, the Soviet military expressed itself clearly and unequivocally in favor of a direct commitment and in fact egged on the initially reluctant political leadership to assume the risk.

The military's position in the spring 1970 debate was consistent with, and appeared to be the epitome of, its conviction that "the USSR is present in the Middle East in

keeping with the state interest of the Soviet Union and the
Arab countries" and was there to stay.[21] This conviction,
evident throughout the period under investigation, was
apparently the fundamental factor in the Soviet military's
attitudes toward the various aspects of the Middle Eastern
nexus. The belief that the foothold gained in the Arab East
was vital to the USSR and should therefore be preserved by
all necessary means seemed to be one of the main motives of
the military's political activity in the course of 1967-1970. In
the spring of 1970, the military considered the change in
scope and quality of the Soviet involvement or, more precisely, the transition from involvement to commitment, as the
means to secure the Soviet position in the area and deter
further threats to it. This opinion was impressed upon the
decision makers through a vigorous public campaign and
presumably through direct approaches through formal
channels. These combined efforts, probably greatly
reinforced by support from the *Izvestiia* group, proved
effective: the military's advice was heeded, and policy
changed accordingly.

The spring 1970 debate threw into sharp relief the theme
recurrent throughout this study, namely, that in the Soviet
political context interest groups form primarily on issues.
Thus, the foregoing analysis offers ground for assuming continuity of perception by the Soviet military that the preservation of the Soviet-Arab alliance was a primary national
interest of the USSR. Moreover, it clearly indicates that this
perception was shared and consistently supported by the
Izvestiia group and served in fact as a rallying point between
this group and the military. The steady alliance between the
Izvestiia and *Krasnaia zvezda* groups may support the hypothesis that a military industrial complex exists in the Soviet
political context. This will be further explored in the concluding chapter, which will analyze possible vertical divisions.

The decision to commit Soviet personnel to the UAR's
defense (coinciding as it did with a change in the CPSU's
approach toward the "progressive" Arab regimes) created a
unity of purpose among the groups represented by *Pravda,*

Izvestiia, and *Krasnaia zvezda.* The ensuing high-risk policy appears to represent the convergence in the attitudes of these groups, with the military taking the lead as the chief proponent of a forward, aggressive policy.

However, at least one group remained outside this "tripartite alliance" and assumed the role of the only opponent of the official policy. The next chapter will focus on the attitudes and role of that solitary dissenter—*Trud,* the press organ of the trade union.

7. The Trade Union Organ: A Case Study in Dissent

Throughout 1966 and the first half of 1967, *Trud* was the foster child of the Soviet press. Both form and content revealed lack of attention, if not outright neglect. For example, typographic errors, virtually nonexistent in the Soviet press, abounded in *Trud*. More important, the reporting, especially of international events, was sporadic, inconsistent, delayed, and lacking in detail and comment. Nearly all international commentaries in *Trud* were written by correspondents or commentators of other press organs. For example, *Izvestiia*'s commentator Demchenko and *Pravda*'s commentator Medvedko appeared to hold part-time jobs on the *Trud* editorial board. Their articles were for the most part random selections from materials that had appeared in *Pravda* or *Izvestiia* a few days or a few weeks earlier. As far as news items were concerned, *Trud* relied heavily on the *APN-Novosti* Press Agency, which is considered in the West to be part of the KGB "disinformation" department, rather than on the more reliable TASS. No independent line or, for that matter, no line at all was elaborated. *Trud* failed to participate or establish any position whatsoever in the prewar public debates.

A few examples will illustrate this point. *Trud* reported the incident of April 7, 1967, in which several Syrian planes were shot down by the Israeli air force as "another ploughing incident." (The reference is presumably to Israeli attempts to cultivate lands on the eastern bank of the Kineret, attempts that provoked recurrent exchanges of fire. Needless to say, the April 7 incident went far beyond that; in retrospect, it marked an important stage in the prewar escalation.) *Trud* accompanied its report of the "ploughing incident" by another dispatch from an unspecified source to the effect that Syrian armed forces had been placed on alert.[1]

The next report on the situation in the Middle East appeared on May 5, 1967, and had to do with gold smuggling from Egypt. On May 19, a sandstorm in Egypt captured *Trud*'s attention. More crucial events were either ignored (e.g. Nasser's request to withdraw the UNEF) or reported in laconic dispatches without any background information, explanation, or comment (e.g., Egypt's decision to mobilize reserves and Nasser's directive to close the Straits of Aqaba, reported on May 23 and 24, respectively).

At the beginning of June, *Trud* joined the other press organs in printing headlines referring to the "Crisis in the Middle East." However, nothing in *Trud*'s reports indicated that a crisis had indeed developed in the region. Sometimes the headline "Crisis in the Middle East" was followed by reports of such unrelated events as the fact that British Premier Harold Wilson was picketed in Ottawa, Canada.[2]

With the outbreak of hostilities, *Trud* aligned itself with the general line of Soviet report and commentary, publishing TASS dispatches and *Pravda* or *Izvestiia* commentaries.

On July 12, 1967, Aleksandr Shelepin was nominated as the Trade Union Chairman. Within a week, a tremendous change occurred in the trade union's press organ. Neat, graphic editing, an abundance of photos and cartoons, the appearance of permanent columns, linear division into seven columns per page (a division typical of all central newspapers)—these were some of the new features. Moreover, *Trud* introduced a new practice: it published a table of contents on its front page, a measure designed to draw attention to central articles in current and forthcoming issues. However, after some five months of being the only Soviet daily to publish a table of contents, *Trud* gave up on its innovation.

This obvious effort to make the paper more attractive and appealing was not limited to form only. As of July 1967, *Trud*'s reporting became more consistent and detailed.

Internal and international events were reported, updated, and followed up. The overall coverage of international events increased significantly. Almost the whole third page of every issue was dedicated to foreign affairs, under the general heading "The Pulse of the Planet." In addition, the last column of the first page was devoted to an international survey. Both innovations made *Trud* similar in both form and content to the three other central dailies.

At the same time, foreign policy issues were more and more frequently dealt with in *Trud*'s editorials. In fact, a regular editorial was an improvement in and of itself; before Shelepin's nomination, *Trud* had featured about one editorial a week.

In September 1967, a new column—"The International Review"—was introduced. It thereafter appeared about twice a week (more often during periods of upheaval) and served as the main platform for *Trud*'s opinions on international developments. Three commentators were assigned to edit the new column. Two of them, Stolpovskii and Tikhonov, made their debut in the "International Review." The third, Rogov, had already published several reports in *Trud*.[3]

From the first day of its appearance (September 12, 1967) and throughout the period under discussion, the "International Review" followed a set pattern: it was divided into three long paragraphs, one on NATO and Europe, another on Southeast Asia, and the third on the Middle East.[4] The commentary examined and explained "the treacherous intrigues of American imperialism throughout the globe," This detailed analysis of the "crimes" of American imperialism was preceded or followed by a summary in bold print, which was generally to the effect that "the intrigues of American imperialism endanger world peace. However, today the nations are able to frustrate these intrigues. The USSR's peace-loving policy serves as an insurmountable barrier on the path of the warmongers." An extremely hostile attitude toward the United States was evident not only in this particular column but also in all *Trud*'s pronouncements.

The correlation between the nomination of Aleksandr

Shelepin to head the trade union and the evident change in *Trud*'s form and content lends itself to the following explanation. After a meteoric rise during Khrushchev's rule and spectacular promotions during the first months of the Brezhnev-Podgornyi-Kosygin reign (when he held the posts of Presidium member, Party secretary, deputy prime minister, and head of the powerful Party-State Control Committee), Shelepin's ascendancy was thwarted, and he began to lose his posts and associates one by one. Finally, in July 1967, he was expelled from the Secretariat and relegated to the trade union leadership.[5] Left with this as his only basis of power, Shelepin apparently decided to exploit it to the maximum in his protracted rivalry with Brezhnev.

This analysis, if correct, would go far to explain the evident effort to turn *Trud* into an appealing, frontline organ, the equal of *Pravda, Izvestiia,* and *Krasnaia zvezda.* Just as a leader involved in a struggle will use the institution he heads as a power base, so too, it may be assumed, will he use the press organ of that same institution as his own mouthpiece or as a platform for his opinions.

Interestingly enough, throughout 1968-1969 Soviet policy toward the Middle East apparently was not a bone of contention between *Trud* and the other three central organs. For most of this period, *Trud* maintained a middle position and did not side with any of the competing factions. In times of crisis or heated debate, it acted as a (self-appointed) arbitrator, attempting to reconcile polarized opinions. Several examples to this effect were cited in chapter 4.

In spring 1970, *Trud* for the first time unequivocally identified itself with the *Pravda* faction and opposed the deepening of Soviet involvement in the UAR through the direct commitment of Soviet military men to combat. *Trud* put its stake on a losing faction. Somewhere between April 16 and 24, 1970, as indicated above, Brezhnev was presumably persuaded by the arguments of the military and its coalition, and made the unprecedented decision to commit Soviet military personnel to the defense of a nonsocialist country. Once the decision was made, *Pravda* immediately shifted its line and sided with *Izvestiia* and *Krasnaia zvezda* to justify and support the new policy. *Trud,* however, in obvious defiance of democratic centralism, persisted in its earlier opinion that this step was inexpedient, unnecessary, and, most important, dangerous.

Thus, the decision to move from involvement to direct commitment precipitated the evolution of an independent, dissenting position on the part of *Trud.* The following will attempt an analysis of *Trud*'s position in 1970-1971. For the sake of clarity and convenience, *Trud*'s position will be compared mainly with that of *Pravda,* i.e., unless indicated otherwise, *Pravda* will serve as symbol for the united line.

In broad terms, *Trud* apparently opposed *Pravda* on two distinct, though intimately interrelated, issues, namely, attitudes toward the "progressive" Arab regimes and the Arab-Israeli conflict.

Trud's Attitudes toward the "Progressive" Arab Regimes

Following the decision to commit Soviet personnel to Egypt's defense, *Pravda*'s attitude toward the ideo-political makeup of the UAR regime and the Ba'th regimes of Syria and Iraq converged with the *Izvestiia* and *Krasnaia zvezda* lines. *Pravda* no longer did ideological "content analyses" of the progressive regimes. Instead, it emphasized, as did *Izvestiia* and *Krasnaia zvezda,* the very fact that these regimes were progressive, that they had an "important place in the avant-garde of the anti-imperialist struggle." Harmonious relations with the ruling elites of these states, which "strive to achieve revolutionary-progressive transformation," were at the center of attention of these three organs.[6]

The Ba'th Regimes of Syria and Iraq

In spite of the marked internal differences between these two states, *Pravda* referred to both as "progressive," i.e., as regimes at the same stage of socioeconomic development. However, despite this "qualitative" equation (itself an expression of a lack of interest in or an ignoring of the deeper ideological content), there is a quantitative difference: a quantitative analysis of articles and news reports dealing with these two states reveals the fact that Syria was given some prominence over Iraq. Of course, this in itself might be considered a sign of preference and a result of otherwise unarticulated qualitative differentiation. Interestingly enough, *Trud,* though it dedicated relatively less space than *Pravda* to both these states, showed the same preferences for articles about Syria.

Pravda, then, was quite prepared to confer on Syria and Iraq the lofty epithets "progressive" and "revolutionary" without taking pains to analyze their internal social or political makeup. One might assume that internal factors were not considered important as long as their foreign policies continued to reflect the antiimperialist line. Two examples may support this hypothesis.

In November 1970 a coup d'etat in Syria led to the ouster of Nur al-Din Atasi, a man considered to be a radical leftist and an avowed friend of the Soviet Union. A few days after Hafiz Asad's ascendancy, *Pravda* published a lengthy commentary on "The Events in Syria." It stated that "the development of events shows that the new Syrian government will continue and intensify the general antiimperialist course. As for various internal changes and reorganizations in the party and governmental apparatus, these constitute an *internal matter* of the Syrian Arab Republic."[7]

This was tantamount to saying that the mere fact of Atasi's ouster was of no concern to the Soviet Union as long as there was no substantial change in Syria's "antiimperialist" policy, i.e., as long as its "fruitful cooperation and friendship with the socialist states"[8] were not endangered as a result of these "organizational changes." *Trud* dealt with this event rather briefly: it printed a short TASS news announcement of Asad's ascendancy.[9] No commentary followed.

One finds a similar attitude to Iraq. *Pravda's* approach may be seen in its commentaries on the peace agreement signed by the Iraqi government and the Kurds. While the war raged (this refers only to the period under discussion), *Pravda* completely ignored the violence and bloodshed. But as soon as the agreement between Bakr and Barzani was signed, it wrote: "The settlement of the problem will further the internal consolidation of Iraq and thereby enable it to fight with increased force in the antiimperialist struggle."[10] Here again *Pravda* referred to the wider context of the international alignment of forces. As with Syria, the Iraqi antiimperialist stand was given prominence over internal events.

Pravda's line thus expressed the official Soviet attitude toward the Arab regimes. There was no declared intention to "export" the revolution or to interfere in any way with the internal structure of a country. Relations focused on the ruling elite of the given "progressive regime," the decisive point being whether and to what extent this elite pursued an antiimperialist policy in the international arena. The existence of such a policy was considered sufficient for the country to receive comprehensive Soviet aid. As long as this policy was pursued, any and all efforts would be made not to alienate the ruling elites.

At the same time, an effort was made to provide an ideological "justification" for the overall system of relations with these regimes. One concrete expression of this effort is to be found in references to Syria and Iraq as "progressive" regimes even in official speeches of Soviet leaders[11] (as well as in *Pravda*, of course). Similarly, *Pravda* often gave a prominent place to leftist measures undertaken by these regimes (such as nationalizations, planned economy, and the like). Its frame of reference in such cases was ideological and found expression in phrases such as "progressive changes complying with the interests of the workers."[12]

Let us now examine *Trud*'s attitude toward these regimes in greater detail. What is immediately striking is that *Trud* did not refer to Syria or Iraq as "progressive" or "revolutionary." Furthermore, as opposed to *Pravda*, it generally did not report on measures undertaken by the ruling elite at the governmental or socioeconomic levels (actions such as the adoption of a new constitution "aiming at further democratization"; a congress of the ruling party; economic planning; or nationalization). Nor, again in sharp contrast to *Pravda*, did *Trud* quote "leftist" declarations of the leaders of these regimes. In fact, it carried what may be called its "policy of silence" much further. For instance, in its articles quoting the speeches of foreign guests invited to the Extraordinary

Joint Session of the CC CPSU and the Supreme Soviet (held in April 1970), *Trud* omitted the speeches of both Izzat Mustafa, head of the Iraqi Ba'th delegation,[13] and al-Tawil, the Syrian minister of the interior.[14]

The smaller space (relative to *Pravda*) that *Trud* dedicated to Syria and Iraq—the fact that *Trud* refrained from calling these regimes "progressive," its systematic neglect of "leftist" measures undertaken by the two states, and its failure to quote the speeches of official leaders invited to an official forum—apparently reflected *Trud*'s dissociation from the Ba'th regimes in Syria and Iraq. A further manifestation of this is seen in the fact that *Trud* quoted only partially the speech delivered by the leader of the Syrian Communist party, Khalid Bakdash, at the Twenty-fourth CPSU Congress. Curiously enough, *Trud* omitted the section of his speech that *praised* the new Syrian regime.[15]

Another significant fact to be noted here was *Trud*'s strong criticism of the persecution of communists by the "progressive" regimes of Syria and Iraq. On July 18, 1970, it published an article entitled "A Well-Founded Fear," signed only "An Observer." This article sharply condemned the arrest, torture, and subsequent death of a prominent Syrian communist. *Trud* emphasized the fact that many more communists were languishing in Syrian prisons, where they were reportedly subjected to incessant brutal torture. *Trud* continued: "It is quite odd that representatives of patriotic, democratic forces are being persecuted. . . . Persecution of democratic activists and the barbarous methods employed against them serve the interests of the enemies of the Syrian nation. Soviet society, which has always been sympathetic to the Syrian nation and its struggle for national liberation, is deeply concerned about the persecution of communists in that country." What is striking here (apart from the criticism itself) is the distinction *Trud* made between the nation, for which it held sympathetic feelings, and the regime.

Iraq also came in for its share of pungent criticism. Again *Trud*'s article was anonymous, and was said to be based on the newspaper's "own information" (*"sobstvennaia informatsiia"*). The title of the report indicated its tone: "The

Crime of the Iraqi Reaction." "How long [the writer asks] will the criminal forces of reaction be able to commit their dark crimes. . . ? The death of two communists in an Iraqi prison, the arrests made from time to time, arouse deep concern. Soviet communists, together with democratic forces in other countries, express their solidarity with the persecuted Iraqi communists and demand an immediate cessation of such crimes."[16] *Trud* thus took upon itself the task of expressing the solidarity and indignation of the "Soviet communists."

These two extremely sharp attacks were *Trud*'s reaction to two campaigns of terror waged by the Syrian and Iraqi regimes—in summer 1970 and winter 1971, respectively. Neither *Pravda* nor any other major Soviet paper reacted to these persecutions and mass arrests. *Pravda*'s silence was consistent with its general policy toward Syria and Iraq—i.e., noninterference in their internal affairs combined with efforts not to alienate their ruling elites, even if this meant the abandonment of the local Communist parties. Still, the anticommunist campaign in Iraq was not entirely ignored by the Soviets, as is seen from the following incident.

Moscow invited three delegations from Iraq to the Twenty-fourth Congress of the CPSU: one from the Iraqi Communist party, one from the Ba'th Party, and a third from the Democratic party of Kurdistan. In terms of Arab-communist solidarity, this triple invitation may have been considered a spectacular achievement. Politically, however, it was a gamble of the first order. Moscow either could not or would not prevent Aziz Muhammad, the first secretary of the Iraqi Communist party Central Committee, from using the Congress as a platform from which to launch a thinly veiled attack on the Ba'th regime of Iraq.[17] It is probable that the failure of the leader of the Ba'th delegation to address the Congress was directly linked to this confrontation of rival Iraqi factions.

But the story did not end there. On May 5, Ponomarev and Suslov met with Aziz Muhammad. Following the meeting, a communiqué was issued; it stressed that "the intrigues of the imperialist agency and reaction, and the persecution of the Communist party . . . hamper the . . . unification of the progressive patriotic forces."[18]

Pravda and *Trud* were the only Soviet papers to publish the communiqué. It is difficult to determine the exact reasons for this deviation from the usual line. In any case, the affair had no apparent impact on overall Soviet-Iraqi relations. During the Congress, prominent Soviet leaders attended a reception at the Iraqi Embassy in Moscow.[19] Shortly afterward (in June 1971) a high-ranking Soviet delegation, headed by Deputy Prime Minister Novikov, visited Iraq, where an agreement was signed providing for substantial Soviet aid.[20] In December 1971, Marshal Grechko visited Iraq on an official mission.[21]

This isolated instance underscored the prevailing silence of the CPSU and its official organ on the subject of the anticommunist campaigns waged by the Ba'th regimes of Syria and Iraq. This silence became even louder, as it were, against the background of *Trud*'s repeated vigorous protests against the "barbarous methods" and "reactionary crimes" of both the Iraqi *and* Syrian regimes.

Trud, in contrast to *Pravda,* was not prepared to tolerate the obvious inconsistency between declarations of friendship for the Soviet Union and the ready acceptance of comprehensive Soviet aid, on the one hand, and such blatantly anti-Soviet actions as the persecution of communists on the other. For *Trud,* friendly relations with the Soviet Union were contingent upon a certain reciprocity. The fact that *Trud* did not publish the official announcement of the Iraqi Embassy in Paris stating that "Soviet aid is given without any political conditions," is perhaps further support for this hypothesis.[22]

We must bear in mind, however, the inherent nature of the Soviet regime. In the Soviet Union, any divergence from or disagreement with the official line must be expressed with extreme caution and within the existing framework: in our case, within the framework of overall relations between the Soviet Union and Syria and Iraq. Thus, *Trud*'s dissociation from the official line meant, in concrete terms, that it would ignore as far as possible the state and the regime in favor of a heavy emphasis on the society and the nation. This distinction in itself constituted a form of disaffection with a given regime, since it is the usual Soviet manner of dealing with *unfriendly* states.

All *Trud's* articles on Syria or Iraq evinced deep sympathy for the nation, the worker, the farmer, and the trade union or communist activist. When it referred to them, it employed loftier ideological language than that *Pravda* reserved for "progressive" regimes. Here, for example, is part of a report by Repin, *Trud*'s Cairo correspondent, on a Syrian textile factory he visited: "The workers address one another as 'comrade.' This lofty title is employed more and more frequently in Syria. . . . The head of the factory committee [*zavkom* in the original] declared that the Syrian working class is firmly determined to strengthen its friendship with Lenin's homeland and with the Soviet nation, which offers the world a way toward peace and socialism. The Syrian workers know that socialism is the only way and [that it is] a necessary condition of social justice."[23] It should again be stressed that *Pravda*'s articles on socioeconomic changes in Syria and Iraq emphasized the role of the "progressive" regimes in these developments and did not even hint at the striving of the working class toward socialism, which the Soviet Union "offers the world."[24]

Political-economic relations with Syria and Iraq were another area in which the differing approaches of *Pravda* and *Trud* may be seen. While *Pravda* assigned a central place to the signing of agreements and the exchange of delegations, *Trud* remained silent. The following examples, beginning with Syria, will demonstrate this difference of attitude.

In January 1970, a delegation of the Soviet-Syrian Friendship Association, headed by B. T. Murataliev, visited Syria. The delegation was received by Atasi, who called the meeting "an important contribution to the strengthening of the friendship between our countries."[25] *Trud* was silent. In April 1970, a Syrian trade delegation visited the Soviet Union and signed a long-term trade agreement.[26] *Trud* was silent. In November 1970 (i.e., after Asad's coup d'etat), an agreement for technical-scientific cooperation was concluded by the Soviet Union and Syria in Damascus.[27] Again, *Trud* was silent.

During the summer of 1971, an important delegation of the Supreme Soviet, headed by N. M. Metchanov, spent two weeks in Syria. *Pravda* provided constant reports about the visit. The delegation was termed "official," and its talks were described as "very successful."[28] At the conclusion of the visit, a joint declaration was issued, stating in part: "The friendly relations between the governments of the Syrian Arab Republic and the USSR serve the interests of both countries and [serve] the cause of peace. . . . The Soviet delegation declared that the USSR is firmly resolved to supply the Syrian Arab Republic with all the aid it needs for the struggle against Israeli aggression. . . ."[29] *Trud* made no mention of the delegation or the joint declaration. It was the only central Soviet paper not to publish a word about the visit. It is true that the joint declaration was rather vaguely worded; and one can neither infer whether any agreement was actually signed nor say for certain what subjects were discussed in these "successful talks." But it may be assumed that systematic neglect of a vital part of the Soviet network of relations with Syria was not a mere oversight. We may be able to arrive at a more solidly grounded conclusion when we consider the case of Iraq.

Before we deal with Iraq, however, a somewhat mysterious meeting should be mentioned. This time, *Trud* was the only Soviet paper that did report it, under a large headline on page one. The report itself was quite brief; it dealt with a meeting between Aleksandr Shelepin and a certain Abdallah Ahmad, a trade union leader and member of the Syrian Ba'th leadership.[30] The reasons for Ahmad's visit to Moscow remain totally obscure, despite all efforts to discover them. Other questions also arise. Was Ahmad connected with the Syrian Communist party? On whose behalf did he come to the Soviet Union? What subjects did he and Shelepin discuss? Most striking of all is the prominence given the meeting by *Trud,* for this report was published only a few days after the signing of the joint declaration in Damascus—an event that *Trud* ignored.

Trud displayed a similar attitude toward Iraq. It carried no report on the Soviet economic delegation that visited Iraq in March 1970 to establish a permanent committee for economic-technological cooperation between the two countries.[31] Nor did *Trud* inform its readers about a long-term Iraqi-Soviet trade agreement.[32]

Again, as in the case of Syria, *Trud* failed to report on a high-ranking Soviet Party and government delegation that visited Iraq. This delegation, headed by Soviet Deputy Prime Minister B. N. Novikov, spent two weeks in Iraq during June 1971. *Pravda* and other Soviet papers published almost daily reports on the various meetings and discussions held during the visit. At its conclusion a joint communiqué was issued; a protocol signed by both sides stated that the "Soviet Union would carry out works necessary to increase Iraqi oil production" and envisioned the construction of a canal from Milekh–Tartar Lake to the Euphrates.[33] *Trud* reported neither the visit, the talks, nor the joint communiqué. (It should be kept in mind that this delegation visited Iraq after the Twenty-fourth CPSU Congress.)

Trud's silence on the delegations that visited Iraq may help clarify and explain its identical reaction (or lack of one) to the delegations that visited Syria. In the case of the latter, no details concerning agreements and commitments, economic or otherwise, were published (not even in *Pravda*). Following the visit of the delegation to Iraq, however, at least some of these details were, as we have seen, explicitly stated. But *Trud*'s reaction to both visits was identical: silence. We may assume, then, that the explanation of the fact that *Trud* ignored both visits lies in its opposition to any further increase of Soviet economic commitments in Syria and Iraq.

If we recall *Trud*'s expressions of general disaffection with these two regimes, we might further assume that its opposition may also partially have derived from its disapproval of the absence of "political conditions to Soviet aid." It would appear that the economic explanation is linked to, or even stems from, the political or ideological explanation. *Trud*'s objection was a dual one: it objected to the ever-growing investments per se and did so, perhaps, because they were being made in countries ruled by unstable regimes, which, far from showing any willingness to introduce any truly Marxist progressive measures into their internal policies, were unwilling even to halt their persecution of communists.

The United Arab Republic

The United Arab Republic was the crux of the matter. The scope of Soviet investment in this country, together with the broad range of connections between the CPSU and the Arab Socialist Union, might well lead one to expect that if the differing attitudes noted above really were of political significance—if, that is, the differences between *Pravda* and *Trud* were a concrete expression of a conflict within the Soviet leadership—then there would be a marked polarization between their approaches to the United Arab Republic. On the other hand, the very nature and degree of Soviet involvement in that country and the concomitant possibility that any divergence in approach may have been interpreted as overt opposition to official policy, may have led *Trud* to adopt a more cautious attitude or at least better camouflage its opinions.

The differences between the two papers are, then, best seen through their handling of the major fluctuations in Egypt during the period under investigation: Nasser's death, the ascendancy of Sadat, the fall of the Ali Sabri faction, and the signing of the Soviet-Egyptian Friendship and Collaboration Treaty. This survey will consequently focus primarily on those events.

The first significant fact to be noted is that the cleavage between *Pravda* and *Trud* over the United Arab Republic was on what might be termed a higher ideological level. We have seen that *Pravda* referred to Syria and Iraq as "progressive-revolutionary" regimes, while *Trud* did not use this terminology. However, *Pravda,* when writing of the United Arab Republic, spoke of socialism; *Trud* spoke, at most, of "progressiveness" and "revolutionism."

A striking instance of this "semantic" gap may be found in a comparison of two articles published by *Pravda* and *Trud* on the same day. Each article was written by the paper's regular correspondent in the United Arab Republic. Both dealt with the same event: Sadat's speech to the National

Assembly shortly after Nasser's death. Yet, while *Pravda*'s correspondent, Glukhov, quoted the speech in its entirety and emphasized Sadat's promise to "defend the socialist (*sotsialisticheskie*) achievements of the Egyptian nation,"[34] Repin, the *Trud* reporter, quoted Sadat's promise to defend the social (*sotsial'nye*) achievements of the Egyptian nation."[35]

Trud adopted a parallel policy toward similar declarations made by top leaders of the Arab Socialist Union. For instance, it ignored Labib Shuqayr's essay, published in *al-Ahram* and quoted extensively by *Pravda*, in which Shuqayr stated: "The revolution cannot proceed without socialism. Socialism is the only way for developing countries to overcome economic retardation." Shuqayr also called for the strengthening of the Arab Socialist Union so that it might "become a true avant-garde movement."[36] Shuqayr's use of Leninist terminology in reference to the ASU was in accordance with *Pravda*'s policy, which ascribed "a leading role" to the ruling parties of progressive regimes. It is therefore highly significant that *Trud* ignored such "bolshevist" declarations made by a prominent ASU leader.

In marked contrast to its dissociation from the United Arab Republic's top leadership, *Trud* developed personal relations with medium-rank and low-rank Arab Socialist Union and trade union activists through its Cairo correspondent, Repin. Socialist declarations made by them were prominently reported.[37] As it did with Syria and Iraq, *Trud* placed great emphasis on Egypt's working class and its striving toward socialism.[38]

Trud's unwillingness to identify itself with the Arab Socialist Union and the ideological role it was supposed to play may be clearly seen from its minimal coverage of Ponomarev's visit to the United Arab Republic in December 1970.[39] Ponomarev was in charge of relations with nonruling Communist parties. One of his responsibilities, however, was Soviet relations with the Arab Socialist Union. The fact that Soviet relations with the Arab Socialist Union were entrusted to the man responsible for relations with Communist parties placed the ruling party of the United Arab Republic in a highly significant category.

When one considers the background outlined above, *Trud*'s attitude to Ponomarev's visit becomes almost self-evident. But another explanation—which does not necessarily nullify the first one—is also possible. Ponomarev also discussed Soviet-Egyptian economic relations and Soviet commitments to Egypt. According to *Pravda,* one of the points emphasized during the talks was that "Soviet aid is granted without any political conditions."[40] *Trud* did not publish this statement. It may be recalled that *Trud* ignored a similar statement about Iraq.[41] Such systematic neglect of this type of announcement may have been tantamount to a fundamental objection by *Trud* to unconditional Soviet aid and investment. Its scant coverage of Ponomarev's visit may thus serve as a good illustration of the interdependence of the economic and political reasons that informed its dissociation from Soviet relations with the progressive Arab states.

The different lines promulgated by *Pravda* and *Trud* also appeared in their coverage of the struggle for succession following Nasser's death. It seems plausible that the Soviet leadership *en bloc* expected that Nasser's death would bring in its wake a "left turn" in Egypt. But such hopes, if they really existed, received no concrete expression in *Pravda. Pravda*'s stress was on continuity; it emphasized the certainty that Nasser's successor would continue the "antiimperialist progressive line,"[42] would aim at "socialist reconstruction,"[43] and would strengthen Egyptian "friendship and cooperation" with the Soviet Union.[44] This emphasis on continuity was so marked that the CPSU organ almost denied Sadat any personal merit. Sadat was expected to be Nasser's faithful follower; as such, and only as such, was he portrayed by *Pravda.*[45]

This perhaps exaggerated stress on continuity may reflect Soviet anxiety about the future of the Egyptian regime and its ties with the Soviet Union. *Pravda*'s emphasis on the "unifying" role of the Arab Socialist Union "in this difficult moment for the Egyptian nation,"[46] along with its extensive quotations from *al-Gumhuriyya*[47] (the Arab Socialist Union organ) may also be seen as expressions of this anxiety; at a moment of instability in the United Arab Republic, *Pravda* put its stress on the most organized and powerful institution in the country, hoping it would not be disappointed.

The new Egyptian leadership was reminded that it was the Soviet Union, and the Soviet Union alone, that had always "extended a friendly hand to Egypt in the country's difficult moments."[48] "The Egyptian nation knows who its real friend is,"[49] stated another article. Alongside this, *Pravda* emphasized Moscow's readiness, for its part, to continue Soviet friendship, support, and aid to the United Arab Republic.[50]

Trud, however, did not repeat the commitments and promises mentioned in *Pravda.* The sense of anxiety that may be felt in *Pravda*'s articles was totally absent from those published by *Trud. Trud* reported Sadat's ascendancy in a detached, unenthusiastic, almost neutral manner. A juxtaposition of the headlines each paper gave to its reports of the event may illustrate the point. *Trud*'s neutral, "A New Government in the United Arab Republic"[51] stood in sharp contrast to *Pravda*'s "No Change of Direction,"[52] or its "Faithful to the Ideas of the Revolution."[53] *Pravda*'s headlines had an ideological connotation that was completely absent in *Trud. Pravda*'s phraseology also implied a sense of relief and self-assurance stemming from the fact that there really would be "no change of direction" in Egyptian policy. The United Arab Republic, it was now apparent, would consistently pursue the antiimperialist, progressive line. The Soviet position in the United Arab Republic was therefore not endangered, all of which *Pravda* saw as sufficient for a continuation of the current Soviet policy.

If Moscow had truly expected a move to the left in Egypt, it is almost certain that its hopes were focused on Ali Sabri. *Trud*'s attitude toward Sabri, who was identified with a leftist line, differed from its attitude toward other Egyptian leaders. This special attitude was evident during Sabri's visit to Moscow in December 1970. *Trud* announced Sabri's imminent arrival a full three days before *Pravda* did so;[54] the latter made its announcement only on the day of Sabri's arrival, December 22. Sabri's visit and his talks with Soviet officials were prominently featured in *Trud,* in contrast to its usually scant coverage of Arab guests in the Soviet Union.[55]

During Sabri's visit, *Trud* published an extraordinarily vitriolic attack on Israel.[56] The bitter tone of this article was a major deviation from the paper's usual stand on the Arab-Israeli conflict. *Trud*'s failure to mention the urgent need for a political settlement was virtually a unique phenomenon for the paper. While its attitude toward the Middle East conflict will be more fully analyzed below, this particular deviation may be explained here. It was suggested above that *Trud*'s opposition to growing Soviet investments in the Arab states stemmed at least partly from its disaffection with those regimes. But if *Trud* considered Ali Sabri to be *the* desirable Egyptian leader, its objections to Soviet involvement and investment in the United Arab Republic would necessarily have lessened. This in fact was the case. *Trud*'s approach underwent an immediate change: from its insistent reiteration of the urgent need for a political settlement (which would reduce Soviet involvement), it moved to a line that conformed to that of its desired leader.

But whatever hopes rested on Sabri, Sadat was the victor in the struggle for Nasser's succession. By May 1971, he was in a position to begin expelling his opponents from their posts. The attitudes adopted by *Pravda* and *Trud* toward Sadat's dismissal of the Sabri group paralleled their approaches to Sadat's election as president. The fact that *Trud*'s attitude toward both events was similar lends further support to the hypothesis that its attitude toward Sadat, as manifested immediately on his election, was neither coincidental nor unique, but part of a consistent and significant policy.

One may assume that the purge of the Sabri faction was a real disappointment to Moscow. However, no mention of it appeared in *Pravda*. *Pravda* reported Sabri's dismissal without delay (on May 4); its headline read: "Organizational Changes in the UAR Government." It should be recalled that this headline implied a principle of policy, namely, that changes in the composition of a government "constitute an internal matter of a given country"[57] and hence are of no concern to the Soviet Union. In fact, shortly thereafter *Pravda* stated explicitly that Sabri's dismissal was an "event . . . of a strictly domestic character."⁵⁸ *Trud,* on the other hand, did not report Sabri's dismissal from office, nor, again in contrast to *Pravda,* did it mention the fall of Sha'arwi Jum'a, the UAR minister of the interior (May 14). From that date, however, *Trud*'s reports paralleled *Pravda*'s short TASS dispatches without commentary.

But as soon as the Egyptian "reorganization" ended, the differences in attitude between the two papers again became evident. On May 20, *Pravda* published Sadat's address to "the Egyptian government in its new composition." Although Sadat did not specifically mention the Soviet Union in his speech, his words—"there is no change in the United Arab Republic's foreign policy . . . which continues to be based on two principles: Arab unity and no territorial concessions"— might have been satisfactory to those in charge of the CPSU organ. For the hard line promulgated in Sadat's speech dissociated him from the American peace initiative and thus bound him to continued dependence on the Soviet Union. This being the case, was it not just as well to ignore the dismissal of the leftist faction and continue to make the best of events? Interestingly enough, we see here the same emphasis on foreign, "antiimperialist" policy as we did when we discussed Syria and Iraq. Moscow's disappointment at Sabri's dismissal notwithstanding, Egypt's consistent antiimperialist line was considered sufficient to guarantee Soviet aid and support. One day later, *Pravda* published Sadat's declaration to the National Assembly in which the Egyptian President stated that "the socialist achievements [of the Egyptian revolution] should be preserved."⁵⁹ Apparently, *Pravda* was willing to tolerate the obvious inconsistency between the "preservation" of "socialist achievements" and the dismissal and trial of anyone suspected of leftist tendencies.

Trud, however, seemed to be more fully aware of the implied contradiction in Sadat's speech. It was not content with verbal declarations presumably aimed at placating the Soviet Union. *Trud* published Sadat's speech but omitted the passage about "socialist achievements."⁶⁰ Yet another instance of *Trud*'s marked disaffection with Sadat's regime after the purge may be seen in the fact that for a full week—from Sadat's last quoted speech until Podgornyi's arrival in the United Arab Republic—there was no mention whatsoever of Egypt on *Trud*'s pages.

Pravda, on the other hand, was throughout this time extensively engaged in preparing the background for Podgornyi's visit and for the treaty to be signed in its course. It constantly stressed the vital necessity for close collaboration between the two countries, basing its arguments on the continuing Israeli threat[61] (here again the emphasis is on foreign affairs). Upon Podgornyi's arrival in the United Arab Republic, *Pravda* told its readers that "all the vicious lies of Western propaganda [which claimed] that pro-Western forces have prevailed in the UAR, have been exposed as sheer absurdities . . . Soviet-Egyptian friendship is based on firm principles and *has nothing to do with persons or events.*"[62]

It is perhaps almost superfluous to note that there was no hint of all this in *Trud.* It did not publish any commentary minimizing the significance of Sabri's ouster.

On May 28 the text of the Soviet-Egyptian Friendship and Collaboration Treaty was published in the Soviet press. On May 29 *Pravda* and *Trud* were again at odds in their reactions to the treaty. *Pravda* gave prominence to the treaty and pointed out its historic and international significance; it viewed the treaty as valid proof of the "utter failure of Western attempts to drive a wedge between the socialist countries and the progressive Arab regimes . . . [which are] striving for social and national progress on the basis of socialist ideas."[63] *Trud,* however, saw the treaty as no more than "an expression of the friendship linking our two nations."[64]

Even after the signing of the treaty, *Trud* refused to grant that the Sadat regime showed socialist tendencies (which *Pravda* had, as we have seen, granted from the first). When *Trud* quoted Sadat's declarations, it continued its policy of omitting "socialist" passages, as may be seen from the following two instances. On June 4, Sadat, in an address to the National Assembly, stated; "Our policy remains unchanged . . . we have chosen the path of socialism and shall not stray from it." *Trud* reported the speech but omitted this passage. On June 11, Sadat declared: "Our friendship with the Soviet Union is . . . a long-range, general policy. We have decided to continue the socialist transformation and to build a socialist society—this is the historic prediction of our state." *Trud* did not vary its usual approach: the speech was quoted—without this passage. These systematic omissions in *Trud*'s quotations of speeches by Sadat lead one to conclude that it objected to official Soviet recognition of Sadat's socialist tendencies, recognition that, according to many observers, was implied in the Cairo Treaty.

The gap between the two papers on the treaty may be seen throughout the entire month of June. Virtually all of *Pravda*'s political and international commentaries referred in one way or another to the treaty, generously praising it (along with Sadat's regime). But *Trud* simply ignored the matter. Only on June 29 did it again mention the treaty, reporting (along with *Pravda*) that it had been submitted to the Presidium of the Supreme Soviet for ratification. But while *Pravda* and other Soviet central papers filled several pages with this story, *Trud* published only a short, purely informative announcement. Nor did *Trud* publish the speeches of Podgornyi, Gromyko, Ponomarev, and Grishin, who addressed the Presidium in support of the treaty. The failure of a paper to report speeches made by such high-ranking leaders is an extraordinary phenomenon in the Soviet Union. Perhaps it can only be explained as the reflection of *Trud*'s deep disaffection with the treaty, with the promises of Soviet aid included in it, and with the political and ideological significance officially attached to it.

Trud's explicit and almost overt objection to the signing of the treaty—a treaty that both formalized Soviet involvement in Egypt and gave de jure recognition to Sadat's regime as one "reconstructing its society along socialist lines"[65]— appeared to epitomize and mark the climax of its consistently dissenting line. For the twelve articles of the treaty embodied all those issues to which *Trud* had hitherto been objecting.

Sudan and Algeria

Sudan is a relative newcomer to the progressive camp. It joined it only in May 1969, when Numayri's "national demo-

cratic revolution" was accomplished. Several characteristics
of this regime may justify its choice as one of the states to
be dealt with in an analysis of the divergent approaches of
Pravda and *Trud*. First, as Sudan is not directly involved in
the Arab-Israeli conflict, it might serve as a touchstone
against which the reasons underlying *Trud*'s dissociation from
the other Arab regimes may be further clarified. Second,
since the Sudanese Communist party and trade unions were
(until the summer of 1971) the strongest in the Arab world, a
special (or different) attitude toward them might be significant. Third, a particular event—the abortive procommunist
coup of summer 1971—might have polarized the different
approaches of *Pravda* and *Trud*. In short, Sudan seemed to be
a useful case study, which might—because of its distinctive
features—shed more light on the fundamental reasons for
Trud's dissociation from both the "progressive" regimes in
Syria, Iraq, and the United Arab Republic in themselves,
and from extensive Soviet relations with these regimes.

In fact, however, *Trud*'s attitude toward Sudan proved
not to be essentially different from its attitude toward
Syria and Iraq. It again ignored the exchanges of Soviet
and Sudanese delegations and the signing of agreements
between the two countries.[66] (It should be stressed that
Soviet aid to Sudan was less extensive than that to Syria
and Iraq, let alone the United Arab Republic.) The fact that
Trud ignored the various announcements about Soviet aid to
Sudan, just as it ignored similar announcements about aid to
Syria and Iraq seems to be very enlightening. One possible
explanation of *Trud*'s objection to extensive Soviet aid to
Syria, Iraq, and the United Arab Republic lies in the fact that
these countries were directly engaged in an ongoing war;
hence, Soviet investments in these countries were constantly
endangered. But if *Trud*'s attitude toward Sudan, a country
not directly involved in the conflict, was the same as its attitude toward the three frontline states, this explanation
necessarily becomes inadequate.

With this hypothesis eliminated, there remain two other
possible explanations for *Trud*'s objection to Soviet aid to
the "progressive" Arab regimes. The first is that it may have

opposed foreign investments as such, on the grounds that
Soviet resources should be allocated differently (perhaps in
such a way as to help solve internal economic problems).
However, at least two facts weaken this argument: (1) *Trud*
ignored both economic *and* political relations with these
countries; and (2) *Trud* did publish information about
Soviet aid granted to other Middle Eastern countries, such as
Iran or Algeria. But the issue is far more complicated than
may appear at first, for it is possible that the considerations
that led *Trud* not to oppose Soviet aid to, and relations with,
Iran were not the same considerations that came into play in
its apparently similar attitude toward Algeria. *Trud*'s approval of Soviet economic relations with Iran may have derived from its concern for the securing of friendly relations
with a country that has a common border with the Soviet
Union, as well as from the economic profitability of such relations; but its approval of Soviet relations with Algeria may
have stemmed from more complex reasons.

The case of Algeria requires more extensive analysis. The
prominence given Algeria in *Trud* is striking: there is a
1:1 ratio between *Trud* and *Pravda* in articles dealing with
Algeria. (It will be recalled that the proportion of articles
between *Pravda* and *Trud* is 2:1 for other Arab countries.)
Except for Egypt, Algeria was the only Arab state in which
Trud maintained a permanent correspondent—V. Shelepin
(Christian name or patronymic never published). Most of
Trud's articles about Algeria concentrated on its internal,
socioeconomic situation.

Trud's unique portrayal of Soviet relations with Algeria
might have been an "ideal model" of Soviet relations with the
"progressive" Arab states. Soviet economic aid, extensive as
it was, was both effective and profitable. (*Trud* stressed the
point that Algeria paid, as it should [*kak pravil'no*], for
Soviet technicians and equipment.)[67] *Trud* also emphasized
Algeria's success in carrying through radical economic
reforms,[68] i.e., Soviet investments here were efficient and not
wasted. Moreover, those investments were not endangered,
for Algeria was even farther from the Arab-Israeli conflict
than Sudan. (The latter country had an army division sta-

tioned at the Suez Canal and intended to join the Tripartite Federation.) Soviet experts in Algeria were mainly engaged in training national cadres;[69] there thus existed the possibility that they might one day carry the main burden of the country's development. Algeria's accelerated industrialization meant that her working class was steadily growing, gathering strength, acquiring "mature class consciousness," and playing an increasingly significant role in the country's political life.[70] The trade unions were strong, independent, well organized, and had a wide range of activities.[71]

As *Trud* saw the situation, Algeria was on the true path of progress. It was building a sound, independent socialist economy, transforming its society, developing a strong, conscious proletariat, and permitting leftist elements unrestricted activity—i.e., Algeria was making all those changes in the base needed for a real change in the superstructure.

The Algerian model, as portrayed by *Trud,* had all the opportunities to make steady progress. Soviet investments and aid to Algeria were therefore worthwhile and would pay off, economically and politically, both in the short run and in the long run. Furthermore, the actions of the Algerian leadership—in allowing the unrestricted political activity of leftist elements and in successfully implementing extensive socioeconomic reforms "according to the Soviet model"[72]—constituted perhaps that reciprocity *Trud* demanded in return for Soviet aid.

However, in *Trud*'s opinion, this did not mean that the ruling party of Algeria should be endorsed on the ideological level or that Soviet-Algerian relations should focus on interparty ties. The moment the Soviet leadership attempted to elevate relations with Algeria to the interparty level, *Trud* dissociated itself from the process through its usual policy of silence. *Trud* did not publish a telegram greeting "Boumedienne, the Algerian Revolutionary Council, and the Front of National Liberation in the name of the Central Committee of the CPSU, the Supreme Soviet, and the Soviet government."[73] This was the first time that *Trud* ignored an announcement concerning Algeria or Soviet relations with Algeria.

Trud's opinions on both the desired model of Soviet relations with the Arab regimes and on the true stage their socio-economic development had reached were further evident from its attitude toward Sudan. *Trud* consistently ignored all the leftist declarations made by the Sudanese leaders; but it was the *only* Soviet paper to publish Numayri's address to "the representatives of the working class," in which he stated that "the path to socialism in a country such as Sudan, which lacks a strong working class, requires a long transitional period."[74] *Trud* apparently agreed with Numayri on this point. As in the case of Algeria, it believed that socialism could not be achieved overnight; the transition to socialism was contingent upon such preconditions as unrestricted political activity and the steady growth of a conscious proletariat. Neither the verbal declarations of leaders professing to be socialists nor Soviet categorization of their regimes as undergoing socialist reconstruction could further the process in the least.

Also significant is *Trud*'s deep concern for the Sudanese Communist party and trade unions. They were described as the "real progressive forces";[75] the paper strongly emphasized the spiritual attachment of their activists to "the language and homeland of Lenin."[76] Before hazarding further hypotheses, however, it might be enlightening to analyze how *Trud* and *Pravda* handled the attempted procommunist coup d'etat of July 1971.

When the procommunist revolt broke out in Sudan, *Trud* did not come out with joyous banner headlines. Its reportage was in fact quite similar to that of *Pravda* (and other Soviet papers), apparently the result of a policy of caution dictated from above. At first it appeared that both papers were simply awaiting further developments. They each reported the initial news about the coup almost identically; each relied on foreign sources, and neither printed commentaries. On the following day (July 22, 1971), both papers were prepared to rely on TASS-Khartoum. They reported that Major Hashim al-Ata, a former member of the Sudanese Revolutionary Command Council and the Sudanese cabinet, had the situation under control and that Numayri had been arrested. Both papers quoted identically Ata's address to the nation, an address in which he explained the ideological and political motivations for the coup.

On July 23, both papers, basing themselves on the *Middle East News Agency,* announced Numayri's countercoup—again without any commentary. But only *Trud* reported the Libyan hijacking of the plane carrying Colonel Babiqar al-Nur. *Trud*'s tone was hostile to Libya; its headline, "All Because of the Libyan Government,"[77] which appeared to place responsibility for the failure of the coup on the Qadhdhafi regime, stood in sharp contrast to *Pravda*'s cautious treatment of the Libyan role in Numayri's restoration to power.

Both papers carried similar reports on the arrests in Sudan; each mentioned the fact that communists too were to stand trial.[78] But on July 27 the change in attitude began and gathered momentum until it became a huge wave of protest. The Soviet press adopted a uniform line, except for three instances when *Trud* distinguished itself.

In the first place, *Trud* actually initiated the wave of protest. While all the other Soviet papers published their stories under headlines such as "Events in Sudan," *Trud*'s headline read "Repressions in Sudan."[79] On this same day (July 27), *Trud* printed a large photograph enclosed by a black frame; above the photograph a caption in heavy print and huge lettering read: "Shaif Ahmad-al-Shaykh Sentenced to Death." On the following day, all the other Soviet papers joined in the protest, apparently on orders from above. All adopted a very tough tone, though *Trud*'s language may be considered even more aggressive.[80]

Trud's second deviation from the general line was its publication of the declaration of the UAR Trade Union Federation expressing protest, shock, and indignation at the repressions in Sudan.[81] The significance of this deviation lies in the fact that Sadat rejected the Soviet demand that he condemn Numayri and was extremely indignant when the Egyptian Trade Union Federation issued its statement. It would appear that *Pravda* preferred not to alienate Sadat and therefore simply ignored the entire matter.

The generally uniform line adopted by all the Soviet papers, including *Trud,* was followed until August 8, 1971. Then the wave of protest subsided abruptly, apparently due to an order from above, with only *Trud* continuing to publish protests for another two days. The culmination came in its publication (on August 10) of the declaration of the World Trade Union Federation. This declaration expressed solidarity "with the Sudanese workers in their struggle for the release of their imprisoned leaders, and with their struggle for the restoration of their fundamental right to organize trade unions." This was the swan song of the great chorus of protests.

On the same day, all the central Soviet papers published Numayri's announcement as it appeared in the *New York Times;* in it the Sudanese leader stated that his country's relations with the United States and China had greatly improved following the successful countercoup. This statement was as a kind of epitaph for the Sudanese affair.

In this particular case, *Pravda* and *Trud* were united in their approach. No polarization occurred. On the contrary, the Soviet press as a whole adopted the very line hitherto promulgated solely by *Trud,* i.e., protesting vigorously against the persecution of communists. Yet, this may be the exception that proves the rule.

Pravda might have been expected to react to the persecution of fraternal Communist parties in the Arab states in the same way it reacted to the persecution of the Sudanese Communist party. Specifically, during the period under investigation, *Pravda* should have made at least two other protests: one in the summer of 1970, when large numbers of communists were arrested and executed in Syria, and another in the winter of 1971, when an anticommunist campaign raged in Iraq. *Pravda* might also have been expected to express disapproval at Sadat's dismissal and trial of the Sabri group (or at least it should not have minimized the significance of the purge as it did). *Pravda's* silence in all these cases and the continued maintenance of friendy relations with

Syria and Iraq (and, of course, with the United Arab Republic, with which the Friendship and Collaboration Treaty was signed almost immediately following Sabri's ouster) seem to support the hypothesis that *Pravda* was prepared to ignore the persecution of communists (or the trial of leftists) as long as there was any possibility of retaining harmonious relations with a ruling elite. But Sudan was a lost cause. The Soviets had no fears of alienating the ruling elite there, for the spate of mutual recriminations between the two countries had far transcended the point at which a rapprochement might have been effected.

Trud's policy, on the other hand, was consistent in all three cases. Nor did it wait for the official protest campaign to begin but published its initial protest before all the other Soviet papers did. One may even hazard a more far-reaching speculation: namely, that those in charge of *Trud* were not certain what the official reaction would be and, consistent with their previous policy, published their protest without waiting for the official campaign to begin (and perhaps in order to trigger such a campaign). The fact that all the other central Soviet papers began and then stopped their protests simultaneously supports this conjecture.

Trud's consistent dissent might have reflected its objection to the official Soviet policy of nonparty orientation, i.e., a policy that "minimizes the role and significance of a distinct communist organization and conceives Soviet interests and communist action mainly in terms of harmonious relations with the ruling Arab elites."[82] *Trud* gave prominence to the working class and to Communist party and trade union activities in Syria, Iraq, Sudan, and Algeria; it held back from giving ideological endorsement to their ruling parties; and it categorically defended persecuted communists in these countries (expressing protest on behalf of Soviet communists). This approach might have been the concrete manifestation of the opposing, party-oriented attitude, "which regards the independence of Arab Communist parties as important for Soviet policy, and which visualizes dialectical relations between the local communists and the incumbent regimes."[83] *Trud*'s unique approach to Algeria seems to support this assumption. Although *Trud*'s disaffection with Soviet relations with the United Arab Republic was less marked than in the case of Syria, Iraq, and Sudan—apparently for reasons of caution—the explanation suggested above may also be applied to Egypt. We have seen *Trud* ignore "bolshevist" references to the Arab Socialist Union and minimize the significance of Ponomarev's visit to Cairo; we have noted *Trud*'s preference for Sabri and its disaffection with Sadat's regime, before and, of course, after the purge. Most crucial of all, *Trud* manifested an almost overt objection to the treaty, the signing of which might be considered the climax and epitome of the nonparty-oriented attitude.

If *Trud* was really objecting to the official policy of nonparty orientation, its dissatisfaction with Moscow's economic support of, and political relations with, these regimes might be seen in a different, perhaps brighter light. In *Trud*'s opinion, Soviet aid should have been reserved for those regimes that were truly able and ready to implement socialist reconstruction. Otherwise, *Trud* might be expected to agree with Hasan Riyad, an Egyptian Marxist living in exile in Paris, who has said that Soviet aid to the Arab states "only prolongs the existence of regimes which are incapable of bringing about the objective conditions necessary for socialist development."[84]

The Arab-Israeli Conflict

The different positions displayed by *Pravda* and *Trud* on the Arab-Israeli conflict seemed to be based on the same principles that governed their attitudes toward the "progressive" Arab regimes. The two subjects are ultimately strands in a larger pattern and are necessarily interdependent.

The ideologization we have seen to be an integral part of *Pravda*'s attitude toward the "progressive" Arab regimes also came into play when the paper dealt with the Arab-Israeli conflict. Its premise was that Israel's aim was and is the destruction of the progressive Arab regimes in the area; Israel strove to deal a blow to the Arab national liberation movement, thereby serving the cause of imperialism.[85] Thus, *Pravda* justified ideologically both Soviet aid to Arab states and the more direct involvement of the Soviet Union in the Middle East. The homeland of socialism was the natural defender of all progressive, revolutionary regimes struggling for their existence.

Since *Trud* did not consider these regimes to be either progressive or engaged in building socialism, it had a different explanation of the essential nature of the Arab-Israeli conflict. Hence, it also had a different view of the overall role of the Soviet Union in the area. *Trud* appeared to object to the view that the conflict in the Middle East was a primary Soviet concern. This stand was expressed concretely in two ways. In contrast to *Pravda, Trud* did not often refer to the Soviet Union as an active partner in the conflict and its settlement. *Trud* usually mentioned the Soviet Union in one summary sentence at the end of its international commentaries, saying only that the Soviet Union was a peace-loving state seeking an international détente.[86] When it quoted the speeches of foreign representatives (other than Arabs) invited to the Twenty-fourth Congress of the CPSU, it systematically omitted all references to the Middle East conflict.[87] (It is of interest that *Trud* followed the same policy for the speeches of several Soviet leaders.)[88] This policy may have been a veiled and cautious expression of *Trud*'s dissociation from the principle that the conflict was of such intimate concern to the Soviet Union that it must be dealt with at its highest ideological forum.

Trud viewed the conflict as one element in a global alignment in which the United States was cast in the role of the devil. For *Trud,* the United States was the same imperialist aggressor as it had been in the past, a country that played a negative role throughout the world, whether in Southeast Asia, Europe, or the Middle East. The United States, in this view, enslaved other states and coerced them into acting against their own vital interests and in subservience to American imperialism.[89]

This point of view was also reflected in the schematic composition of *Trud*'s commentaries. In contrast to *Pravda,* the commentaries in *Trud* generally did not deal with the Middle East as an isolated phenomenon. They had a fixed pattern;

they reviewed the negative role played by the United States in Southeast Asia, the Middle East, Europe, or Africa. From this point of view, Israel or, say, Thailand were mere puppets of the United States and were forced into dangerous military adventures initiated by the latter for its own imperialist aims: "The United States prefers its satellite states such as Israel or Thailand to fight its imperialist wars for it, [wars] that cause nothing but suffering and harm to these nations."[90] And *Trud* stated explicitly that "the conflagration in the Middle East was ignited and continues to rage only because it serves the interests of the American monopolies."[91]

As opposed to *Trud*'s active view of the "satanic" global role of the United States, *Pravda* saw the United States as a kind of toothless lion. The United States had lost most of its position and influence in the Middle East; its only remaining ally there was Israel. Thus, the United States could play only a passive role in the area, responding to the onslaught of the "national liberation movement, [which is] united with the socialist states in one mighty front."[92]

The two papers seemed to approach the problem from diametrically opposed positions. *Trud* considered the United States to bear the main burden of responsibility for having pushed Israel into a military adventure (in order to secure American interests).[93] *Pravda,* however, focused its attack on Israel, accusing the Golda Meir government of primary responsibility for the conflict; it correspondingly viewed the United States as dragged along under Israeli and Zionist pressure.[94] In this view, the United States was at fault for supporting Israel and supplying her with arms, but not for being the actual initiator of the conflict.

The divergent approaches of *Pravda* and *Trud* were of crucial significance. The danger of the eruption of a global conflict, in which the superpowers would find themselves involved, would be demonstrably lessened if the Middle East crisis were a limited one initiated mainly by Israel, rather than one in which the United States played the main role. Obviously, the first view, *Pravda*'s, left a much wider scope for Soviet activity in the area without endangering the overall Soviet-American relations.

It may well be that this view of the conflict was responsible for the shift in *Trud*'s approach, which began in May 1970. From January 1970 until that time, *Trud* had promulgated a stringent anti-Israeli line, using harsh terms and demanding total Israeli withdrawal from all the occupied territories. *Trud*'s vitriolic attacks against Israel reached a climax following the Israeli air raids on Abu-Zahbal and Al-Bakr. Then, at the beginning of May, Israel made public the facts that Soviet pilots were flying operational missions for the United Arab Republic and that the ultramodern missile complex being supplied to Egypt was manned by Soviet crews.[95] Shortly thereafter, Soviet papers, including *Trud*, began to hint at measures being employed by the Soviet Union to defend Egyptian air space.[96] Within a few days of the publication of these reports, *Trud*'s shift became apparent: reports about military operations in the Suez Canal zone virtually ceased to appear in the paper. This new editorial policy came into effect after *Trud* published a page-one report on an Israeli Skyhawk that had been downed by "the United Arab Republic's antiaircraft fire."[97] After the publication of this item, *Trud* repeatedly stated that "now Israel is no longer able to penetrate deep into UAR territory without suffering severe losses."[98] This was perhaps *Trud*'s "justification" for its new line. What seems to be implied in these statements is that, in *Trud*'s opinion, the Soviet Union had done enough to *defend* Egypt. With both Egyptian air space and the civilian rear now adequately protected, there was no reason to supply the United Arab Republic with more arms or deepen Soviet involvement in the country.

If this was *Trud*'s opinion, it was not shared by those actually responsible for official Soviet policy. The CPSU continued to publish announcements of further Soviet military aid to Egypt.[99] *Trud* systematically omitted references to the subject of military aid. As if to reinforce its new, divergent line, *Trud*'s commentaries began to speak of the need for an urgent political solution to the Middle East crisis and for a lasting peace in the area.[100] The correlation between this change of line and the escalation in Soviet involvement in the conflict seems clear. A *Trud* commentary of June 3, 1970, left few doubts about the reasons for its shift: "The Soviet threat [i.e., Soviet involvement in the Middle East] . . . may pull the United States directly into the conflict." *Trud's* approach to the conflict was thereafter perceptibly more moderate.

In this connection it should be recalled that the official Soviet line supported a political settlement in the Middle East on the basis of Resolution 242 of the United Nations Security Council. Both *Pravda* and *Trud* favored such a solution. But this common meeting ground of the two papers became a very tenuous one the moment an interpretation of the resolution became necessary.

The *Pravda* line faithfully reflected Brezhnev's demand for "a total withdrawal of Israeli forces from all the occupied Arab territories."[101] As though it wished to dispel any doubts about the exact meaning of "all the occupied territories," *Pravda* sometimes specified them, insisting on Israeli "withdrawal from all the occupied territories, including Jerusalem, the West Bank, the Golan Heights, Sinai, and Gaza."[102]

On the other hand, *Trud,* though it also demanded an Israeli withdrawal, systematically left the word *all* out of commentaries referring to the occupied territories. More crucial still, the word *all* appeared neither in *Trud's* quotations of official speeches made by Arab leaders nor in articles that partially quoted joint communiqués signed by the Soviet Union with various other countries.[103] (Of course, when *Trud* publishes the complete text of a joint communiqué, it cannot and does not omit anything.)[104]

Pravda and *Trud* also differed on another key point arising from the interpretation of the Security Council resolution: the part to be played by negotiations between the disputants. *Pravda* insisted that an Israeli withdrawal was the precondition of, and the only basis for, a political solution; *Trud* saw negotiations as the starting point and basis for a settlement. This may be illustrated by two quotations from articles published by *Pravda* and *Trud* immediately after the first cease-fire came into effect. *Pravda* stated: "The cease-fire is the first step toward the political settlement of the crisis caused by the Israeli criminal aggression. The UAR . . .

agreed to the cease-fire in order to permit the full and unconditional realization of the Security Council resolution, which
is the only basis for peace [and which] demands an immediate, unconditional withdrawal . . . from all the occupied territories."[105] Two days later, *Trud* wrote: "The UAR's peaceful initiative aims at solving the conflict through negotiations.
The cease-fire has created a real basis for a just and lasting
peace, in compliance with the Security Council resolution. A
withdrawal from [the] occupied territories as well as the
rights of the Palestinian nation should be secured."[106]

These two formulations illustrated the substantial difference between the two papers. If one recalls the discussion
above, one may conclude that *Trud* was interested in a quick
political settlement in order to halt the ever-widening Soviet
involvement in the Middle East. It therefore tended toward
an interpretation of the Security Council resolution that
would be acceptable for Israel as well as for the Arab states
and thus make possible the termination of the conflict. *Trud*
constantly reiterated its opinion that a "solution to the conflict and an end to the state of war serve the vital interests
of the Arab states as well as those of Israel."[107] Yet, there
was another difference between the two papers: *Trud* insis-
tently stressed the *urgent* need for a political solution:
"There is not a day to be lost; it is imperative that the actu-
alization of the idea of a political settlement begin immediately."[108] Hence its impatience in September 1970, when
Israel withdrew from the talks conducted by Dr. Jarring.
Trud intensified its attacks on Israel, which it saw as sabotaging a possible political settlement. "The sides involved in
the conflict have agreed to renew their contacts through Dr.
Jarring. Yet day after day passes and no progress is made.
The situation is deteriorating, time is passing. . . . Israel should
understand that the termination of the conflict will serve her
vital interests as well as those of the Arab states."[109] *Trud's*
interest in a political solution that would put a brake on
Soviet involvement in the Middle East was also evident in its
negative attitude to the initiative aimed at partial settlement
to reopen the Suez Canal. The impatience that had characterized *Trud*'s stand until that time (February 1971) was now to

be found in pronouncements made by *Pravda* and the Soviet government. Their attacks on Israel were now sharpened; Israel was condemned for its unwillingness to agree to "this constructive initiative."[110] In contrast to these unrestrained and virulent attacks, *Trud*'s dissociation from the idea of a partial settlement may be seen in the paper's almost total lack of reference to the new program. Throughout February 1971, *Trud* did not publish a single article dealing with the idea of a partial settlement and the concomitant chances and prospects for reopening the Suez Canal; during this same period, *Pravda* published nine articles on this subject.

Apparently, *Trud* did not consider a partial settlement to be a guarantee of a "stable and lasting peace," i.e., a guarantee of a decrease in Soviet involvement in the area. The re-opening of the Suez Canal might even have the opposite, undesirable effect of leading to the expansion of Soviet activities. (*Trud*'s negative attitude to the United States, the initiator of the idea of a partial settlement, may also be seen as a determining factor in its attitude.) It is thus obvious why *Trud* did not participate in the Soviet press campaign against "the racist, egoistic Zionist state."[111] Israel's "obstructionist position"—its refusal to allow Egyptian forces to cross the Suez Canal, thus apparently blocking a partial settlement—coincided with *Trud*'s own opposition to such a solution.

Against this background, *Trud*'s attitude toward the visit of U.S. Secretary of State Rogers to the Middle East in May 1971 should be self-evident and not require extensive discussion. *Trud* was very close to *Pravda* in its negative approach to the Rogers mission. But it should be stressed again that each paper approached the event from a different angle and that the reasons for the negative attitude of each were different. *Pravda* saw the visit as a propaganda measure aimed at restoring American influence in the Middle East and called the visit a "futile attempt to drive a wedge between the socialist states and the progressive Arab regimes."[112] It emphasized throughout that "the full and unconditional evacuation of the Israeli troops from all the occupied Arab lands is the primary and indispensable condition of a political settlement."[113] *Trud,* on the other hand, viewed the mission as simply unnecessary, for "the UAR is ready . . . to conclude a peace treaty with Israel at the time of [*pri*] an Israeli withdrawal," and therefore "all the objective conditions for a political settlement already exist."[114] This was tantamount to stating that since the parties to the conflict were able to solve the problem by themselves, there was no need for *either* of the superpowers to intervene. Of course, *Trud* made no reference to what *Pravda* called "futile" American efforts "to reactivate the pro-Western elements in the Middle East."

The Rogers mission seems to be a point at which this survey may justifiably be concluded. The manner in which the two papers dealt with this issue serves both to pinpoint their divergent attitudes toward the Arab-Israeli conflict and possible solutions to it and to illuminate further the reasons underlying their opposing points of view. *Pravda*'s explicit linking of the American initiative to Soviet relations with the "progressive" Arab regimes supports the hypothesis, suggested above, that there was a fundamental and intimate connection between the divergent attitudes of these two papers toward the Arab regimes and their views of the Arab-Israeli conflict.

Political Implications of *Trud*'s Dissent

Before any political significance may be attached to the differences noted, one must try to eliminate, as far as possible, two possible sources of these differences. The first is that there may be a division of areas of interest, one that stems from the very nature or purpose of each of the two papers under discussion. One is the CPSU press organ and official Soviet mouthpiece, i.e., it is intended for both domestic and foreign readers. The other, since it is the trade union organ, may concern itself with more socially oriented subjects and contain fewer reports on economic agreements or foreign relations; this type of paper is intended mainly for internal consumption. Yet, as was indicated above, *Trud* does deal with foreign affairs. In fact, relative to the number of pages in each paper, the amount of space *Trud* gives to articles and news items that deal with international events is no less than what *Pravda* gives. There is no marked division of areas of interest between the two.

There may also be a division of labor, directed from above, in which *Trud* is given the task of expressing views and opinions that *Pravda,* being the official Soviet organ, cannot permit itself to print. Although this possibility cannot be completely refuted, one may suggest that it does not fully explain the divergent lines seen in *Pravda* and *Trud.* It may provide reasons for some differences—for instance, the way each paper views the role of the United States or the persecution of communists by the Arab "progressive" regimes—but it leaves other aspects of *Trud*'s line unaccounted for. Why does *Trud* publish its criticism and denunciations anonymously? Why does it leave significant passages out of its quotations of high-ranking leaders' speeches? Why does it make such semantic and lexical distinctions as its emphasis on "social" rather than "socialist" or "occupied territories" rather than "all the occupied territories"? In sum, why should *Trud* express—if that is its function—legitimate and officially sanctioned dissenting opinion in such a cautious, almost surreptitious manner? Moreover, it hardly seems logical to suppose that a central Soviet paper would be assigned the role of consistently expressing dissenting views and suggesting policies that significantly deviate from and contradict the official line.

Our survey has tried to discover the probable reasons for the divergent attitudes manifested by *Pravda* and *Trud.* Several political and economic explanations have been suggested, and with the aid of two "touchstones"—Sudan and Algeria—most of them were eliminated as inadequate.

Trud advocated a more uncompromising, "dogmatic" line toward the United States and the "progressive" Arab regimes. It objected to both the pragmatic compromise upon which the official nonparty orientation is based and to the ideologization of this compromise. Instead, it suggested a more revolutionary, party-oriented approach. By the same token, *Trud* expressed disaffection with the USSR's extensive economic and political relations with the "progressive" Arab regimes (which in its opinion were not progressive at all), demanding instead a different allocation of resources and proposing that these be directed to countries (such as Algeria) where there were possibilities for adequate economic and political returns for Soviet aid.

Trud's special attitude toward Algeria may also have derived from its opinion (or perhaps have camouflaged its opinion) that Soviet attention should be diverted from the Arab East and directed to Africa and the western Mediterranean. *Trud*'s unequivocal position in favor of a quick political settlement of the Arab-Israeli conflict and its opinion that Soviet involvement in the conflict was unnecessary, not worthwhile, and, above all, risky, may well support this hypothesis. In any event, *Trud* disengaged itself from overly intimate relations with the ruling elites of the Arab regimes, relations that led the Soviet Union into a highly vulnerable position. The differences between *Pravda* and *Trud* apparently stemmed from divergent doctrinal criteria based on and combined with divergent political, economic, and strategic considerations.

8. Epilogue: The Soviet Military as the Chief Proponent of a Forward Policy in the Arab East

The decision to commit Soviet personnel to the UAR's defense, coinciding as it did with a change in the CPSU's approach toward the "progressive" Arab regimes, created a unity of purpose among the *Pravda, Izvestiia* and *Krasnaia zvezda* groups. The ensuing assertive Soviet policy evidently represented the convergence in these groups' attitudes, with the military emerging as the chief proponent of a high-risk, aggressive approach.

Perhaps a brief assessment of the military's political activity in 1970-1973 would help to illustrate this point and provide an epilogue to this part of the study.

In spring 1970, the change in the scope and quality of Soviet involvement created a joint deterrent predicated upon a substantial defensive capability and Soviet presence. This joint deterrent at first limited Israeli airstrikes to the Suez Canal zone and subsequently, with the introduction of SAM-3 sites into the zone, helped to induce Israel to accede to a cease-fire and standstill agreement on the Suez Canal.

When the cease-fire went into effect on August 7, 1970, *Krasnaia zvezda* embarked upon a three-part campaign. It presented the cease-fire as a major Soviet-Arab achievement, effected by "the severe losses Israel suffered during the War of Attrition, especially during the hot summer of 1970."[1] Such a claim may well have been aimed at proving the soundness of the military's evaluations to those in the Soviet leadership who, as suggested above, opposed the deepening involvement and commitment of Soviet military personnel.

Concomitantly, *Krasnaia zvezda* attempted to impress upon the decision makers its opinion that the truce should be used as a breathing space to entrench and fortify the Soviet position in Egypt. For, "the balance of power should continue to shift in favor of the forces of socialism and progress."[2] Finally, as if to buttress its opinion, *Krasnaia zvezda* repeatedly pointed to the dangers of being lulled by the "temporary cease-fire" and to the fact that the Middle East conflict was "still simmering and endangering world peace."[3] Thus, the Soviet Ministry of Defense may have been trying to prevent a détente in the Middle East and the possible concomitant diversion of Soviet attention from the area.[4]

Since the cease-fire agreement was originally designed to lead quickly to negotiations through a mediator, with the ultimate possibility of direct talks between the parties, this may be the appropriate place to analyze the attitude of *Krasnaia zvezda* toward the idea of a political settlement.

Krasnaia zvezda took great pains to emphasize the irreconcilability of the Arab and Israeli stands. On the one hand, according to *Krasnaia zvezda,* Israel would never agree to a political settlement, because that, meaning a total withdrawal, would be tantamount to a "conscious renunciation of the Zionist ideology." On the other hand, the Arabs, and "justly" so, were not ready to give up "a single inch of their territory."[5] Therefore, the Jarring mission, debates in the UN Security Council, and the two- and four-power talks were a "mere exercise in verbosity" that could not, and would not, have any results.[6]

Thus, the circle was closed: on the one hand, *Krasnaia zvezda* assumed a priori that Israel would never agree to a total withdrawal; on the other hand, it presented the "immediate unconditional withdrawal of all the Israeli forces from all the occupied territories" as the *conditio sine qua non* of any political settlement.[7] Obviously, this was a vicious circle, from which war was the only way out. As the Soviet military organs deferred such a solution, they emerged, if only by elimination, as the standard-bearers of the status quo.[8] As long as it could possibly be maintained, the impasse of "neither war nor peace" would have been suitable. The continued simmering of the Arab-Israeli conflict would have provided the raison d'être for the perpetuation of the Soviet-Arab alliance.

A partial settlement would not have altered the status quo in this respect. It could also have furthered Soviet strategic interests in Afro-Asia by permitting the reopening of the Suez Canal.[9] If acceptable to all parties, a partial settlement could also have minimized the risk of a military showdown. Therefore, the Soviet military's organs favored such a solution, provided it would not mean détente in the area or an Arab-American rapprochement.[10]

Disenchantment

In May 1971, the Treaty of Friendship and Cooperation between the UAR and the USSR was signed in Cairo. The Soviet media heralded the treaty as an "historical event" and the "dawn of a new era."[11] The Soviet position in the UAR seemed legalized and secured for at least the fifteen years of the treaty.

However, even a brief survey of the official Soviet and Egyptian commentaries on this document reveals the seeds of a future rift. First and foremost, the Arab media played up the military aspects of the treaty. Egyptian leaders made it completely clear that they had signed the treaty with the understanding that "the Soviet Union will help us to liberate the land" (i.e., the territories lost to Israel in 1967).[12] These pronouncements were completely ignored by Soviet "political" organs, including *Pravda*. Interestingly enough, however, this Arab attitude was echoed and supported by the Soviet military organs. In contrast to *Pravda* and other "civilian" papers, which stressed that the treaty was not directed against anyone and constituted, in fact, the epitome of peace-loving Leninist policy,[13] the military organs emphasized that the treaty was directed against Israel and, by implication, against the United States. "The signing of the Treaty of Friendship and Cooperation causes anxiety to Israel and the United States, for it is directed at supporting the just struggle of the Egyptian nation."[14] The treaty "exerts pressure on Israel and the United States in order to

force them to comply with the Egyptian demand for withdrawal of all the Israeli forces from the occupied territories."[15] "The treaty has a substantial effect on the situation
in the Middle East, since it includes Soviet commitments to
continue military support of the UAR."[16]

This extremely interesting alignment between the Egyptian leadership and the Soviet military, as opposed to the
Soviet political leaders, lends itself to the following explanation. In view of the already evident strains in Soviet-Egyptian
relations—as manifested in the period immediately preceding
and immediately following the conclusion of the Cairo
Treaty—the Soviet military may have deemed it necessary to
state unequivocally the Soviet commitment to the Arab national goal (i.e., liberation of the territories lost to Israel in
1967), thereby attempting to secure the Soviet position in
the Arab East. The Soviet military (and perhaps also Arab
leaders) might have hoped that the treaty would exert
pressure on Israel (and the United States) and make it feasi-
ble to extort concessions from them. In other words, the
military presumably hoped to be able to use the threat of
military power included in the treaty to advance Soviet goals
without the need of actually committing this power to battle
over the Middle East.

If so, these hopes were futile. A partial settlement proved
unattainable. The prospects for an overall peace settlement
were as remote as ever. The impasse of "neither war nor
peace," which in many respects suited the Soviet Union,
became less and less tolerable to the Arabs. President Sadat
declared war the only alternative. Moscow, engaged at first
in the Indo-Pakistani conflict and later in preparations for the
Soviet-American summit, did not consider a military
solution to be in the current interests of the USSR. The situation was further exacerbated by mounting strains between
the Soviet advisers and their Egyptian trainees, strains that
culminated in General Sadiq's ordering a Soviet general out
of the UAR for calling Egypt an "unfaithful mistress."[17]

Marshall Grechko traveled to Egypt in February and
again in May 1972, presumably in an attempt to silence the
rising disaffection by injecting increasing doses of promises

and commitments.[18] The fact that Grechko was entrusted with a mission better suited to a foreign minister (or, in the tradition of Soviet-Arab relations, the President of the Supreme Soviet) could be interpreted as follows. The appointment may indicate that Moscow considered the strains to be mainly on the military level, concerning arms supplies, training schedules, and friction between Soviet advisers and Egyptian officers. This, however, does not seem to be an adequate justification for sending an officer of Grechko's seniority. (It may be recalled that the delegation sent to the UAR to assess its military needs in the wake of the 1967 defeat included "only" the first deputy defense minister, Marshal Zakharov.) Another explanation, not necessarily excluding the former, seems plausible, namely, that the visit was at Grechko's own initiative. Presumably most aware of the gap dividing Moscow and Cairo and considering a rift harmful to Soviet interests, Grechko might have volunteered to travel to Cairo on a reconciliatory mission. This hypothesis appears to be validated by the fact that throughout this period the political press organs manifested disenchantment with the Middle Eastern venture, virtually ceasing to publish articles on this subject. The military press not only continued to manifest its interest in the Middle East, but also went to great pains to stress the continuous vitality of the Soviet-Arab alliance. On this basis one may further surmise that the disenchantment, as evident in the political organs, reflects the creation and ascendancy of a coalition opposing any further commitment to the Arabs. Outweighed by such a coalition, Grechko might have decided to utilize his personal relationship with Brezhnev to gain his approval for a mission of goodwill.

Following Grechko's return from his May visit to Cairo, *Krasnaia zvezda* markedly shifted its interest from the UAR to Syria and Iraq. This may imply that Grechko (and his followers within the military) had been convinced that the situation was beyond repair and a rift unavoidable. If this assessment is correct, it could be assumed that a contingency plan for withdrawal was then prepared. The relatively early elaboration of such a plan would go far to explain the swiftness and totality of the Soviet pullout immediately after Egypt's request on July 19, 1972.

Recommitment

Starting in the immediate wake of the exodus from Egypt, Soviet military organs engaged in an effort to bring home again the vital importance of the Soviet-Arab alliance. Recurrent and inordinately detailed references were made to the steadily growing Israeli military power. Israel, said *Krasnaia zvezda*, enjoyed free access to the American arsenals, which provided it with such sophisticated "offensive weapons as Lance missiles, laser-guided and TV-guided bombs, heavy Cobra helicopters, and Phantom aircraft."[19] "Foreign volunteers serve in the Israeli army as officers and technical advisers. . . . One-third of the Israeli air force is composed of foreigners, mainly Americans."[20] In fact, Israel was supplied with "greater generosity than any other of the US allies."[21]

By manifesting preoccupation with and concern over the growth of Israel's military potential, the Soviet military was presumably lobbying for increased arms supplies for the Arabs. This acquires particular significance in the light of the pronounced Arab criticism concerning the scope and quality of Soviet military aid. It may be recalled that both Arab and Western commentators considered the Soviet refusal to supply Egypt with modern offensive weapons as an important factor in the rift.[22]

As if to lend urgency to its demand for stepped up arms supplies to the Arabs, *Krasnaia zvezda* warned that "the progressive Arab regimes are in the Pentagon's sights (*pritseli*) . . . their very existence is threatened by American imperialism."[23] The implication is clear if one bears in mind the Soviet military's view that the preservation of those regimes was in the immediate Soviet interest.

Soviet interests were even more directly imperiled by the "dangerous reactivization of NATO in the Mediterranean," which the military organs repeatedly pointed out. For example, *Soviet Military Review* gave a detailed description of the Pentagon's efforts to strengthen its network of military bases, which serve as "bridgeheads of aggression against the Soviet Union, the socialist states, [and] the national liberation movement."[24] *Krasnaia zvezda* flatly reported alleged NATO plans to lay nuclear mines along Yugoslav shores.[25]

The references to NATO's "offensive" in the Mediterranean (sharply contrasting with previous claims that NATO was on the retreat) may have been a thinly veiled warning that the Soviet strategic position had been weakened as a result of the pullout from Egypt. The reader may recall that the USSR had been granted port facilities in Alexandria and Port Said as well as the use of several Egyptian airfields for its TU-16 and MIG-23 squadrons.[26] Denial of these privileges would have created obvious logistic difficulties for the Mediterranean flotilla and, more significantly, deprived it of the naval reconnaissance flights and air cover provided by Egyptian-based Soviet aircraft.

The Soviet military's attempt to impress upon the political leadership the harmful effects of the rift was mirrored in Cairo. Radio Amman reported an "increased disaffection in the Egyptian military, with the recognition that the expulsion of Soviet advisers had brought nothing positive to Egypt in its confrontation with Israel."[27] A Lebanese newspaper mentioned a petition signed by a hundred Egyptian senior officers requesting reconciliation with Moscow and swift restoration of the Soviet advisers to their duties.[28] These reports acquire more credibility if seen against the background of the totality of Soviet withdrawal. According to Western reports, the advisers "left ahead of the deadline set by Sadat, taking with them supplies, heavy equipment and weapons, thus leaving much of the Egyptian Army in shambles. Simultaneously, the flow of ammunition and spare parts was virtually stopped."[29] Cairo was thus given an ample lesson of its total dependence on Soviet military aid.

The realization that preserving the Soviet-Egyptian alliance was of mutual interest and, at least for the time being, indispensable for the attainment of their national goals had evidently been promoted by the military establishments of both parties.[30] The path of rapprochement was thus opened. Initial reconciliatory overtures were followed by intensive and unprecedently frequent exchanges of military and political delegations. These were accompanied by unequivocal pledges of "all-out support"[31] and overt references to military aid and "strengthening cooperation between the respective armed forces."[32] Before long, Soviet military organs could again state with confidence that "the balance of power is steadily shifting in favor of the forces of socialism and progress."[33] Furthermore, it was asserted that "today [late September 1973] the content of the entire revolutionary process consists in a joint *offensive* against imperialism and capitalism."[34] The pendulum thus completed its full swing.

9. Divergences between Institutions or within Institutions?

Hitherto we have addressed ourselves to broad categories, analyzing the divergences discerned among the four Soviet newspapers in terms of the divisions between and among institutions.

Clearly, some credence must be given to the possibility that the issue of Soviet involvement in the Middle East and the vast array of related problems produced a horizontal polarization, i.e., polarization along institutional lines. Thus, for example, *Trud*'s opposition to the policy of commitment may be seen as deriving from the trade union's institutional function and as representing the Soviet workers' disaffection with the economic burden imposed on them by the costly military and economic aid programs.

By the same token, *Krasnaia zvezda*'s advocacy of a forward, high-risk policy may be explained in terms of the military establishment's functional interests. The functional interests and objectives of the military derive from the nature of its primary role—to defend the country against aggression. As this enjoys top priority whenever international tensions are high, the military is naturally inclined to perceive the world situation in terms of constant crisis, thus reinforcing its claim to resources and political status. In addition, involvement in extensive military aid programs could secure a high level of resource allocation to the armed forces in general and thus could be a vested interest of the military establishment as a whole.

Similarly, *Pravda*'s insistence on the "ideological purity" of the progressive Arab regimes, its campaigns to exhort them to adopt the Soviet model of "scientific socialism," and attempts to draw these regimes into the socialist camp may be explained in terms of the functional interests and objectives, both internal and international, of the Communist party of the Soviet Union.

However, not all of the divergences discerned among the four newspapers may be attributed to interinstitutional polarity. To give but one example, *Trud*'s evident opposition to the official nonparty approach and its counterproposals of concentration on local Communist parties and other revolutionary elements can hardly be seen as inherent to the trade union's institutional function.

Furthermore, the institutional-functional approach does not really explain the various zigzags and shifts in the lines of the various newspapers. For instance, the institutional-functional approach may explain *Pravda*'s insistence on an ideologically sound basis for the Soviet relations with the Arab progressive regimes; it cannot explain, however, *Pravda*'s gradual shift (starting in August 1968 and becoming predominant in 1970) to a line favoring harmonious relations with the Arab ruling elites at the expense of local Communist parties.

Thus, a more differentiated approach is necessary, an approach dictated by the "logic of the situation." We have dealt here with newspapers officially representing such vast and heterogeneous institutions as the military or the Party. Though these institutions probably differ in terms of their internal cohesion and in terms of their vested interest in the specific policy issue, an issue of such far-reaching political, economic, strategic, and ideological ramifications as the Soviet involvement in the Middle East may well produce some vertical divisions, i.e., divisions *within* a given institution.

However, no conclusive evidence for this was found. At any given moment, each of the four press organs presented a uniform and consistent line vis-à-vis the others. Never was an editorial position challenged from within.

Hence, we may hypothesize that a press organ is not controlled by and does not serve as a mouthpiece for an institution as a whole, but rather the group currently in ascendancy within the institution. In other words, it appears that the group currently in power uses the institution's organ as its exclusive platform, denying it to opposition within the institution. Though it is virtually impossible to determine the precise composition of these groups, several hypotheses may nevertheless be ventured.

Any attempt to attribute support for the positions advanced by *Pravda* to a group or several groups within the Communist party of the Soviet Union poses a whole complex of methodological and conceptual problems, most of which cannot be solved within the framework of this study.

On the methodological level, we are faced with a problem of definition. Most Western scholars, including those who admit the possible existence of interest groups in the USSR, regard "the Party" as the key group. Few, however, bother to define to whom the term *Party* might refer. Clearly, the CPSU, composed of some twelve million members coming from all walks of life, can hardly be perceived as an interest group. Membership in the Party is, for many Soviet citizens, tantamount to membership in an exclusive social club, entitling them to the various privileges reserved for members of "the new class." Moreover, a Party card is a necessary prerequisite for a position of responsibility and a successful career. Thus, the CPSU appears to be a political and sociological elite, rather than a political interest group.

Further narrowing the definition, one may attempt to apply the term *Party* (connoting a political interest group) to the *apparatchiki,* i.e., the professional party employees. However, it is almost impossible to point to any common interest shared by a group composed of anywhere between 100,000 and 200,000 men working in all territorial units of the country, many in specialized positions with narrow functional responsibility. Even a cursory survey of some biographical data reveals several potential sources of cleavage among the *apparatchiki.* In terms of their age distribution, for example, officials at the lower level of the apparatus are quite different from those in higher positions. There is also a considerable ethnic diversity among the party officials. Other potential sources of cleavage are those associated with the differentiated structure of the apparatus itself. A number of officials work in the center, but most are scattered across the country. Some work in rural *raikomy* (regional Party committees), others in industrialized areas. More significantly, the local party organs are organized along branch lines, with officials working within specialized subunits. Obviously, this structural differentiation is accompanied by specialization in the career patterns of the personnel.[1]

This inherent diversity is transposed onto, and compounded by, the structure of the Party's instrument of decision making, the Central Committee.

The Central Committee is composed of persons with key occupational assignments, most of whom have acquired reputations as successes in their respective areas of specialization. Most are also associated with an important functional group in the Soviet system.[2]

Within Party *apparatchiki,* some joined the apparatus rather late in their careers,[3] some hold party posts that require technical training and special skills[4] as well as administrative ability, still others have spent all their adult lives in party administration, in propaganda, or in the security organs. The data compiled by Gehlen and McBridge clearly indicate the wide range of experiences and attitudes the *apparatchiki* may carry into the Central Committee.

Thus, to cite Jerry F. Hugh:

> If we are to treat the party apparatus as a unified interest group . . . we must assume that the agriculture department and the defense industry department of the Central Committee (with their leaders of quite different backgrounds) have greater community of views and interests than do the agriculture department of the Central Committee and the Ministry of Agriculture. . . . We must assume that the construction engineer whose party and Soviet work in urban areas apparently warranted his appointment as Minister of Industrial Construction has a set of interests and outlooks basically in common with the agronomist whose party and Soviet work in rural regions earned him appointment as Minister of Agriculture.[5]

On the conceptual level, these data shatter the traditional image of the CPSU as a tightly knit, homogeneous, single-minded entity. The realities of sustaining an ideological structure in an industrial state facing the complexities of a highly technological era, suggest that monolithism in the CPSU and in its Central Committee may have given way to diversity. Loyalties to the Party may have to be shared with overlapping and often conflicting loyalties to other entities and sectors.

On the methodological level, there is an implicit admission of failure: the overlapping associations, the divided loyalties, the very diffusiveness of the party apparatus, compounded by our inability to ascertain the relative value of any of these factors—all make it extremely difficult to ascertain where vertical divisions may occur. In the case of a foreign policy issue, it is virtually impossible to categorize any definite subgroups within the party apparatus, since a lack of supportive data makes it virtually impossible to determine the "party interest" in any specific issue or to indicate the points at which dual loyalties may clash.

Nevertheless, we may speculate that the *Pravda* line in fact represents the attitudes and positions of a narrow group at the apex of the party hierarchy. Specifically, we would conjecture that *Pravda* is the mouthpiece of the CPSU's general secretary, Leonid Brezhnev, and a group of his followers and protégés (Kirilenko, Andropov, Kulakov, Mazurov, to name but a few). Our assumption that *Pravda* serves as the platform for this group is based on a virtually absolute correlation between Brezhnev's public pronouncements and the *Pravda* line at any given moment, as well as on the fact that *Pravda* is regarded both inside and outside the USSR as *the* official organ of Soviet policy.

Though little can be said about the broader "constituency" of the group presumably responsible for and represented by *Pravda,* it seems plausible that they share one pirmary interest—to perpetuate and augment their power.

This group may assume, or claim, the role of the supreme arbitrator of conflicting interests, maneuver between the various interest groups, and enter into temporary alliances of convenience with one or more of the incumbents. (Several possibilities of alliances consisting of party *apparatchiki* and members of other political institutions will be discussed below.)

The attribution of *Trud*'s positions to a group or several groups within the trade unions is no less problematic. First, *Trud*'s opposition to a policy of involvement in the frontline Arab states and its evident disaffection with the economic and military aid programs granted to these regimes may reflect the position of the Soviet trade unions as an institutional recoiling against the economic burden imposed by foreign commitments.[6] *Trud*'s doubts about the soundness of a policy diverting finances, equipment, manpower, and other resources from domestic projects to investments in a politically and militarily unstable region may, however, be shared by other elements and institutions associated with the consumer demand sector. It is quite possible that in the USSR, no less than in Western countries, foreign aid allocations prove highly vulnerable to austerity moves at home and political fortunes abroad. It may well be that *Trud*'s arguments serve as a rallying point for, and constitute the base of, an interinstitutional coalition of elements disaffected with official economic priorities and with the resulting resource-allocation policy.

As we have seen, however, *Trud*'s dissociation from the policies of involvement and commitment was accompanied by an obvious objection to the ideological premises upon which this policy was based, namely, the nonparty approach.

Trud's emphasis upon the importance of local communists and other revolutionary elements and its solitary championing of their rights and, in fact, their very survival, may indicate the existence of yet another alliance (or set of alliances).

The CPSU's decision to renounce local Communist parties and to embrace, for pragmatic reasons, the ruling elites of the "progressive" Arab regimes might have encountered intraparty opposition, resulting in the alienation of at least some of the CPSU's ideologues and doctrinaires. Unable to voice their dissenting views in *Pravda,* they might have adopted *Trud* as their platform. The possible influence of such a group may be further traced in *Trud*'s uncompromising attitudes toward the United States and its intolerant attitude toward the internal politics of the "progressive" Arab regimes.

Admittedly, at first glance it is extremely difficult to envision an alliance between "doctrinaires" and proponents of the consumer demand sector. However, these groups' interest in opposing a certain policy line—in this case, Soviet involvement in the frontline Arab states—though based on entirely different motivations, may be a common denominator for at least a temporary alliance. Moreover, the group (or groups) using *Trud* as the platform for their dissent may choose, or have to advocate, a line that at least partially conforms to the interests of the institution with which their mouthpiece is officially associated.

As far as personalities are concerned, Aleksandr Shelepin appears to be closely tied with *Trud*. His 1967 nomination as the chairman of the trade unions resulted in an immediate and highly visible change in *Trud*'s appearance and general editorial line. Moreover, there is a close correlation between Shelepin's public pronouncements and the *Trud* line. For example, Shelepin's speech delivered during the electoral campaign for the Supreme Soviet in June 1970 contained a far more militant attack on the United States than the speeches of other candidates did. Shelepin described American policy as "a course aimed at escalating armed, aggressive conflicts." He saw the aggressive, ominous role of the United States playing its part throughout the world, in Southeast Asia, the Middle East, and Latin America.[7] Unlike Brezhnev, Shelepin did not mention the need for rapprochement with the United States. "It would be a dangerous delusion to present the situation as though imperialism were dying," he added. This was explicit criticism of *Pravda*'s line that imperialism was on the wane; Shelepin thus placed himself firmly behind *Trud*.[8]

Another very interesting comment in Shelepin's speech may at first glance appear irrelevant to our subject. While the speeches of all candidates, and especially Brezhnev's, included a sharp attack on the People's Republic of China, Shelepin not only failed to assault China but, in a statement that "the international community of socialist states constitutes 25.9 percent of the land area of the world and 34 percent of its population," actually included China in the socialist commonwealth.[9] It is only logical to suppose that Shelepin's attitude toward China[10] was related to his position vis-à-vis the United States on the one hand and the party-oriented approach advocated by *Trud* on the other hand. While this is not the place to develop such a hypothesis and thus risk unwarranted speculations, the correlation seems an interesting one and certainly requires further investigation.

The intention here has been to point out the similarities between Shelepin's stand (as evident from his speeches) and the *Trud* line. The evidence indicates that Shelepin played a significant role in the formulation of the *Trud* line. Systematically expelled from all his strongholds, Shelepin seemed to exploit his sole remaining power base—the Soviet trade union and its newspaper, *Trud*.

As suggested above, it is possible that Shelepin was not alone in his struggle against the 1966-1973 line of Soviet foreign policy. The trade union may well have been the organizational basis of a heterogeneous group united by its disaffection with Brezhnev's policies on both the domestic and international levels. This group may have been joined by those who opposed the present leadership on personal as well as ideological grounds, with Suslov, Shelest, and Podgornyi the likely possibilities. Unfortunately, lack of tangible evidence precludes further exploration of this point.[11]

Let us now move to the other pole of the political spectrum in an attempt to assess the position of the Soviet military. In broad terms, the Middle Eastern issue may produce a division within the military establishment along the following lines.

1. The "strategic forces group," i.e., the Strategic Rocket Forces, Strategic Air and Air Defense Command. This group, naturally inclined to consider the thermonuclear ICBM and ABM balance to be of utmost importance, may well consider the whole Middle East venture a sheer waste of time and resources. The attitudes of this group may be inferred from

indirect references published by *Krasnaia zvezda.* These references generally take the form of criticism of or argument against an "invisible" opponent's view. Thus, for example, *Krasnaia zvezda* of September 24, 1969, printed an article signed by Major General N. Kupenko in which he argued that maintenance of air and naval bases in the Mediterranean is highly significant "even in the era of ICBMs." Rejecting the claim that "the Middle East has lost its strategic significance with the introduction of intercontinental nuclear delivery systems," General Kupenko pointed out that the United States and NATO attribute "particular importance to the Middle East in their global strategy, seeing it as a possible theater of military activity and a staging area to launch an attack against the USSR."[12] All these references seem to indicate that the "strategic forces group" harbored doubts about the expediency and necessity of establishing a military presence in the Middle East and the eastern Mediterranean.

2. The GRU (military intelligence) and other institutions responsible for foreign military assistance might, in view of the recurrent poor performance of the Arab armies, have opposed increasing involvement, on the grounds that it damaged the prestige and reputation of Soviet training and equipment. The recurrent references by *Krasnaia zvezda* and *Kommunist vooruzhennykh sil* to the effect that the Arab soldier was potentially a good fighter and that it was therefore worthwhile to invest in raising his operational skills may be construed as a revealing sign of as well as a rebuttal to such doubts.[13] At the same time, Soviet military intelligence might have had misgivings about the expediency of placing ultramodern weapons so close to the West's backyard, where they could be easily captured intact by the enemy. Though the latter problem still remains, the greatly improved Arab military capability, as demonstrated in the October War, might have contributed to disperse, if not eliminate completely, the GRU's misgivings.

3. The Soviet "theater forces" logically make up the group most interested in a forward policy in the Middle East, a policy that secures high levels of resource allocation to the Navy and Tactical Air Force and increases concomitantly their prestige at both the national and international levels.

The Naval and Tactical Air Commands might have considered the increasing involvement and the accompanying assumption of risks by the Soviet Union a fair price for the acquisition of naval and air facilities in Egypt, Syria, and Iraq. Thus, the Soviet "theater forces" appear to be the chief standard-bearers of a forward policy in the Middle East and the Mediterranean. Most probably, *Krasnaia zvezda,* the official press organ of the Ministry of Defense, is dominated by, and serves as the exclusive platform for, this group.

As far as personalities are concerned, the "theater forces group" is probably led by Admirals Gorshkov and Kasatonov, and by the commander of the Tactical Air Force, General Kutakhov. The late minister of defense, Marshal Andrei Grechko, may be identified with this group on the basis of his public pronouncements and essays published in the military press.[14] Marshal Epishev, the head of the Main Political Administration (MPA), may perhaps be added to this group. Though the MPA did not seem to have any vested parochial interest in involvement in the Middle East, its main organ, *Kommunist vooruzhennykh sil,* sided consistently and unequivocally with the forward line advocated by *Krasnaia zvezda.* This fact may lead to the assumption that Marshal Epishev (and an unidentified group of followers within the MPA) chose to support the group then in ascendancy within the Ministry of Defense for personal reasons.

The foregoing study allows us to assume continuity of perception by the Soviet "theater forces" that the preservation of the Soviet-Arab alliance was a primary national interest of the USSR. This group might well have been egging on the decision-makers to assume risks whenever these were deemed necessary to secure the Soviet position in the Arab East. As we have seen, the "theater forces group" was consistently and unequivocally supported by the *Izvestiia* goup. Whose organ is *Izvestiia?*

Izvestiia is the official press organ of the Soviet Council of Ministers. That is to say, it officially represents one of the most diversified and heterogeneous political institutions of the USSR. Composed of some fifty-four ministries (plus twelve state committees), the Council is probably an arena of competition, rivalry, and conflict among its intrinsically diverse elements. It can hardly be perceived as a unified political interest group or a unitary decision-maker.

The internal heterogeneity characteristic of the Soviet Council of Ministers may produce divisions along the following lines: (1) the security demand sector (including the police, the armed forces, and the defense industries); (2) the producer demand sector (including heavy industry, construction, and transportation); (3) the consumer demand sector (including light industry, consumer goods industry, trade, and housing); (4) the agricultural demand sector; and, (5) the public services and welfare sector.[15]

In broader terms, the principal dichotomy appears to be traditional: consumer demand sector versus producer demand sector.

However, these inherent intrainstitutional diversities could not be detected in *Izvestiia*'s attitudes toward the various aspects of the Middle Eastern nexus. The fact that *Izvestiia* was able to elaborate a consistent, coherent, and, in some cases, independent line toward the issues examined in this study goes far to substantiate our hypothesis that a press organ serves as a mouthpiece for the groups in ascendancy within a given institution, rather than for the institution as a whole.

Izvestiia's alignment with *Krasnaia zvezda*'s advocacy of a high-risk policy of commitment to the frontline Arab states may have been dictated by and reflected the interests of the defense/producer demand sector. This sector, composed of some thirteen ministries and a vast network of related research and development agencies—an *imperium in imperio* within the Soviet economic structure—may well be the Soviet equivalent of a military-industrial complex.

Of the fifty-four ministries composing the Soviet (All-Union) Council of Ministers, eight are devoted almost exclusively to production for the military. Five other ministries and one state committee also consign a substantial share of their output to the military.

The following eight ministries are responsible for the bulk of Soviet military production, including defense-related equipment manufactured by space and nuclear industries:

1. The Ministry of Defense Industry, under S. A. Zverev; conventional arms and military equipment
2. The Ministry of Aviation Industry, under P. V. Dementev: aircraft, aircraft parts, and some missile equipment
3. The Ministry of Shipbuilding Industry, under B. E. Butema: naval ships, ship parts, and ship repair
4. The Ministry of Electronics Industry, under A. I. Shokin: electronic components and parts, which are supplied to the Ministries of Radio Industry, Communications, Instrument Building, Means of Automation and Control Systems, and Electrotechnical Industry, all of which use the components to produce finished electronic equipment
5. The Ministry of Radio Industry, under V. D. Kalmykov: supervises the production of electronic systems and radiotechnical equipment for military uses.
6. The Ministry of General Machine Building, under S. A. Afanas'ev: development and production of strategic ballistic missiles and space vehicles
7. The Ministry of Medium Machine Building, under Ye. P. Slavskii: atomic energy program, production of fissionable materials, and construction of nuclear weapons
8. The Ministry of Machine Building, under V. V. Bakhirev: established in 1968, probably responsible for supervision of the civilian space program

Other ministries oriented toward civilian production but responsible for a substantial share of military production include:

1. The Ministry of Instrument Manufacturing, Means of Automation and Control Systems, under K. M. Rudnev

2. The Ministry of Tractor and Agricultural Machine Building, under I. F. Sinitsyn
3. The Ministry of Chemical Industry, under L. A. Kostandov
4. The Ministry of Automobile Industry, under A. M. Tarasov
5. State Committee for Science and Technology, under the chairmanship of V. A. Kirilin, also a deputy chairman of the Council of Ministers

All these ministries and state committees are constitutionally subordinate to the Council of Ministers. Although legally subject to the administrative control of Premier Kosygin, the work of the first eight was in fact highly centralized under Dmitrii F. Ustinov, until April 1976 a secretary of the Central Committee and a candidate member of the Politburo.[16]

The defense industries as a group are characterized by a greater continuity of personnel and organization than any other comparable sector of the Soviet economy. The executives involved in the defense industries have spent most of their careers in this area and are among the most experienced, efficient, and dynamic managers in the Soviet economic structure.[17]

Although there is little or no overlapping, interlocking, or rotation of personnel between the military bureaucracy and the defense industrial bureaucracy in the USSR, they are nevertheless uniquely intertwined.[18]

Without the business generated by an extensive and sophisticated military establishment, the share of resources assigned to heavy industry and the prestige it now enjoys would decline significantly. "A redirection of heavy industry toward consumer production would cause considerable reorganization, disorientation, and dislocation among personnel who are among the best paid in the country."[19] Thus, heavy industry as a whole exists in a symbiotic relationship with the military establishment.

The mutuality of interest may produce shared attitudes toward various policy issues. Specifically, in the realm of foreign policy, both the military and the defense-producer sector might be interested in maintaining a certain level of international tensions to legitimize and provide the rationale for large defense budgets. Conversely, both groups might have a shared interest in preventing détente, an interest based on the common fear that in a more relaxed international context their claim to the nation's resources would decline in priority. Furthermore, expansion of Soviet political and military commitments to allied and client states may be in the interest of the military-industrial complex, since it provides an ever-widening market for defense-related industries and a testing ground for new types of equipment.

Thus, *Izvestiia*'s consistent alignment with and support for *Krasnaia zvezda*'s advocacy of a forward policy in the Middle East may reflect the symbiotic relationship between the group currently in ascendancy within the military establishment and the heavy industry "lobby."

Although the defense-related industries as a whole benefit from an "aggressive," high-risk foreign policy, some internal rivalries might nevertheless emerge. Presumably, the division within the heavy industry sector would occur along lines paralleling those dividing the military. Thus, for example, units involved in the manufacture and development of ballistic missiles may establish subgroup alliances with the "strategic forces group." By the same token, subgroup interest may unite the aviation industry and the Ministry of Shipbuilding with the "theater forces group." It should be stressed that we do not have any evidence whatsoever to substantiate this speculation.

Izvestiia's advocacy of a policy of involvement in the Middle East and its obvious efforts to bring home the need to preserve the strategic position in the Arab East by all necessary means may reflect the parochial interests of the military industrial complex, but certain other aspects of the *Izvestiia* line may point to the existence of a broader coalition.

First, *Izvestiia*'s pragmatism—its perception of interest (economic, strategic, or otherwise) as the sole criterion upon which relations with the "progressive" Arab regimes and presumably with other states should be based—may represent the common credo of a group that, for lack of a more precise definition, we shall term "the state technocrats."

Furthermore, *Izvestiia*'s advocacy of noninterference in the internal affairs of the "progressive" Arab regimes and its consistent dissociation from attempts to impose on them the Soviet model of "scientific socialism" may reflect the specific interests of the Foreign Ministry and related institutions. These institutions, which are engaged in and responsible for the actual conduct of foreign relations, may have a vested interest in establishing foreign relations on a more manageable, interstate basis, rather than on ideological considerations.

The specific interest of yet another group can be traced in at least one conclusive instance of *Izvestiia*'s behavior. *Izvestiia*'s appeal to ignore Iraq's politics and embrace that country for the economic payoffs it could offer may reflect the parochial interests of the "oil lobby," i.e., institutions connected with the petrochemical industries, as well as other "lobbies" interested in an economically sounder basis for Soviet relations with client states.

Thus, *Izvestiia*'s position on the intricate issue of commitment to the frontline Arab states may well reflect a more complex set of alliances than a linear coalition between the military and the producer demand sector. As we have seen, at least two groups within the state bureaucracy may well project their interests onto *Izvestiia*'s line. In addition, a broader group, imprecisely defined as "state technocrats," appears to share at least some of the postulates espoused by the above-mentioned political interest groups.

Cutting even further across institutional lines, alliances may emerge between the military-industrial complex and conservative elements within the CPSU apparatus, who may share a wide spectrum of views, perceptions, and policy positions with the military and its supporters. The KGB may perhaps be added as another possible component of such an alliance.

However, whereas a policy that assigns priority to capital-goods production and perceives the international situation as an inevitable confrontation between the socialist and imperialist camps may enjoy the support of both the Party conservatives and the security organs, these same elements would probably anathematize any attempts to undermine ideological purity, condone ideological deviations, or renounce the messianic credo of Marxism-Leninism as the basis of foreign policy.

This analysis, if correct, leads to the conclusion that the Soviet political system is probably characterized by many crisscrossing, interinstitutional alliances. The various groups are presumably in a state of constant flux, coalescing on the basis of a similarity of views on one issue and changing sides when another issue is concerned. Based on a low common denominator, the Soviet political groupings may be established to tip the scales of decision making on a specific issue. Once the issue is decided, the alliance may be dissolved, and the groups previously comprising it often find themselves on opposite sides of the political barricade.

The temporary nature of Soviet political coalitions is presumably the reason for the numerous instances of "conceptual incoherence" on the part of a given press organ, that is to say, the promulgation of "hawkish" attitudes on an issue with strategic implications as opposed to lenient attitudes on an issue with ideo-political ramifications, or vice versa.

This "conceptual incoherence" was particularly apparent in *Pravda* and *Izvestiia* in 1968-1969. The former espoused a moderate approach toward the Arab-Israeli issue together with stringent ideo-political demands; and the latter took the position of a "hawkish liberal," i.e., it combined rigidity on the Arab-Israeli issue with tolerance of the domestic politics of the "progressive" Arab regimes.

Throughout this same period, *Krasnaia zvezda* successfully oscillated between the two lines, manifesting perceptibly more consistency than *Pravda* or *Izvestiia*.

Krasnaia zvezda's ability to elaborate a more coherent line than *Pravda* or *Izvestiia* may indicate that the group responsible for and represented by *Krasnaia zvezda* is more tightly knit and more cohesive than the groups represented in the three remaining newspapers. Moreover, it is possible that the military is the pivot of the Soviet political balance, i.e., the group whose support must be mobilized to tip the scales of decision making one way or another. Conversely, should the military attempt to initiate a policy decision or change the existing policy line, it may have to enlist the support of at least one additional political interest group.

Thus, the Soviet political process may be portrayed as a parellelogram of pressures and counterpressures, with shifting, temporary alliances of convenience as its vectors. A policy decision may represent a compromise between conflicting arguments, a compromise achieved on a *quid pro quo* basis and preceded by bargaining and maneuvering for and between alliances or positions.

10. Toward A New Model of Soviet Decision Making

The ensuing remarks should be placed in their proper context. To a certain extent, our research is a pilot study, one that attempts to test a certain research method and ascertain its usefulness in the analysis of Soviet decision making. The research was limited in both scope and purpose; it analyzed the attitudes of four groups, presumably represented by four press organs, toward one facet of Soviet foreign policy over a limited period of time.

In our particular case study—Soviet involvement in the frontline Arab states in the crucial period of 1966-1973—the examination of press pronouncements generally proved to be a useful analytic tool for the study of Soviet political interest groups and their role in the decision-making process. Clearly, the research method itself, as well as both the premises and conclusions of this study, would be validated only if a similar research method were applied to other case studies in the realm of both foreign and domestic policies.

Its obvious limitations and reservations notwithstanding, the foregoing analysis allows several broad conclusions to be drawn.

First and most obvious, it has been seen that the Soviet attitude toward the complex of Middle East issues is not monolithic. Differences in attitudes and approaches and even suggestions of alternative political lines do exist and are implicitly—at times explicitly—argued in the Soviet press. The bringing to light of such differences would perhaps in and of itself justify a survey such as the present one.

The general conclusion to be drawn from the discovery of such far-reaching divergences is that a more discriminating approach to the study of Soviet foreign policy is vitally necessary.

On the basis of the evidence presented in this study, foreign policy does not seem to be the exclusive domain of the CPSU or its topmost leaders. Political interest groups, affected directly or indirectly by the outcomes of foreign policy decisions, were seen to press their point of view upon the decision-makers in an apparent attempt to secure a policy line that would best serve their own interests and what they perceive to be the national interest of the USSR. Consequently, the decision makers may not enjoy an absolutely free hand in matters of foreign policy. Rather, they may have to act within a parallelogram of pressures and counterpressures exerted by various political interest groups. In the cases here examined, the actual policy decisions were more often an obvious compromise between divergent arguments than unilaterally imposed fiats.

In saying this we do not deny that the ultimate power to make final decisions probably rests in the hands of the very few; nor do we say that during a crisis abroad, for instance, the leadership cannot in effect ignore "outside" opinion and function as an authoritative decision-maker. This, however, is by no means unique to the Soviet Union. A similar situation prevails in most democratic regimes.

Our study points not only to the broadening basis of elite participation in the formulation of foreign policy, but also to a somewhat shifted center of gravity in Soviet politics. Traditionally, the Communist party was viewed as the fount of all power; elite participation, if it was discerned at all, was deemed to come at the Party's initiative, through a process of cooptation. Though we do not have sufficient evidence to refute the cooptation model, several of the case studies presented above may well indicate a genuine *pressure* for participation on the part of the interested groups.

Moreover, the CPSU itself appeared to act as an interest group in some cases, competing with others in a relatively free market of ideas and attempting to summon support for its argument (see, in particular, the case of the January 1969 peace initiative). The fact that the CPSU had to argue its policy with other incumbent groups, that it was faced with a sustained and vocal opposition, and that it was often compelled to modify its line in order to accommodate the opposition—all this may attest to the gradual emergence of additional centers of power in the Soviet political context. Several cases suggest that the military-industrial complex may be emerging as a second, if not alternative center of power. Thus, the monistic model, which regards the CPSU as the fount of all power, may have to be replaced by a new structural model that would allow for an emerging poly-centrism.

In our opinion, the political interest groups examined in this study and, in particular, the emerging military-industrial complex do not attempt to challenge the Party's ultimate authority. On the basis of circumstantial evidence, we would venture that the pressure exerted by the political interest groups examined here is for participation *together* with the Party in decision making, rather than for the replacement of the Party.

On the other hand, it should be stressed that the very existence of publicly articulated policy alternatives may increase the accountability of the ultimate decision-makers. Though one can hardly argue that the Soviet leaders are accountable to their "constituencies," "public opinion," or formally responsible bodies (such as the Party Congress or the Supreme Soviet), it is nevertheless plausible that in case of failure a leader associated with a certain policy line would be held responsible by his Central Committee or Politburo colleagues. This may be particularly true under conditions of leadership conflict, when disagreements over policies are closely intertwined with the dynamics of power struggle. Thus, in case of failure, not only the opposition's line but the opposition itself may become a viable political alternative.

The policy process in the USSR has often been described by Western scholars as a unidirectional phenomenon. Brzezinski and Huntington, for example, make a very clear distinction between the initiation of policy in the United States and the USSR. Their general conclusion is that decision making "bubbles up" in the United States and "trickles down" in the Soviet Union. Moreover, they assert, in the United States interest groups, social forces, and lower-ranking government agencies initiate all policy proposals, while in the USSR the topmost leadership does all the important initiating.[1] However, our research dealt with at least four fairly conclusive cases in which the initiative to change or modify the official policy came from groups other than the Party.[2] Furthermore, in retrospect and on evidence available, in all but one of these cases the pressure was successful, and the official policy was adjusted accordingly.

Obviously, we do not deny that initiative often comes from the inner circle of the topmost Party leaders. We do argue, however, that the unidirectional model and the "bubble up—trickle down" dichotomy are too restrictive, if not too simplistic.

Traditionally, disputes and struggles in the communist countries were analyzed along the lines of "left" versus "right," "conservatives" versus "liberals," "dogmatists" versus "pragmatists." In our opinion, these dichotomies are much too narrow to be used as adequate analytical models. As has been seen, the spectrum of opinion is relatively wide and includes numerous variations in the intermediate area between the two poles.

More crucially, the traditional dichotomous approach presupposes a certain totality, or consistency, of opinion. Our study, however, presented numerous cases of liberal hawks and dogmatic doves, i.e., cases in which a certain position on one issue was not accompanied by an analogous posture on another issue. Thus, it appears that ideological or conceptual consistency is an exception rather than the rule in the USSR, as it is, incidentally, anywhere else.

Our study, limited as it might be, presents the Soviet political process as a complex, highly diversified phenomenon. The political forces appear to be in a state of constant flux, with groups tending to coalesce into temporary, shifting alliances, based on low common denominators. Consequently, it is the opinion of this author that any attempt at an a priori categorization of Soviet political groupings and alliances is utterly useless. Similarly, attempts to elaborate structural models divorced from empirical realities are tantamount to placing analysis in a procrustean bed.

The data presented in this study tend to refute yet another stereotype, namely that pertaining to the character and functions of the Soviet press. Anthony Buzek in his book *How the Communist Press Works* attributes four functions to the Soviet mass media: propaganda, agitation, organization, and criticism. He presumes that the press is wholly an instrument of authority and is used for the mobilization and manipulation of the general public, both in the USSR and outside its borders.[3] Similar views are presented by such prominent students of Soviet affairs as Inkeles, Barghoorn, and Fainsod, to name but a few.

The evidence presented throughout this study suggests that it might be appropriate to revise the list of functions traditionally attributed to the Soviet press. This research goes far to substantiate its initial hypothesis that in the Soviet political context the press organs serve as channels of input, as the means through which political interest groups attempt to impress their views upon the decision-makers, summon support for their arguments, and affect the general climate of opinion.

As this study indicates, disagreement and dissent may be voiced only in a cautious, oblique, and sometimes almost surreptitious manner. Fundamental divergences have to be couched in marginalistic terms. Access to the mass media is limited for the general public and presumably for the various splinter groups within the political institutions. The Soviet press is not free. Yet, neither is it the strictly controlled, highly centralized, monolithic, and monotonous instrument of mass manipulation portrayed by most Western scholars.

Notes

Notes

Chapter 1

1. W. Zimmerman, "Elite Perspectives and the Explanation of Soviet Foreign Policy," in *The Conduct of Soviet Foreign Policy,* ed. Erik P. Hoffmann and Frederic J. Fleron, Jr. (Chicago, 1971), pp. 18-19.

2. Roger E. Kanet, ed., *The Behavioral Revolution and Communist Studies* (New York, 1972), pp. 1-8.

3. Carl J. Friedrich and Zbigniew Brzezinski, *Totalitarian Dictatorship and Autocracy* (Cambridge, Mass., 1956), pp. 16-17.

4. Ibid., pp. 9-10.

5. H. Gordon Skilling and Franklyn Griffiths, *Interest Groups in Soviet Politics* (Princeton, N.J., 1971), p. 3.

6. Zbigniew Brzezinski, "Totalitarianism and Rationality," *American Political Science Review* 50 (September 1956): 761. Quoted in Skilling and Griffiths, *Interest Groups in Soviet Politics,* p. 5.

7. Skilling and Griffiths, *Interest Groups in Soviet Politics,* p. 8.

8. Roman Kolkowicz, "Interest Groups in Soviet Politics: The Case of the Military," *Comparative Politics* 2, no. 3 (April 1970): 447.

9. Alexander Dallin, "Soviet Foreign Policy and Domestic Politics," in Hoffmann and Fleron, *The Conduct of Soviet Foreign Policy,* pp. 42-43.

10. Ibid., p. 43.

11. William Keech and Joel Schwartz, "Group Influence in the Policy Process in the Soviet Union," *American Political Science Review* 62 (September 1968): 847.

12. Skilling and Griffiths, *Interest Groups in Soviet Politics,* p. 17. In the communist countries of Eastern Europe, there was a clear indication of the growing importance of groups in the political process. This fact was acknowledged by some communist theorists, such as

Djordjević, Lakatos, Ehrlich, and Šik. See Skilling and Griffiths, *Interest Groups in Soviet Politics,* pp. 12-16.

13. The term *interest group* is more often used than defined. Following David Truman, we shall consider a political interest group an aggregate of persons who have certain characteristics in common, share certain attitudes on public issues, adopt distinct positions on these issues, and make definite claims on those in authority. For a thorough discussion of the applicability of group theories to the USSR, see Skilling and Griffiths, *Interest Groups in Soviet Politics,* pp. 3-45.

14. Zbigniew Brzezinski and Samuel P. Huntington, *Political Power USA/USSR* (New York, 1964). See especially chapter 4.

15. Jeremy R. Azrael, *Managerial Power and Soviet Politics* (Cambridge, Mass., 1966).

16. Kolkowicz, "Interest Groups in Soviet Politics." See also Roman Kolkowicz, *The Soviet Military and the Communist Party* (Princeton, N.J., 1967).

17. John Erickson, *Soviet Military Power* (Tel Aviv, 1972). Hebrew translation by the Israeli Ministry of Defense.

18. Alfred G. Meyer, *The Soviet Political System* (New York, 1965), pp. 233-237.

19. Frederick C. Barghoorn, *Politics in the USSR* (Boston, 1966), p. 216.

20. Wolfgang Leonhard, *The Kremlin Since Stalin* (New York, 1962), pp. 15-17ff.

21. Skilling and Griffiths, *Interest Groups in Soviet Politics,* chapters 1 and 2.

22. Brzezinski and Huntington, *Political Power,* p. 196; Barghoorn, *Politics in the USSR,* pp. 214-215; Azrael, *Managerial Power,* pp. 9-10.

23. Meyer, *Soviet Political System,* pp. 114, 187-193; V. Aspaturian, "The Soviet Union," in *Modern Political Systems,* ed. Roy C. Macridis and R. E. Ward, 2 vols. (Englewood Cliffs, N.J., 1968), pp. 550-551; Skilling and Griffiths, *Interest Groups in Soviet Politics,* chapters 1 and 2.

24. Brzezinski and Huntington, *Political Power,* pp. 196-197; Azrael, *Managerial Power,* p. 9; Barghoorn, *Politics in the USSR,* pp. 213-215.

25. Meyer, *Soviet Political System,* pp. 110-111.

26. Skilling and Griffiths, *Interest Groups in Soviet Politics,* chapters 1 and 2; Boris Meissner, "Totalitarian Rule and Social Change," *Problems of Communism* 15, no. 6 (November-December 1966): 58.

27. Skilling and Griffiths, *Interest Groups in Soviet Politics,* p. 9.

28. See Azrael, *Managerial Power;* Erickson, *Soviet Military Power;* Kolkowicz, *The Soviet Military;* Aspaturian, "The Soviet Union."

29. V. Aspaturian, "The Soviet Military-Industrial Complex: Does It Exist?" *Journal of International Affairs* 26, no. 1 (1972): 7-8; Malcolm Mackintosh, "The Soviet Military—Influence on Foreign Policy," *Problems of Communism* 22, no. 5 (September-October 1973): 4-5.

30. Alexander Dallin, "Soviet Foreign Policy," p. 39.

31. Arthur Bentley, *The Process of Government* (Evanston, Ill., 1949), p. 204.

32. These aspects of policy making have been termed by some specialists in comparative politics the "articulation" and "aggregation" of group interests and "rule application." See G. A. Almond and J. Coleman, eds., *The Politics of the Developing Areas* (Princeton, N.J., 1960), p. 33f.

33. H. Gordon Skilling, in his contribution to the pioneering study he edited together with F. Griffiths, divided Soviet political interest groups into two broad categories: (1) occupational groups, which include certain "intellectual" groups, whose task is primary research or creative work, for example, writers, economists, and lawyers, and certain groups that can be called "official" or "bureaucratic" and that occupy key positions in the power structure, namely, party *apparatchiki,* state bureaucrats, trade union officials, and military men; (2) opinion groups. Since the occupational aggregates are likely to be divided in their attitudes on certain issues, it is assumed that within occupational categories (both official and nonofficial), certain opinion groups may be identified. The members of such a group share, it is assumed, a common viewpoint on specific issues, usually one that is in sharp conflict with that held by other members of the same occupation. For a more thorough analysis, see Skilling and Griffiths, *Interest Groups in Soviet Politics,* pp. 24-32.

34. July 1971, i.e., the month following the signing of the Soviet-Egyptian Friendship and Cooperation Treaty, which institutionalized the Soviet presence in the UAR, was initially chosen as the closing of this research. However, since this date proved very quickly to be only a minor point on the continuum of Soviet-Arab relations, one of the later chapters will attempt to follow up and update the developments in the period July 1971–September 1973.

35. Jan Triska and David D. Finley, *Soviet Foreign Policy* (New York, 1968), pp. 116-117.

36. Triska and Finley, *Soviet Foreign Policy,* pp. 118-120.

37. Robert Levine, *The Arms Race* (Cambridge, Mass., 1963), pp. 28-29.

38. Alexander Dallin, "Soviet Foreign Policy," pp. 39-41.

39. Alex Inkeles, *Social Change in Soviet Russia* (New York, 1968), pp. 265-291.

Chapter 2

1. Roman Kolkowicz, "The Soviet Policy in the Middle East," *The USSR and the Middle East,* ed. M. Confino and S. Shamir (Jerusalem, 1973), p. 79.

2. B. Pinchuk, "Soviet Penetration into the Middle East in Historical Perspective," in ibid., pp. 65-66.

3. C. B. Joynt and O. M. Smolansky, *Soviet Naval Policy in the Mediterranean,* Lehigh University Department of International Affairs, Research Monograph no. 3 (Lehigh, Pennsylvania, 1972), pp. 1-7.

4. Ibid., p. 7.

5. *Pravda* and *Izvestiia,* 24 February 1966; *Pravda* and *Izvestiia,* 25 February 1966.

6. *Pravda,* 26 February 1966.

7. *Izvestiia,* 20 March 1966. Emphasis added. See also ibid., 13 March 1966. (In succeeding quotations, all emphasis has been added unless otherwise noted.)

8. *Pravda,* 18 March 1966; see also *Pravda,* 17 April 1966.

9. Ibid., 18 March 1966. However, *Pravda* of 30 March 1966 did cite a Syrian paper to the effect that the extraordinary regional conference of the Ba'th (held in Damascus March 10-27) agreed "to develop further and deepen the socialist transformation."

10. Ibid., 24 April 1966; *Izvestiia,* 24 April 1966; *Krasnaia zvezda,* 24 April 1966.

11. The construction of the Euphrates High Dam could have resulted in political problems between Syria (and the USSR) and Turkey, with the latter threatening to interfere with the project by building a dam of its own. Moreover, the Syrian dam could have caused extensive damage to Iraq's agriculture. See Walter Laqueur, *The Struggle for the Middle East* (London, 1969), p. 96. Thus, in embarking upon the project, the USSR was taking a significant risk.

12. *Pravda,* 4 December 1966.

13. Ibid., 4 November 1966; ibid., 9 November 1966.

14. *Izvestiia,* 10 November 1966.

Chapter 3

1. See, for example, *Pravda,* 12 February 1967, commenting on Salah Jadid's Moscow visit.

2. A. Levy, "Communism in Syria," in *The USSR and the Middle*

East, ed. M. Confino and S. Shamir (Jerusalem, 1973), p. 398.

3. *Izvestiia,* 8 January 1967.

4. Ibid. See also ibid., 2 February 1967; *Pravda,* 23 April 1967; *Krasnaia zvezda,* 30 April 1967.

5. Levy, "Communism in Syria," p. 398; see also *Pravda,* 6 February 1967; ibid., 10 May 1967.

6. F. J. Khouri, *The Arab-Israeli Dilemma* (Syracuse, 1968), p. 245.

7. *Izvestiia,* 17 May 1967.

8. *Krasnaia zvezda,* 17 May 1967.

9. *Pravda,* 18 May 1967. Nasser claimed in his speech of 9 June 1967 that the Soviets supplied him with information about an Israeli plan to invade Syria through the parliamentary delegation. This was confirmed by Sadat, who headed the delegation, in a speech of 28 September 1975. According to some Western and Israeli observers, however, Soviet warnings about Israeli troop concentrations intended for an invasion of Syria on the morning of 17 May 1967, were officially delivered to the UAR through the Soviet ambassador in Cairo as early as 12 May. See D. Dishon, ed., *Middle East Record, 1967* (Jerusalem, 1971), pp. 189-191.

10. M. Howard and R. Hunter, "Israel and the Arab World, the Crisis of 1967," *Adelphi Papers,* no. 41, pp. 16-17.

11. See *Pravda,* 22 May 1967; ibid., 24 May 1967; ibid., 25 May 1967; *Izvestiia,* 24 May 1967; ibid., 25 May 1967; ibid., 27 May 1967; *Krasnaia zvezda,* 25 May 1967; ibid., 30 May 1967.

12. *Izvestiia,* 21 May 1967.

13. See also *Izvestiia,* 28 May 1967, referring to the "Egyptian Rights in the Straits of Aqaba."

14. Ibid., 28 May 1967.

15. *Krasnaia zvezda,* 25 May 1967.

16. *Pravda,* 27 May 1967; ibid., 28 May 1967; ibid., 31 May 1967; ibid., 1 June 1967; ibid., 4 June 1967.

17. Ibid., 28 May 1967; ibid., 29 May 1967.

18. Ibid., 28 May 1967.

19. Ibid., 27 May 1967.

20. Ibid., 5 June 1967.

21. A good illustration of how those strands were actually presented and intertwined is found in Alexander Kushnir, "Truth about Israel's Aggression," *Soviet Military Review,* no. 8, August 1967, pp. 56-57.

22. See, for example, the Soviet government's declaration of 7 June 1967; the Moscow Declaration, issued after a joint session of members of the central committees of the Soviet and East European communist parties, 9 June 1967; the resolution of the CC CPSU

Plenum of 22 June 1967; Brezhnev's speech before the graduates of the Frunze Military Academy on 5 July 1967; the Budapest Declaration of Soviet bloc leaders, issued on 13 July 1967; Kosygin's speech at the UN General Assembly on 19 June 1967.

23. *Izvestiia* editorial, 16 June 1967.

24. Ibid., 26 July 1967; see also *Krasnaia zvezda*, 22 July 1967.

25. *Krasnaia zvezda*, 11 June 1967.

26. Ibid., 15 June 1967; see also ibid., 14 June 1967; ibid., 23 June 1967; *Izvestiia*, 26 July 1967.

27. *Krasnaia zvezda*, 16 June 1967. See also ibid., 22 June 1967; ibid., 23 June 1967; ibid., 6 July 1967; ibid., 15 July 1967; ibid., 30 July 1967; ibid., 20 August 1967.

28. Ibid., 22 June 1967; ibid., 23 June 1967; ibid., 4 July 1967.

29. Ibid., 4 July 1967.

30. See, in particular, the *Krasnaia zvezda* editorial of 30 December 1967; and two lengthy articles published in ibid., 27 December 1967, and ibid., 30 December 1967, under the title "A Ship Entered the Mediterranean."

31. *Krasnaia zvezda* editorial, 22 June 1967.

32. For example, ibid., 9 June 1967.

33. See also ibid., 23 June 1967.

34. Ibid.

35. Ibid.

36. See ibid., 23 June 1967; ibid., 4 July 1967.

37. *Pravda*, 6 September 1967.

38. *Izvestiia*, 14 July 1967.

39. Ibid.; *Pravda*, 9 August 1967.

40. *Pravda*, 9 August 1967.

41. *Izvestiia*, 24 July 1967.

42. *Pravda*, 11 July 1967.

43. Ibid., 11 June 1967; ibid., 6 August 1967.

44. *Izvestiia*, 21 June 1967; ibid., 28 June 1967; ibid., 14 July 1967.

45. Ibid., 12 June 1967.

46. *Pravda*, 25 August 1967.

47. Ibid., 18 June 1967.

48. Ibid., 25 August 1967.

49. *Izvestiia*, 27 June 1967.

50. *Pravda*, 25 August 1967.

51. Ibid., 11 June 1967; *Izvestiia*, 11 June 1967; *Krasnaia zvezda*, 11 June 1967.

52. See, for example, *Pravda*, 13 June 1967; *Izvestiia*, 14 June

1967; *Krasnaia zvezda,* 14 June 1967.

53. *Pravda,* 9 August 1967.

54. See, for example, ibid., 24 June 1967; ibid., 6 July 1967; *Izvestiia,* 15 June 1967; ibid., 27 June 1967; *Krasnaia zvezda,* 20 August 1967.

55. See, for example, *Pravda,* 29 June 1967; ibid., 10 July 1967; ibid., 14 July 1967; ibid., 9 August 1967; *Izvestiia,* 11 June 1967; ibid., 13 June 1967; *Krasnaia zvezda,* 14 June 1967; ibid., 15 July 1967.

56. *Izvestiia,* 11 June 1967; *Krasnaia zvezda,* 22 June 1967.

57. *Pravda,* 10 July 1967; ibid., 12 July 1967; ibid., 14 July 1967; *Izvestiia,* 8 July 1967; *Krasnaia zvezda,* 14 July 1967.

58. *Pravda,* 19 June 1967; ibid., 16 July 1967; ibid., 23 July 1967; *Izvestiia,* 27 June 1967; ibid., 30 June 1967; *Krasnaia zvezda,* 22 June 1967; ibid., 15 July 1967.

59. *Pravda,* 14 June 1967; ibid., 15 June 1967; ibid., 16 June 1967.

Chapter 4

1. *Pravda,* 29 July 1967.

2. Ibid.

3. Ibid. In view of this reference to "seizures after" the 1948-1949 war, *Pravda*'s definition of annexation appeared to apply only to the results of the June 1967 war.

4. Ibid.; see also ibid., 3 August 1967.

5. Ibid., 3 August 1967.

6. Ibid.

7. Ibid.

8. Ibid., 29 July 1967.

9. Ibid.; ibid., 3 August 1967.

10. Ibid., 19 June 1967; ibid., 23 June 1967; ibid., 12 July 1967; ibid., 16 July 1967. In a commentary published on 9 August, *Pravda* went as far as to relegate the solution of the Arab-Israeli dispute to the course of history itself, stating that "in the final account, Israel would have to leave the Arab lands since it attempts to go against the irreversible trend of history."

11. Ibid., 14 July 1967; see *Pravda*'s editorials of 25 June and 30 June 1967.

12. *Pravda*'s editorials of 14 July and 3 August 1967.

13. Ibid., 29 July 1967; see also ibid., 2 August 1967 and ibid., 28 August 1967. Refuting "allegations" that the Soviet Middle East policy stems from anti-Semitism, *Pravda* may have been pursuing yet another goal, namely, to prevent total alienation on the part of the

Soviet Jewish population, whose identification with Israel and Zionism increased significantly after the Six-Day War. It is noteworthy that *Izvestiia* sided with this aspect of *Pravda*'s line. In an article signed by Yurii Ivanov and published on 2 July 1967, the Zionist ideology and leadership were subjected to virulent criticism. However, Ivanov emphasized that "the nationalistic ruling elite of Israel . . . should not be confused with the Israeli nation."

14. See, for example, *Izvestiia,* 28 June 1967; ibid., 25 July 1967; *Krasnaia zvezda,* 23 July 1967; ibid., 24 July 1967.

15. See, for example, *Izvestiia,* 23 June 1967; ibid., 24 June 1967; ibid., 27 June 1967; ibid., 28 June 1967; ibid., 25 July 1967; ibid., 24 August 1967; *Krasnaia zvezda,* 23 July 1967; ibid., 24 July 1967; ibid., 20 August 1967; ibid., 24 August 1967; ibid., 23 September 1967; ibid., 25 September 1967.

16. *Izvestiia,* 25 July 1967.

17. This explanation presupposes that those responsible for *Krasnaia zvezda* and *Izvestiia* were equally well aware of the fact that, at least in the near future, the Arabs would not be able to regain their lost territories by military means. *Izvestiia*'s and *Krasnaia zvezda*'s pronounced support of Arab extremism may be taken literally, i.e., as an advocacy (or pledge) of direct Soviet involvement on the Arab side in a new military round. However, in view of the scope of the Soviet presence at that time, this explanation seems somewhat farfetched.

18. *Krasnaia zvezda* refrained from adopting any position toward the summit, publishing only infrequent, laconic TASS reports of the proceedings.

19. See, for example, *Pravda,* 8 August 1967; ibid., 16 August 1967; ibid., 19 August 1967; and ibid., 31 August 1967. All were written by Beliaev and Primakov.

20. Beliaev and Primakov in *Pravda,* 6 August 1967. See also ibid., 19 August 1967; ibid., 30 August 1967; and ibid., 31 August 1967.

21. *Pravda,* 4 September 1967; *Izvestiia,* 5 September 1967.

22. *Pravda,* 5 September 1967; *Izvestiia,* 5 September 1967. See also *Izvestiia,* 19 December 1967.

23. *Izvestiia,* 5 September 1967.

24. *Pravda,* 5 September 1967.

25. *Pravda,* 4 September 1967.

26. Beliaev and Primakov in *Pravda,* 5 September 1967.

27. In a later commentary, *Izvestiia*'s correspondent Matveev stated that peace in the Middle East was impossible without a "just solution of the Palestinian problem." *Izvestiia,* 11 November 1967.

28. *Pravda*, 4 November 1967; *Izvestiia*, 4 November 1967; and *Krasnaia zvezda*, 4 November 1967.

29. *Pravda*, 11 November 1967; *Krasnaia zvezda*, 11 November 1967; *Izvestiia*, 12 November 1967.

30. See also the Soviet press quotation of the Egyptian media's reaction to the meeting; it appeared under the headline "Brezhnev Required Full Liquidation." *Pravda*, 24 November 1967; *Krasnaia zvezda*, 24 November 1967; *Izvestiia*, 25 November 1967.

31. Presumably the one proposed by the Soviet representative Kuznetsov. See *Pravda*, 11 November 1967; *Izvestiia*, 11 November 1967; *Krasnaia zvezda*, 11 November 1967; ibid., 22 November 1967.

32. Vishnevskii in *Pravda*, 27 November 1967. See also Kudriavtsev in *Izvestiia*, 24 November 1967; and Zavilov in *Krasnaia zvezda*, 28 November 1967.

33. Kudriavtsev in *Izvestiia*, 24 November 1967. See also Maevskii in *Pravda*, 24 November 1967; Vishnevskii in *Pravda*, 27 November 1967; *Krasnaia zvezda*, 28 November 1967.

34. *Pravda*, 27 November 1967.

35. The English version of Security Council Resolution 242 called for "withdrawal from the occupied territories." The French translation added the definite article *les*, thus referring to withdrawal from *the* occupied territories. Since Russian has no definite article, Soviet official interpretation immediately added the word *all*, thus clarifying its stand on this seemingly semantic dispute.

36. See, for example, *Pravda*, 18 February 1968; ibid., 6 June 1968; ibid., 21 June 1968; ibid., 19 August 1968; ibid., 30 September 1968.

37. Ibid., 21 June 1968. See also ibid., 28 January 1968; ibid., 23 March 1968.

38. Ibid., 13 April 1968. See also ibid., 8 March 1968; ibid., 5 June 1968; ibid., 24 July 1968.

39. Ibid., 12 February 1968. See also ibid., 18 February 1968; ibid., 18 April 1968; and ibid., 28 April 1968.

40. Ibid., 12 February 1968. See also ibid., 19 February 1968; ibid., 6 March 1968; ibid., 18 April 1968; ibid., 13 May 1968.

41. *Le Monde*, (Paris) 12-13 May 1968.

42. Primakov in *Pravda*, 20 May 1968.

43. Ibid.

44. Ibid., 29 May 1968. See also ibid., 25 June 1968.

45. Ibid., 25 June 1968; ibid., 24 July 1968.

46. Ibid., 26 May 1968; ibid., 3 June 1968.

47. Ibid., 3 June 1968.

48. *Izvestiia,* 2 February 1968; ibid., 24 February 1968; ibid., 27 April 1968.

49. Ibid., 27 March 1968.

50. See, for example, ibid., 24 Feburary 1968; ibid., 14 April 1968.

51. Ibid., 7 January 1968. See also ibid., 16 January 1968; ibid., 24 February 1968; ibid., 26 March 1968; ibid., 4 June 1968; ibid., 9 September 1968.

52. Ibid., 24 February 1968.

53. Ibid., 20 August 1968. See also ibid., 19 September 1968; ibid., 22 September 1968.

54. Ibid., 14 May 1968.

55. Ibid. See also ibid., 15 May 1968.

56. Demchenko in ibid., 23 May 1968.

57. No patronymic given. It is interesting that several Soviet journalists bear the same surnames as top officials. However, it is almost impossible to establish the existence of family ties.

58. Lieutenant-Colonel Popov in *Krasnaia zvezda,* 15 November 1968. See also ibid., 15 July 1968; and ibid., 4 December 1968.

59. Ibid., 24 April 1968; ibid., 3 July 1968; ibid., 15 November 1968.

60. Ibid., 19 July 1968; ibid., 9 August 1968.

61. Colonel Leont'ev in ibid., 15 July 1968. See also ibid., 23 February 1968; ibid., 29 March 1968; ibid., 23 May 1968; ibid., 19 July 1968; ibid., 12 September 1968; ibid., 9 December 1968.

62. Ibid., 25 July 1968; ibid., 15 November 1968.

63. Ibid., 15 November 1968; ibid., 4 December 1968.

64. Ibid., 21 May 1968.

65. See also ibid., 3 July 1968.

66. On June 4, *Izvestiia*'s commentator Kudriavtsev wrote that "the Soviet Union supports the Arabs' readiness to liquidate the results of the Israeli aggression by political means. This is the only reasonable way to normalize the situation." Yet, except for this isolated instance, *Izvestiia* did not side with *Pravda.*

67. In Soviet parlance, the term *frank* usually connotes lack of agreement. Western comment following the visit stressed "mutual disappointment from the talks." *Daily Telegraph* (London), 10 July 1968; *Times* (London), 11 July 1968.

68. *Al-Ahram,* 12 July 1968, as quoted in Daniel Dishon, ed., the *Middle East Record, 1968* (Jerusalem, 1973), pp. 49-50.

69. See, for example, *Pravda,* 19 July 1968; ibid., 21 August 1968; ibid., 13 October 1968; ibid., 17 November 1968; ibid., 24 November

1968; ibid., 10 December 1968.

70. Ibid., 24 November 1968.

71. Ibid., 3 November 1968. See also ibid., 14 November 1968; ibid., 29 December 1968.

72. Ibid., 6 November 1968. *Pravda* seemed to play on the assonance between Mos'ka and Moshe, the former being the Russian popular, often derogatory, form of the latter.

73. *Izvestiia*, 6 November 1968; *Krasnaia zvezda*, 6 November 1968.

74. This statement was in sharp contrast with *Izvestiia*'s pronouncement following the Khartoum conference (see above) as well as with its later statements (see below).

75. *Izvestiia* added the explanation that the reference was to the "Palestinian problem."

76. Popov in *Izvestiia*, 28 December 1968. In Arab parlance, the term *restoration of justice* frequently connotes the solution of the Palestinian problem.

77. Cf. Dishon, *Middle East Record, 1968,* p. 56.

78. It is interesting that the second stage of the plan referred only to the Israeli-Egyptian issue.

79. *Pravda*, 7 February 1969; *Izvestiia*, 8 February 1969; *Krasnaia zvezda*, 8 February 1969.

80. See, for example, *Pravda*, 11 January 1969; ibid., 2 March 1969; ibid., 23 March 1969; ibid., 8 April 1969; ibid., 10 April 1969; *Izvestiia*, 26 February 1969; ibid., 27 September 1969; ibid., 9 October 1969; *Krasnaia zvezda*, 10 January 1969; ibid., 5 February 1969; ibid., 14 February 1969.

81. *Pravda*, 2 June 1969; ibid., 6 June 1969; ibid., 7 June 1969; ibid., 10 June 1969; ibid., 7 July 1969; ibid., 9 July 1969; *Izvestiia*, 26 February 1969; ibid., 4 June 1969; ibid., 5 June 1969; ibid., 14 September 1969; ibid., 5 October 1969; ibid., 27 November 1969; *Krasnaia zvezda*, 10 January 1969; ibid., 14 February 1969.

82. See references in preceding note. See also official pronouncements such as Gromyko's speech at the UN General Assembly on 20 September 1969; Podgornyi's speech of 7 November 1969; the Warsaw Pact resolution on the Middle East, 27 November 1969.

83. *Pravda*, 11 January 1969; ibid., 22 January 1969; ibid., 2 March 1969; ibid., 23 March 1969; ibid., 8 April 1969; ibid., 10 April 1969; ibid., 1 May 1969; ibid., 2 June 1969; ibid., 6 June 1969; ibid., 7 June 1969; ibid., 10 June 1969; ibid., 7 July 1969; ibid., 9 July 1969; ibid., 13 July 1969; ibid., 27 July 1969; ibid., 31 August 1969; *Izvestiia*, 5 June 1969; ibid., 29 June 1969; ibid., 10 August 1969;

ibid., 27 September 1969; ibid., 9 October 1969.

84. *Izvestiia,* 5 June 1969. See also the previous references and ibid., 16 April 1969; ibid., 20 June 1969; ibid., 29 June 1969; *Pravda,* 2 March 1969.

85. See, for example, *Krasnaia zvezda,* 7 January 1969; ibid., 10 January 1969; ibid., 14 February 1969; ibid., 26 April 1969.

86. *Pravda,* 30 August 1969.

87. Ibid., 8 April 1969. See also *Izvestiia,* 27 July 1969; *Krasnaia zvezda,* 5 February 1969; ibid., 2 February 1969; ibid., 16 April 1969.

88. See, for example, N. Bragin in *Pravda,* 23 March 1969; V. Rumiantsev in ibid., 6 June 1969; Academician B. Gafurov in ibid., 4 September 1969.

89. Rumiantsev in *Pravda,* 6 June 1969. See also Bragin in ibid., 23 March 1969.

90. *Izvestiia,* 16 April 1969.

91. *Pravda,* 14 March 1969; *Izvestiia,* 27 March 1969; *Krasnaia zvezda,* 14 April 1969.

92. *Pravda,* 9 May 1969. Interestingly enough, the author, *Pravda*'s Middle East correspondent Primakov, added that "Egypt, for its part, is aware of the dangers of underestimating the enemy and will not allow itself to be dragged into any adventure." Neither *Izvestiia* nor *Krasnaia zvezda* presupposed such "political wisdom" and self-restraint on Egypt's part. See also *Pravda,* 14 March 1969; ibid., 1 May 1969; ibid., 23 July 1969; ibid., 30 July 1969; *Izvestiia,* 27 March 1969; ibid., 25 April 1969; ibid., 30 April 1969; ibid., 11 May 1969; ibid., 22 May 1969; ibid., 25 June 1969; ibid., 2 July 1969; ibid., 13 September 1969; *Krasnaia zvezda,* 5 February 1969; ibid., 14 April 1969; ibid., 16 May 1969; ibid., 12 September 1969; ibid., 21 November 1969.

93. *Krasnaia zvezda,* 15 April 1969. See also ibid., 10 January 1969; ibid., 24 January 1969; ibid., 14 February 1969; ibid., 15 March 1969; ibid., 16 April 1969; ibid., 26 April 1969; ibid., 7 June 1969; ibid., 2 August 1969.

94. *Krasnaia zvezda*'s editorial of 4 September 1969. See also ibid., 15 March 1969; ibid., 15 April 1969; ibid., 24 December 1969.

95. Ibid., 2 February 1969; ibid., 14 March 1969; ibid., 16 May 1969; ibid., 2 August 1969; ibid., 11 September 1969; ibid., 12 September 1969; ibid., 2 November 1969.

96. Ibid., 21 November 1969. See also the editorial of 4 September 1969.

97. Colonel Ponomarev and R. Vasil'ev in ibid., 10 January 1969. See also ibid., 24 January 1969; ibid., 5 February 1969; ibid., 15 March 1969; ibid., 11 April 1969; ibid., 15 April 1969; ibid., 16 April 1969;

ibid., 26 April 1969; ibid., 2 August 1969; ibid., 8 August 1969; ibid., 14 August 1969; ibid., 12 September 1969; ibid., 27 September 1969; ibid., 7 October 1969; ibid., 9 October 1969.

98. *Krasnaia zvezda*'s "International Military Review" of 24 January 1969 claimed that apart from thirty Hawk surface-to-air missiles, Israel was developing a surface-to-surface seaborne missile named Gabriel and a two-stage, guided, surface-to-surface rocket MD-660. This rocket, according to *Krasnaia zvezda*'s report, "uses solid fuel and can carry conventional or nuclear warheads."

99. *Krasnaia zvezda,* 10 January 1969; ibid., 24 January 1969; ibid., 16 April 1969.

100. Ibid., 2 August 1969. See also ibid., 11 September 1969; ibid., 12 September 1969; ibid., 12 October 1969. This appraisal of the Chieftain is extremely interesting, particularly in view of the fact that in 1967 Soviet tanks proved unsuitable to desert conditions. Thus, this reference may indicate pressure to develop a model better adapted to desert warfare or a new antitank weapon or both. Both may have seemed needed not only for the Middle East but also for Soviet use, especially in view of the clashes with China.

101. Ibid., 5 February 1969.

102. See, for example, *al-Ahram* of 27 April 1969 warning that "all-out war" was imminent unless the Big Four "take action."

103. See the *Daily Telegraph* (London), 2 March 1969.

104. The full text of the speech is quoted in *Record of the Arab World* pp. 1848-1860.

105. Ibid., p. 3008. Moscow preferred not to acquaint the Arab public with the fact that Nasser was facing internal opposition. This seems clear from the way parts of Rumiantsev's article were broadcast by Radio Moscow in English and other foreign languages but omitted from the Arabic version.

106. *Izvestiia,* 31 May 1969.

107. Ibid., 5 June 1969.

108. *Izvestiia* published four more articles to the same effect. Interestingly enough, the later articles were even more unequivocal in refuting "malicious psychological warfare waged by the imperialists" and aimed at "discrediting the USSR," driving a wedge between the USSR and its Arab allies, and changing the existing balance of power. All these articles included strongly worded pledges of Soviet support. See ibid., 26 July 1969; ibid., 7 October 1969; ibid., 27 November 1969; ibid., 4 December 1969.

109. See the *New York Times,* 11 June 1969; ibid., 15 June 1969; ibid., 18 June 1969; *The Economist,* 14 June 1969.

110. The Soviet-Egyptian communiqué of 14 June 1969 employed a new formula—to the effect that "the efforts to achieve a peace settlement in the Middle East require the implementation of the Security Council resolution of November 22, 1967, in all its provisions *and* the withdrawal by Israel of its forces from all Arab territories occupied as a result of the June 5, 1967, aggression." Hitherto, Soviet and joint Arab-Soviet statements asserted that the Security Council resolution "envisages" or "presupposes" an Israeli withdrawal.

111. *New York Times,* 18 June 1969.

112. Cf. *Record of the Arab World,* pp. 2308-2310.

113. See *MENA,* 23 July 1969. Several sources place the beginning of the War of Attrition in spring 1969.

114. Ibid. For a full text of both statements, see *Record of the Arab World,* pp. 2299-2313.

115. *Pravda,* 15 June 1969.

116. *Izvestiia,* 26 July 1969.

117. *Krasnaia zvezda,* 11 September 1969.

118. See, for example, *Izvestiia,* 26 July 1969; ibid., 14 September 1969; ibid., 27 September 1969; *Krasnaia zvezda,* 2 August 1969; ibid., 12 September 1969; ibid., 14 September 1969.

119. *Pravda,* 15 July 1969.

120. Associated Press report from Beirut, quoted by *Record of the Arab World,* p. 2318.

121. Ibid.

122. Ibid.

123. Radio Moscow in Arabic referred on two separate occasions to this "hostile campaign," without, however, mentioning Sabri's name. Reference was made only to "false rumors" about pro-Soviet elements being purged." "Those who circulate such rumors will end in a filthy swamp," warned Radio Moscow on 18 September. See also Radio Moscow, 22 September, quoted by the BBC Summary of World Broadcasts, 20 September and 24 September 1969.

124. See also *Pravda,* 16 September 1969.

125. In the same article, *Pravda* urged the UN to employ sanctions against Israel in order to "compel it to carry out the UN decisions. Continued tension is fraught with danger, first and foremost danger to Israel itself. In challenging the peace-loving countries . . . the Israeli extremists are playing with fire, putting the nations' patience to a hard test."

126. See, in particular, Medvedko in *Pravda,* 5 October 1969; ibid., 23 October 1969. See also *Izvestiia,* 9 October 1969; ibid., 21 October 1969; *Krasnaia zvezda,* 14 October 1969; ibid., 21 October

1969; ibid., 30 October 1969.

127. Full text of Nasser's speech quoted in *Record of the Arab World*, pp. 3071-3076.

128. Ibid., p. 3078.

129. As a further illustration of the hardening of Egypt's stand, one may cite the following events. On 25 September 1969, Egyptian Foreign Minister Riyad told reporters at the UN that his government was ready to negotiate with Israel through Dr. Jarring according to the Rhodes formula. The reference was probably to the 1949 negotiations conducted on Rhodes by UN mediator Ralph Bunche with the Israeli and Arab delegates separately. Confusion immediately set in when other Egyptian sources claimed that Riyad's declaration was misinterpreted. Egypt's indecision, which lasted for about two weeks, indicated that there were opposing currents pulling in different directions. Finally, after two weeks of statements and counterstatements, the negative, uncompromising influence predominated. On 12 October, the Rhodes formula and, in fact, any possibility of negotiations with Israel were officially rejected. Ibid., pp. 3710-3715. On 28 October, the United States presented the Soviets with a ten-point plan for the settlement of the Israeli-Egyptian dispute. On 10 November, *Agence France du Presse* reported from Cairo that the UAR government had received the text of the American proposal from Ambassador Vinogradov. On 18 November, Egypt categorically rejected the peace proposal. Ibid., pp. 3689-3691.

130. *Izvestiia,* 28 November 1969. See also ibid., 29 November 1969.

131. See also *Krasnaia zvezda,* 28 November 1969.

132. *Agence France du Presse,* 27 November 1969, quoted in *Record of the Arab World,* p. 3673.

133. UPI report quoted in ibid., p. 3674. See also Radio Cairo commentary of 2 December 1969, quoted in ibid., p. 3679.

134. *Pravda,* 9 December 1969.

135. The so-called Rogers Plan has never been made public. According to the *New York Times* of 13 January 1970, Rogers' speech of 9 December 1969 contained the essence of the American proposal.

136. *Izvestiia,* 26 December 1969. See also ibid., 18 December 1969.

137. *Krasnaia zvezda,* 24 December 1969.

138. See the *New York Times,* 13 January 1970. See also *Record of the Arab World,* pp. 3704-3705.

139. See, for example, *Pravda,* 7 January 1968; ibid., 31 March 1968; ibid., 13 April 1968; ibid., 10 May 1968.

140. *Izvestiia*, 25 January 1968; ibid., 27 November 1968.

141. Ibid., 28 March 1968. See also *Krasnaia zvezda*, 11 October 1968.

142. *Izvestiia*, 25 January 1968; ibid., 3 February 1968; ibid., 28 March 1968; ibid., 6 May 1968; *Krasnaia zvezda*, 7 February 1968; ibid., 11 February 1968; ibid., 6 May 1968; ibid., 12 May 1968.

143. *Krasnaia zvezda*, 12 March 1968. See also ibid., 10 October 1968; ibid., 11 November 1968; *Izvestiia*, 25 January 1968. *Izvestiia*'s commentary of 25 January 1968 stated that by attacking the Arabs, Israel eased the conduct of the Vietnam war. No explanation or further details were given. *Pravda* also repeated the notion that the increasing tension in the Middle East "diverts world attention from the US crimes in Vietnam." *Pravda*, 10 May 1968; ibid., 19 July 1968; ibid., 21 August 1968; ibid., 28 October 1968. For *Krasnaia zvezda*, see below.

144. *Izvestiia*, 25 January 1968.

145. Ibid. See also ibid., 25 April 1969; ibid., 4 June 1969; ibid., 2 July 1969; ibid., 3 August 1969.

146. *Krasnaia zvezda* went as far as to claim that Israel was, for all intents and purposes, a NATO member. *Krasnaia zvezda*, 13 October 1968; ibid., 15 November 1968; ibid., 5 December 1968. Moreover, in a commentary published on 15 November, Lieutenant-Colonel Leont'ev cited American press reports about the existence of a US-Israeli agreement that "envisages the possibility" of direct US intervention in the Arab-Israeli conflict. In the paragraph immediately following these revelations, Leont'ev drew attention to the "steadily increasing combat readiness" of the Arab states and to their "resolve to defend their rights." Thus, few doubts were left as to the course the USSR should adopt in view of the alleged existence of this agreement.

147. See, for example, *Izvestiia*, 3 August 1968; ibid., 4 October 1968; *Krasnaia zvezda*, 13 October 1968; ibid., 15 November 1968; ibid., 5 December 1968.

148. *Krasnaia zvezda* editorials of 23 March 1968, 8 September 1968, 29 September 1968; Marshal Grechko's article in ibid., 16 February 1968; Marshal Zakharov's article in ibid., 17 February 1968. See also *Krasnaia zvezda*'s "International Military Commentaries" of 23 January 1968 and 4 February 1968. These commentaries almost invariably followed a set pattern: attack on the American aggression in Southeast Asia was followed by an indignant condemnation of the current "crime" committed by the "imperialists" (such as the *Pueblo* incident, support of the "black colonels" in Greece, and the loss of an atomic bomb around Greenland). Then the "increasing tension and deteriorating situation" in the Middle East were examined. Thereupon

followed the conclusion that all these developments were links in the chain of imperialist assault, necessitating "constant vigilance and increased combat preparedness on the part of the Soviet armed forces."

149. *Krasnaia zvezda* editorial, 4 February 1968. See also ibid., 23 January 1968; ibid., 7 November 1968; *Izvestiia* editorial, 28 March 1968; Demchenko in ibid., 2 June 1968; Popov in ibid., 5 September 1968.

150. See, for example, *Krasnaia zvezda,* 15 March 1968; ibid., 29 March 1968; ibid., 15 July 1968; ibid., 19 July 1968.

151. See, for example, *Izvestiia,* 10 November 1968; ibid., 18 December 1968; ibid., 29 December 1968. Interestingly, *Izvestiia's* one and only reference to Israeli efforts to achieve nuclear capability was included in an article condemning the raid on Naj' Hamadi. *Izvestiia,* 10 November 1968.

152. *Krasnaia zvezda,* 17 February 1968. See also ibid., 28 July 1968; ibid., 29 September 1968; ibid., 2 November 1968; ibid., 12 November 1968; ibid., 24 November 1968; ibid., 27 November 1968; *Izvestiia,* 28 July 1968.

153. Admiral Kasatonov mentioned, without any further elaboration, the presence of Soviet "surface ships and submarines in the Mediterranean."

154. The notion that the Soviet Union's naval stature in the Black Sea made it a Mediterranean power was first introduced by Gromyko in an interview with the Italian *Unita* on 12 May 1968. See Y. Ro'i, *From Encroachment to Involvement* (Jerusalem, 1974). The Soviet press completely ignored Gromyko's statement.

155. The elaboration of a joint position on the issue of the Soviet presence in the Mediterranean was reflected in a proliferation of articles analyzing the problem along the lines established in the November statement. See, for example, *Pravda,* 8 December 1968; ibid., 9 December 1968; ibid., 13 December; *Krasnaia zvezda,* 27 November 1968; ibid., 30 November 1968; ibid., 8 December 1968; *Izvestiia,* 26 November 1968; ibid., 9 December 1968; ibid., 17 December 1968.

Chapter 5

1. Uri Ra'anan, "Moscow and the Third World," *Problems of Communism* 14, no. 1 (January-February, 1965): 22.

2. See Roger Kanet, "The Recent Soviet Reassessment of Developments in the Third World," in *The Conduct of Soviet Foreign Policy,* ed. Erik P. Hoffmann and Frederic J. Fleron, Jr. (Chicago, 1971), p. 399.

3. For details, see ibid.

4. Ra'anan, "Moscow and the Third World," p. 24; Kanet, "Recent Soviet Reassessment," pp. 403-404.

5. Ra'anan, "Moscow and the Third World," p. 24.

6. For a detailed analysis of this controversy, see Oded Eran, "Soviet Perceptions of Arab Communism and its Political Role," in *The USSR and the Middle East,* ed. M. Confino and S. Shamir (Jerusalem, 1973), pp. 109-123.

7. Ibid., p. 114.

8. Marshall Shulman, "Recent Soviet Foreign Policy, Some Patterns in Retrospcet," in Hoffman and Fleron, *Conduct of Soviet Foreign Policy,* pp. 467-468.

9. Brezhnev's speech quoted in *Pravda,* 30 March 1966.

10. *New Times,* 19 April 1967, quoted by Ya'acov Ro'i, "The USSR and the Middle East," in *Middle East Record, 1967,* ed. D. Dishon (Jerusalem, 1971) p. 7.

11. Ibid.

12. *Aziia i Afrika Segodnia,* March 1967, quoted by Ro'i, "The USSR and the Middle East," p. 7.

13. Radio Moscow, 21 April 1967, quoted by Ro'i, "The USSR and the Middle East," p. 3.

14. *Pravda,* 6 June 1969. See also ibid., 7 July 1969; ibid., 23 July 1969; *Izvestiia,* 14 March 1968; ibid., 2 April 1968; ibid., 3 July 1968; ibid., 23 July 1969; *Krasnaia zvezda,* 23 July 1968; ibid., 25 September 1969.

15. *Pravda*'s commentator E. Primakov in *International Affairs,* March 1968. See also Primakov in *Za rubezhom,* 5-11 July 1968; *Pravda,* 26 April 1968; ibid., 28 April 1968; ibid., 25 July 1968; ibid., 16 September 1968; *Izvestiia,* 23 July 1968.

16. Volskii in *Krasnaia zvezda,* 3 July 1968.

17. *Izvestiia,* 25 September 1969.

18. *Pravda,* 23 July 1968. See also *Krasnaia zvezda,* 3 July 1968.

19. *Pravda,* 23 July 1968. See also *Izvestiia,* 23 July 1968; *Krasnaia zvezda,* 3 July 1968.

20. *Pravda,* 22 January 1969; ibid., 7 May 1969; ibid., 6 June 1969; ibid., 23 July 1969; ibid., 27 August 1969; *Izvestiia,* 21 June 1968; ibid., 4 June 1968; *Krasnaia zvezda,* 25 September 1969.

21. Beliaev in *Pravda,* 23 July 1968. Implied here is an admission that there is a Soviet influence over the region. In this sense, this citation is unique. See also ibid., 1 April 1968; ibid., 25 July 1968; *Izvestiia,* 4 July 1968; ibid., 17 December 1968; *Krasnaia zvezda,* 3 July 1968.

22. R. Hrair Dekmejian, *Egypt under Nasir* (Albany, New York,

1971), p. 253.

23. *Pravda,* 27 February 1968.

24. *Pravda,* 28 February 1968.

25. *Izvestiia,* 28 February 1968.

26. Ibid.; *Pravda,* 28 February 1968.

27. *Pravda,* 5 March 1968; *Izvestiia,* 5 March 1968; *Krasnaia zvezda,* 5 March 1968. According to Dekmejian, "Nasir skillfully placed himself on the side of the demonstrators by castigating the police for initially resorting to force and blamed a handful of reactionary agents for the disturbances." Dekmejian, *Egypt under Nasir,* p. 258.

28. Kudriavtsev in *Izvestiia,* 6 March 1968.

29. Dekmejian, *Egypt under Nasir,* p. 258.

30. Ibid.

31. *Pravda,* 7 March 1968.

32. Dekmejian, *Egypt under Nasir,* pp. 258-259.

33. Ibid., pp. 259-261.

34. *Pravda,* 20 April 1968; ibid., 28 April 1968; *Izvestiia,* 27 April 1968; ibid., 5 May 1968; *Krasnaia zvezda,* 5 May 1968.

35. *Izvestiia,* 5 May 1968.

36. *Pravda,* 20 April 1968.

37. Ibid.

38. Ibid., 11 May 1968.

39. See, for example, *Krasnaia zvezda,* 2 April 1968; ibid., 20 April 1968; ibid., 4 May 1968; ibid., 5 May 1968.

40. Though the attitudes of the fourth newspaper, *Trud,* will be analyzed in detail in a separate chapter, it might be interesting to note here that *Trud* remained neutral in this discussion. Neither democracy nor the ASU's leading role was presented as the main goal of the program. *Trud* referred to the program in such noncommittal terms as "widening the social basis," and "deepening the progressive transformation" without providing any further elaboration. See Repin in *Trud,* 4 July 1968. In all, *Trud* referred only three times to the March 30 Program.

41. Dekmejian, *Egypt under Nasir,* p. 264.

42. *Izvestiia,* 26 November 1968.

43. *Pravda,* 4 December 1968.

44. *Krasnaia zvezda,* 4 December 1968.

45. *Izvestiia,* 3 December 1968.

46. *Trud* again maintained a neutral position. In its only reference to the November events, it made every effort to bridge over the two conflicting interpretations. "Whatever the motives of the demonstrators might have been, they worked against the cause [for which] Egypt is

fighting, against the soldier in the front, against the partisan in the occupied territories," wrote *Trud* on 4 December. Despite this attempt to maintain neutrality, *Trud* was closer to *Pravda* than it was to *Izvestiia*.

47. Demchenko was appointed *Izvestiia*'s Cairo correspondent in July 1968. During that year several of his reports were published in *Izvestiia*. In 1969 Demchenko was apparently busy traveling throughout the Middle East; most of his reports in that year dealt with Syria, Iraq, or the Arab-Israeli conflict.

48. Emphasis in the original. For a similar statement, see Beliaev in *Pravda*, 27 August 1969.

49. Primakov in *Pravda*, 7 May 1969. See also Rumiantsev in ibid., 6 June 1969.

50. Rumiantsev in ibid., 6 June 1969.

51. For further references, see Miasnikov in ibid., 22 January 1969; and Beliaev in ibid., 27 August 1969.

52. Miasnikov in ibid., 22 January 1969.

53. Ibid., 7 May 1969.

54. See, for example, Miasnikov in *Pravda*, 22 January 1969; Primakov in ibid., 7 May 1969.

55. Glukhov in ibid., 7 July 1969. See also ibid., 7 May 1969; ibid., 6 June 1969; ibid., 27 August 1969.

56. This position was diametrically opposed to *Izvestiia*'s argument that the achievement of the Arab national goal presupposed the transition to socialism. See above, p. 116, and below pp. 125-127.

57. Miasnikov in *Pravda*, 22 January 1969.

58. When he introduced the New Economic Policy (NEP), Lenin described it as taking one step back in order to take two steps forward.

59. Ibid. For similar pronouncements, see Rumiantsev in ibid., 6 June 1969; and Beliaev in ibid., 27 August 1969.

60. Savin in *Krasnaia zvezda*, 25 September 1969. Savin's name appears very infrequently in *Krasnaia zvezda*. It is impossible to determine whether he is a military man or what his affiliation may be.

61. Ibid.

62. Beliaev in *Pravda*, 27 August 1969.

63. Primakov in ibid., 13 May 1969; Rumiantsev in ibid., 6 June 1969.

64. Beliaev in ibid., 27 August 1969. See also Primakov in ibid., 13 May 1969.

65. Beliaev in ibid., 23 July 1968.

66. Ibid. See also Primakov in ibid., 13 May 1969.

67. This analysis by *Pravda*'s senior commentators was diametrically opposed to Mirskii's theories. Mirskii, the chief ideologist of Soviet

relations with the Third World, considered the military in national democratic regimes a force of progress, capable of leading the country to socialism. See G. Mirskii, "Klassovaia bor'ba v razvivaiushchikhsia stranakh," in *Mirovaia ekonomikai mezhdunarodnye otnosheniia,* 1966, no.3

68. See, for example, Demchenko in *Izvestiia,* 17 December 1968; Koriavin in ibid., 23 July 1969.

69. In an article signed by Kudriavtsev and published on 4 June 1968, *Izvestiia* stated that "the main cause of the defeat . . . was the basic incompatability between the social basis of the Egyptian revolution and the tasks currently facing the country. The task of liquidating the consequences of the Israeli aggression necessitates the strengthening of the progressive regime and widening its social basis." This was the only time *Izvestiia* deviated from its otherwise consistent line of non-interference in internal affairs, military or otherwise.

70. There are several excellent sources providing a chronology and analysis of the Soviet-Arab official exchanges. The present research does not attempt a historical survey of USSR–Arab states relations. Therefore, various visits and political, economic, or military agreements concluded in the period under discussion will be analyzed only if they were disputed in the press.

71. Cf. Sizov in *Pravda,* 3 September 1968; Demchenko in *Izvestiia,* 28 August 1968; Sgibnev in *Krasnaia zvezda,* 16 April 1968.

72. *Izvestiia,* 29 August 1968; See also *Pravda,* 3 September 1968.

73. The article was signed by G. Drambiants, who "has recently returned from a trip to Syria." This was the first and only time Drambiants's name appeared beneath an article dealing with the Middle East. Reading his article, one gets the irresistible, though obviously unconfirmed, impression that its author is a military man.

74. Since *Izvestiia* did not publish any detailed commentaries on the Egyptian army, no comparative analysis is possible. However, *Izvestiia's* preferences may perhaps be inferred from the fact that it chose to evaluate the Syrian, rather than the Egyptian, armed forces.

75. See, for example, *Pravda,* 9 March 1968; *Izvestiia,* 29 August 1968.

76. Colonel Sgibnev in *Krasnaia zvezda,* 16 April 1968.

77. See also *Pravda,* 4 May 1968; ibid., 5 May 1968; *Izvestiia,* 5 May 1968; *Krasnaia zvezda,* 5 May 1968.

78. See A. Levy, "The Syrian Communists and the Ba'th Power Struggle," in Confino and Shamir, *The USSR and the Middle East,* pp. 395-407.

79. Levy cites claims by Lebanese newspapers that the Soviet embassy in Damascus "threw all its weight behind and did everything possible to support the radical wing." Ibid., p. 405.

80. Two communist ministers sat in the Syrian cabinet from 1966. At the Ba'th Party Congress of September-October 1968, the communists demanded two more portfolios, specifically, the Ministry of Health and the Ministry of Labor and Social Affairs. Ibid., p. 404.

81. According to the Beirut newspaper *al-Sayyad,* the Syrian Communist party called upon its members to prepare themselves to take up arms in support of Jadid's faction against Asad in the eventuality of a civil war. It is clear from the Lebanese press report that the communists regarded the outbreak of a civil war as imminent. *Al-Sayyad,* 6 March 1969, as quoted in Levy, "Syrian Communists and the Ba'th Power Struggle," p. 409.

82. *Krasnaia zvezda,* 6 March 1969.

83. The Soviet position in Syria was especially important after the latter granted the USSR port facilities in Lataqia. *Krasnaia zvezda* underlined this obvious interest with extensive coverage of the calls by Soviet naval squadrons at Syrian ports. See, for example, *Krasnaia zvezda,* 21 April 1968; ibid., 22 April 1968; ibid., 23 April 1968; ibid., 24 April 1968.

84. *Al-Hayat,* as quoted by Levy, "Syrian Communists and the Ba'th Power Struggle," p. 409.

85. *Pravda's* appeal to maintain "national unity" was in sharp contrast with the Syrian Communist party's appeals to take up arms against the military faction. According to *al-Hayat,* Khalid Bakdash, the leader of the Syrian Communist party, left for Moscow in the midst of the crisis. *Al-Hayat,* 22 March 1969, quoted by Levy, "Syrian Communists and the Ba'th Power struggle," p. 409. It is possible that Bakdash was summoned to Moscow and asked to curb communist activity, which was causing increasing resentment in both factions. It is also possible that Bakdash flew to Moscow on his own initiative to demand greater support for the Jadid faction against the military wing.

86. *Krasnaia zvezda* might have been particularly outraged by the fact that Salah Jadid, apparently realizing how unpopular cooperation with the communists had become, launched an unprecedented attack against "communist infiltration of the government" and tried to dissociate his group from any collusion with the communists. See Levy, "Syrian Communists and the Ba'th Power Struggle," p. 410. This development might have reinforced the Soviet military in its position that this and any further "retreats" could have been prevented if the

Soviet Union had decided to throw more weight behind Jadid's faction.

87. See Levy, "Syrian Communists and the Ba'th Power Struggle," pp. 409-410.

88. UPI, quoted by *Arab Report and Record,* 1-15 April, 1969.

89. Generally, *Pravda* refrained from using the term *usurper* with reference to Israel. This instance of employing a term typical of Syrian militant parlance may be seen as a gesture toward Syria.

90. See a similar reference in *Izvestiia,* 17 April 1969.

91. *Pravda,* 12 April 1969. See also ibid., 17 April 1969; ibid., 23 April 1969; *Izvestiia,* 17 April 1969.

92. *Pravda* was the only one of the three newspapers to print this item. Its solitary apology may support the hypothesis ventured above: that the military's opinion was to some extent supported and heeded by the *Pravda* group and that some action, probably less vigorous than that proposed by the military, was indeed undertaken. *Izvestiia's* failure to publish this item may indicate that it was consistently of the opinion that developments in Syria did not necessitate any Soviet intervention.

93. Speaking at a Kremlin dinner given in Atasi's honor, Podgornyi stated that "we have struggled and shall continue to struggle for a just political settlement in the Middle East. [Such a settlement] should provide for, and state as its primary condition, the withdrawal of Israeli forces from all territory occupied during the 1967 aggression." Atasi, however, was perceptibly more militant when he stated: "We find ourselves at the stage of resolutely confronting the enemy and [we] are getting ready for the liberation of the occupied lands." See *Pravda,* 6 July 1969; *Izvestiia,* 6 July 1969; *Krasnaia zvezda,* 6 July 1969.

94. Levy, "Syrian Communists and the Ba'th Power Struggle," pp. 413-414.

95. Medvedko in *Pravda,* 24 January 1968. This direct reference to Egypt was unique. Generally, the similarity between the shortcomings in Iraq and those evident in other "progressive" regimes was only implicit. See, for example, Medvedko in *Pravda,* 14 July 1968.

96. These three items reported the July coup d'etat.

97. According to *Krasnaia zvezda,* the Soviet ships visited Iraqi ports "within the framework of an agreement between the Soviet and Iraqi general staffs." *Krasnaia zvezda,* 11 May 1968.

98. See, for example, A. Pol'shchikov in *Izvestiia,* 18 January 1968; ibid., 2 February 1968; A. Stupak in ibid., 13 July 1968.

99. A. S. Becker, "Oil and the Persian Gulf," in Confino and Shamir, *The USSR and the Middle East,* p. 185.

100. Ibid., pp. 173-185.

101. Ibid., p. 189.

102. B. Rachkov in *Izvestiia,* 12 July 1969.

103. *Pravda,* 18 July 1968; *Izvestiia,* 18 July 1968; *Krasnaia zvezda,* 18 July 1968.

104. *Pravda,* 20 July 1968; ibid., 23 July 1968; *Izvestiia,* 20 July 1968; ibid., 23 July 1968; *Krasnaia zvezda,* 20 July 1968; ibid., 23 July 1968.

105. *Pravda,* 24 July 1968; ibid., 26 July 1968; ibid., 2 August 1968; ibid., 10 August 1968.

106. Medvedko in ibid., 12 August 1968.

107. Ibid.

108. Ibid.

109. *Pravda* listed only one "positive step" of the new regime, namely, the closure of "the terrible prison Nukrat al-Salman," in which "many patriotic heroes have been rotting for years." Yet even when listing this "positive step," *Pravda* hastened to voice indignation about the fact that "many Nukrat prisoners were merely transferred to another prison."

110. See also Primakov in *Pravda,* 20 September 1968.

111. *Pravda*'s public pressure could have been meant to reinforce the vigorous activity of the Iraqi Communist party, which demanded participation in the government, licensing of the CP daily, and reinstatement of all communist officers retired since 1959. None of these demands was granted. The communists were given only basic and limited toleration, such as general absence of persecution, freedom of movement, and toleration of conventions and clandestine publications. U. Dann, "The Communist Movement in Iraq," in Confino and Shamir, *The USSR and the Middle East,* p. 385.

112. *Pravda,* 30 August 1968. *Pravda* was evidently oblivious to the irony of the situation: the Iraqi regime, only recently condemned for its brutality, was being cited for refuting "allegations that the Soviet Union trampled upon human liberty."

113. *Pravda* did subject Iraq's position on the Arab-Israeli issue to vitriolic criticism: "One cannot but voice indignation at the tendency to reject the Security Council resolution [242] as the basis for a political settlement. Proponents of such an approach lack any political realism." *Pravda,* 29 September 1969. Interestingly, Iraq was not mentioned by name as adhering to this "unrealistic" course. Hence, it may be assumed that *Pravda* again used Iraq as a symbol and a forum for criticism applicable to other Arab states.

Chapter 6

1. International Institute for Strategic Studies, *Strategic Survey* (London, 1970), p. 46.

2. Nasser's speech of 23 July 1970, as quoted in *Arab Report and Record,* July 1970, pp. 424-425; see also Haykal in *al-Ahram,* 18 September 1970. Some eighteen months later, Sadat revealed that Nasser had asked for SA-3 missiles to be accompanied by Soviet operators. Radio Cairo, 30 August 1971, BBC Summary of World Broadcasts, pt. 4, 1 September 1971.

3. Ibid.

4. *Strategic Survey,* 1970, p. 47.

5. *Arab Report and Record,* March 1970, p. 167.

6. Moshe Dayan's speech of 20 March 1970, as quoted in the *New York Times,* 21 March 1970. Some Western reports indicated that the new SA-3 missiles were initially deployed around Alexandria, around the airfields near Cairo, and in the vicinity of the Aswan High Dam. *New York Times,* 19 March 1970. If correct, these reports could indicate that the Soviets intended to use these missiles primarily to protect bases in which they had gained de facto rights. The Soviets might thereby have attempted to create some sort of "neutral zone" from whch Israeli aircraft would be deterred by the mere presence of a Soviet-manned defense system.

7. Soviet pilots had been sent to Egypt as early as 1968 to train Egyptian airmen. Contingency plans to activate Soviet personnel in Egypt for combat missions must have extended at least since early 1969. The more militant line advocated by *Krasnaia zvezda* and *Izvestiia* throughout 1968-1969 may well suggest who the proponents of such plans were. Thus, the debate described here may reflect the divergent views of the protagonists over the execution of a decision that had already been adopted.

8. *Krasnaia zvezda,* 14 March 1970. The fact that the Soviet press debate did not start until mid-March may indicate that the initial decision to step up arms supplies to Egypt was adopted unanimously. This premise is further supported by the logic of the situation. In view of the evident collapse of the Egyptian defense system, the Soviet Union could not possibly deny weapons to Egypt. Commitment of Soviet personnel to active combat was, however, a different matter. The concluding sentences of this article are rather interesting. The author, Colonel Bushin, related a legend about the Urals town of Irbit, which took its name in commemoration of the victory of Urals tribes against a foreign invader who won three battles but was defeated in the fourth. The town's name means "Ir was beaten" (*Ir byl bit*). Then Bushin stated with assurance,

"It is quite possible that very soon a town will be built somewhere in the Middle East, the name of which will be *Dayanbit* ("Dayan was beaten") or perhaps *Izrabit* ("Israel was beaten")."

9. *Krasnaia zvezda,* 15 March 1970.

10. The ambiguity is in the original. The Russian syntax makes it impossible to determine whose interests should be secured—those of the Arabs or those of "their friends."

11. See, for example, *Krasnaia zvezda,* 18 March 1970; ibid., 24 March 1970; 29 March 1970.

12. See, for example, *Pravda,* 3 March 1970; ibid., 7 March 1970; ibid., 9 March 1970.

13. Ibid., 21 March 1970.

14. *Izvestiia,* 21 March 1970.

15. *Krasnaia zvezda,* 24 March 1970.

16. See, for example, *Izvestiia,* 28 March 1970; ibid., 29 March 1970.

17. *Ma'ariv* (Tel Aviv), 29 April 1970.

18. *New York Times,* 30 April 1970.

19. See, for example, *Pravda,* 4 May 1970; ibid., 5 May 1970; *Izvestiia,* 5 May 1970; ibid., 6 May 1970; *Krasnaia zvezda,* 5 May 1970; ibid., 13 May 1970. *Trud* maintained silence.

20. Later in the speech, Nasser pointed out (somewhat out of context) that more and more people with secondary and higher education were joining the Egyptian armed forces. This may have been meant as a reassurance to the USSR that their ultramodern equipment was in good hands and that the Soviet investment was not in vain.

21. *Krasnaia zvezda,* 25 April 1970; *Soviet Military Review,* 1971, no. 12, p. 51.

Chapter 7

1. *Trud,* 8 April 1967.

2. Ibid., 3 June 1967.

3. Unfortunately, there is no way to determine whether *Trud*'s editorial board was reorganized and who was nominated as the responsible editor.

4. Southeast Asia and the Middle East were virtually permanent features. The focus of the third section varied, reflecting current world events.

5. For a more detailed description of Shelepin's career and rivalries, see Michael Tatu, *Power in the Kremlin* (New York, 1970), pp. 197-200, 503-508.

6. See, for example, *Pravda,* 19 March 1971; ibid., 17 July 1970.

7. Ibid., 30 November 1970.

8. Ibid.

9. *Trud,* 22 November 1970.

10. *Pravda,* 13 March 1970; see also ibid., 5 April 1970. Ahmad Hasan al-Bakr was president of Iraq and Mulla Mustafa Barzani the leader of the Kurdish rebels.

11. See, for example, Brezhnev's speech at the Twenty-fourth CPSU Congress, as quoted by ibid., 31 March 1971; *Trud,* 31 March 1971.

12. See, for example, *Pravda,* 26 September 1970. See also ibid., 1 February 1971.

13. Cf. ibid., 25 April 1970; *Trud,* 25 April 1970.

14. Cf. *Pravda,* 30 April 1970; *Trud,* 30 April 1970.

15. Cf. *Pravda,* 7 April 1971; *Trud,* 7 April 1971.

16. *Trud,* 11 February 1971.

17. See Aziz Muhammad's speech as quoted by *Pravda,* 9 April 1971; *Trud,* 9 April 1971.

18. *Pravda,* 7 May 1971; *Trud,* 7 May 1971.

19. *Pravda,* 8 April 1971; ignored by *Trud.*

20. *Pravda,* 26 June 1971; ignored by *Trud.*

21. *Pravda,* 14 December 1971; ignored by *Trud.*

22. *Pravda,* 2 June 1970.

23. *Trud,* 4 March 1971.

24. See, for example, *Pravda,* 30 November 1970.

25. Ibid., 16 January 1970.

26. Ibid., 3 April 1970.

27. Ibid., 23 November 1970.

28. Ibid., 21 June 1971.

29. Ibid., 22 June 1971.

30. *Trud,* 26 June 1971. During the period under investigation, Ahmad was mentioned twice in the Soviet press. *Sovetskaia Kirgiziia* of 23 May 1971 reported: "At a meeting of the Syrian society held in Damascus, Abdallah Ahmad, member of the regional Ba'th leadership and member of the Syrian delegation to the Twenty-fourth CPSU Congress, delivered a lecture summing up the results of the Congress."

31. *Pravda,* 23 March 1970.

32. Ibid., 23 January 1971.

33. Ibid., 26 June 1971.

34. Ibid., 9 October 1970. The term used in the Arabic original, *ishtirakiyya,* means socialist.

35. *Trud,* 9 October 1970.

36. Labib Shuqayr, chairman of the UAR National Assembly, as

quoted by *Pravda,* 2 November 1970.

37. See, for example, *Trud,* 9 January 1970; ibid., 18 March 1970; ibid., 16 March 1971.

38. See, for example, ibid., 4 October 1970; ibid., 10 October 1970.

39. Cf., for example, *Pravda,* 12 December 1970; *Trud,* 12 December 1970.

40. *Pravda,* 11 December 1970.

41. See chapter 6, note 21.

42. See, for example, *Pravda,* 5 October 1970; ibid., 6 October 1970. See also Sadat's telegram to Brezhnev, Podgornyi, and Kosygin, as quoted in ibid., 16 October 1970.

43. See, for example, ibid., 2 October 1970; ibid., 6 October 1970; ibid., 9 October 1970; ibid., 17 October 1970.

44. See, for example, ibid., 4 October 1970; ibid., 5 October 1970; ibid., 9 October 1970; ibid., 17 October 1970.

45. See, for example, ibid., 15 October 1970; ibid., 16 October 1970; ibid., 17 October 1970.

46. See, for example, ibid., 2 October 1970; ibid., 6 October 1970; ibid., 8 October 1970; ibid., 15 October 1970.

47. Ibid.

48. See, for example, ibid., 4 October 1970; ibid., 5 October 1970; ibid., 6 October 1970. See also Kosygin's speech on Cairo radio and television, as quoted in ibid., 2 October 1970.

49. Ibid., 6 October 1970.

50. See, for example, the telegram of Brezhnev, Podgornyi, and Kosygin to Sadat, as quoted by ibid., 30 September 1970. See also Kosygin's telegram to the UAR government, as quoted by ibid., 9 October 1970; ibid., 10 October 1970.

51. *Trud,* 22 October 1970.

52. *Pravda,* 22 October 1970.

53. Ibid., 9 October 1970.

54. *Trud,* 19 December 1970.

55. It may be instructive to compare *Trud'*s coverage of Sabri's visit with its coverage of Nasser's last visit to the Soviet Union in July 1970. On that occasion, *Pravda* dedicated a large part of its front page to Nasser's visit, including photographs and large headlines. *Trud* at that time also published a large photograph on its front page. But the picture and the headlines, no smaller than *Pravda'*s, heralded the arrival of the president of the Central African Republic, who happened to be in Moscow concurrently with Nasser. Cf. *Pravda,* 1 July 1970; *Trud,* 1 July 1970.

56. *Trud,* 22 December 1970.

57. See note 6.

58. *Pravda,* 5 June 1971.

59. Sadat's speech, as quoted by ibid., 21 May 1971.

60. Sadat's speech, as quoted by *Trud,* 21 May 1971.

61. See, for example, *Pravda,* 22 May 1971; ibid., 23 May 1971; ibid., 24 May 1971; ibid., 25 May 1971. Cf. *Trud's* coverage of the same period.

62. *Pravda,* 26 May 1971.

63. Ibid., 30 May 1971. See also ibid., 31 May 1971.

64. *Trud,* 1 June 1971.

65. *Pravda's* editorial, 2 June 1971.

66. See, for example, ibid., 28 May 1970 (this is a very interesting report stating that twenty Soviet experts were attached to various Sudanese ministries). See also ibid., 26 May 1970; ibid., 10 December 1970; ibid., 8 January 1971.

67. See, for exampe, *Trud,* 5 October 1971. See also ibid., 24 January 1971.

68. See ibid., 24 January 1971; ibid., 6 July 1971; ibid., 27 July 1971.

69. See, for example, ibid., 23 May 1971; ibid., 6 July 1971; ibid., 3 October 1971.

70. See, for example, ibid., 21 May 1971; ibid., 11 November 1971.

71. See, for example, ibid., 31 March 1970; ibid., 14 March 1971; ibid., 21 May 1971.

72. Ibid., 27 July 1971. See also ibid., 24 January 1971.

73. Cf. *Pravda,* 1 November 1971; *Trud,* 1 November 1971. Previous telegrams that greeted "the Algerian nation" were quoted by *Trud.* See, for example, ibid., 7 July 1971.

74. Numayri's speech, as quoted in *Trud,* 18 June 1970.

75. See, for example, ibid., 19 March 1970. See also ibid., 26 May 1970.

76. Ibid.

77. Ibid., 23 July 1971. *Trud* mistakenly stated that Muhammed Abd-al Khaliq Muhjub, secretary general of the Sudanese Communist party, was also on the plane.

78. *Trud,* 25 July 1971; *Pravda,* 25 July 1971.

79. Cf. *Pravda,* 27 July 1971; *Trud,* 27 July 1971.

80. Cf. *Pravda,* 28 July 1971; *Trud,* 28 July 1971. Cf. also *Pravda,* 31 July 1971; *Trud,* 31 July 1971. Ahmad-al-Shaykh was secretary general of the Sudanese trade unions and vice-chairman of the World Federation of Trade Unions.

81. *Trud,* 3 August 1971.

82. Oded Eran, "Soviet Perceptions of Arab Communism and Its

Political Role," in *The USSR and the Middle East,* ed. M. Confino and S. Shamir (Jerusalem, 1973), p. 1.

83. Ibid.

84. Hasan Riyad, as quoted in *Problems of Communism* 15, no. 5 (September-October 1966): 45.

85. See, for example, *Pravda*'s editorial of 14 January 1970. See also *Pravda*'s "International Review" of 1 February 1970.

86. See, for example, *Trud*'s commentaries of 14 July 1970 and 8 September 1970.

87. Cf. the speeches of N. Ceausescu as quoted by *Pravda,* 3 April 1971; *Trud,* 3 April 1971; T. Zhivkov as quoted by *Pravda,* 3 April 1971; *Trud,* 3 April 1971; G. Hall, as quoted by *Pravda,* 4 April 1971; *Trud,* 4 April 1971; W. Kashtan, as quoted by *Pravda,* 7 April 1971; *Trud,* 7 April 1971.

88. Cf. the speeches of Marshal Grechko, as quoted by *Pravda,* 3 April 1971; *Trud,* 3 April 1971; A. B. Chakovskii, as quoted by *Pravda,* 6 April 1971; *Trud,* 6 April 1971.

89. *Trud*'s "International Review" of 30 June 1970. See also *Trud*'s commentaries of 16 June 1970, 14 July 1970, and 20 September 1970.

90. Ibid., 14 July 1970.

91. Ibid., 13 May 1970.

92. *Pravda*'s editorial of 27 January 1970. See also *Pravda*'s commentary of 15 November 1970.

93. See, for example, *Trud*'s "International Review" of 22 July 1970.

94. See, for example, *Pravda*'s commentary of 1 February 1970. See also ibid., 19 September 1970; ibid., 9 December 1970.

95. See *Ma'ariv* (Tel Aviv), 1 May 1970.

96. See, for example, *Pravda,* 5 May 1970; *Trud,* 5 May 1970.

97. *Trud,* 27 May 1970.

98. See, for example, *Trud*'s editorial of 5 June 1970.

99. See, for example, *Pravda,* 30 May 1970; ibid., 5 June 1970; ibid., 10 July 1970.

100. See, for example, *Trud*'s editorial of 5 June 1970; and *Trud*'s "International Review," of 22 July 1970.

101. Brezhnev's speech, as quoted by *Pravda,* 13 June 1970; *Trud,* 13 June 1970.

102. See, for example, *Pravda,* 18 June 1970.

103. See, for example, *Trud*'s quotation of M. Riyad's speech, 3 March 1971; Nasser's speech, 17 June 1970; Nasser's speech, 30 July 1970. See also *Trud*'s "International Review," 31 July 1970, quoting

the Soviet-Egyptian joint communiqué.

104. This point—withdrawal from "the territories" or from "territories"—is a bone of contention among the great powers and between Israel and the Arab states. See chapter 3, note 35. The difference here between *Pravda* and *Trud* is not at once apparent. Nevertheless, *Trud*'s position was clear. Although *Pravda* took pains to stress its demand for a total withdrawal of all Israeli forces from all (the) occupied territories, emphasizing that this is the only meaning of the Security Council resolution, *Trud* spoke only of withdrawal from (the) territories and did not further define, qualify, or elaborate on this vital issue.

105. *Pravda*, 9 August 1970. See also ibid., 27 June 1970.

106. *Trud*, 11 August 1970.

107. Ibid., 16 June 1970. See also ibid., 27 July 1970.

108. Ibid., 25 August 1970.

109. Ibid., 15 September 1970. See also ibid., 1 September 1970; ibid., 3 September 1970; ibid., 8 September 1970.

110. See, for example, *Pravda*, 3 March 1971. See also the announcement of the Soviet government, as quoted by ibid., 28 February 1971.

111. Ibid., 3 March 1971.

112. Ibid., 14 May 1971. See also ibid., 5 June 1971.

113. Ibid., 14 May 1971.

114. *Trud*, 6 May 1971.

Chapter 8

1. *Krasnaia zvezda*, 23 August 1970. See also ibid., 6 September 1970.

2. Ibid., 23 August 1970. See also ibid., 28 August 1970; ibid., 2 September 1970.

3. Ibid., 23 August 1970. See also ibid., 28 August 1970; ibid., 2 September 1970; ibid., 6 September 1970.

4. It is also possible that the campaign waged by *Krasnaia zvezda* served a further purpose, namely, to constitute part of the pressure (and a pretext) for the "relocation" of Soviet missile complexes. On 9 September 1970, *Krasnaia zvezda* announced that the missiles had been moved closer to the Suez Canal "in order to prevent them from being damaged by an Israeli attack." This admission was in sharp contrast to the categorical denial voiced by *Pravda*. The pressure presumably delivered by the Ministry of Defense and *Krasnaia zvezda*'s subsequent revelation that the missiles were in fact moved forward (in obvious violation of the standstill agreement) may have been an integral

part of their policy of deterrence. The "relocation" of the missiles strengthened Soviet credibility and reinforced its deterrent power. The "leaking out" of this information may also be explained as an attempt to test American credibility. This is a classic practice in Soviet foreign policy: trying to press or provoke the adversary in order to test his reactions, always leaving room for retreat in case of an actual response. Such a deliberate provocation may also serve to convince the Arabs, as well as the "soft-liners" in the Soviet leadership, that the United States is nothing but a "broken reed" and a "paper tiger": there is no reason for the Arabs to seek rapprochement with the United States nor for the "soft-liners" to fear its reaction.

5. *Krasnaia zvezda,* 2 February 1970; ibid., 23 August 1970; ibid., 6 May 1971; ibid., 11 November 1972; ibid., 6 March 1973; 29 April 1973.

6. Ibid., 23 August 1970; ibid., 5 May 1971; ibid., 6 May 1971.

7. Ibid., 2 February 1970; ibid., 11 February 1971; ibid., 5 March 1971; ibid., 12 May 1971; ibid., 9 November 1972.

8. Ilana Dimant, "Die arabischen und israelischen Streitkräfte im Spiegel der sowjetischen Militärpresse," *Osteuropa* no. 10 (October 1973): 805-813.

9. *Krasnaia zvezda,* 3 February 1971; ibid., 11 February 1971; ibid., 7 March 1971; ibid., 15 April 1971.

10. *Krasnaia zvezda*'s fear of a US-UAR rapprochement may be inferred from its hostile attitude to the Rogers mission. William Rogers' visit to Egypt in May 1971 was equated with that of John Foster Dulles, "who came to the Middle East in 1953 to form the aggressive Baghdad Pact." See *Krasnaia zvezda,* 6 May 1971. See also ibid., 5 May 1971; ibid., 7 May 1971.

11. See, for example, *Pravda,* 2 June 1971; *Krasnaia zvezda,* 5 June 1971; *Izvestiia,* 2 June 1971.

12. Sadat's speech, as quoted in *al-Ahram,* 2 June 1971.

13. *Pravda,* 13 June 1971; ibid., 18 June 1971.

14. *Krasnaia zvezda,* 1 June 1971.

15. Ibid., 30 May 1971.

16. Ibid. See also ibid., 4 June 1971; ibid., 19 June 1971.

17. *Le Soir* (Beirut), 16 February 1972.

18. See Grechko's speeches on both occasions. Each visit was accompanied by a demonstration of strength and support, including the anchoring of a Soviet squadron in Alexandria and the overflight of Israeli-held Sinai by two MIG-23s.

19. *Krasnaia zvezda,* 11 November 1972. See also ibid., 29 September 1972; ibid., 22 October 1972.

20. Ibid., 24 November 1973.

21. Ibid. See also ibid., 19 September 1972.

22. See, for example, Sadat's speech at the ASU National Congress, broadcast by Radio Cairo, 24 July 1972; President Hafiz al-Asad's press interview, Radio Damascus, 10 August 1972; Haykal's *al-Ahram* articles broadcast by Radio Cairo, 11 August 1972 and 18 August 1972. See also *The Guardian,* 20 July 1972; *Le Monde,* 20 July 1972.

23. *Krasnaia zvezda,* 11 October 1972. See also ibid., 6 October 1972; ibid., 7 October 1972; ibid., 11 October 1972.

24. *Soviet Military Review,* 1972, no. 12, p. 44.

25. *Krasnaia zvezda,* 15 October 1972. See also ibid., 21 October 1972; ibid., 24 October 1972; ibid., 28 October 1972; ibid., 24 November 1972.

26. *Strategic Survey,* 1970 and 1971. See also *The Guardian,* 31 August 1972.

27. Radio Amman, 23 October 1972, as quoted by *USSR and the Third World* 11, no. 10 (1972).

28. *Al-Nahar* (Beirut), 31 October 1972, as quoted in ibid.

29. *Newsweek,* 23 October 1972.

30. On 27 October 1972, the "resignation" of the Egyptian war minister, Muhammad Sadiq, was announced in Cairo. It might well be that Sadiq, famous for his pronounced anti-Soviet stance, was offered as a sacrificial lamb to Moscow. Interestingly enough, his successor, General Ismail Ali, pointed in his inauguration speech to the vital importance of the Soviet-Arab alliance, based upon "mutual interest of fighting against imperialism, colonialism, and Zionism." See *Krasnaia zvezda,* 1 November 1972.

31. Kosygin's speech, as quoted in ibid., 17 November 1972. See also Grechko's speech, as quoted in ibid., 9 November 1972; and the Soviet-Egyptian joint communiqué, as quoted in *Pravda,* 2 February 1973.

32. *Krasnaia zvezda*'s summary of the results of Ismail Ali's talks with Grechko, 25 March 1973.

33. *Soviet Military Review,* 1973, no. 1, p. 53.

34. Ibid., 1973, no. 10, p. 11.

Chapter 9

1. See Jerry F. Hugh, "The Party Apparatchiki," in *Interest Groups in Soviet Politics,* ed. H. Gordon Skilling and Franklyn Griffiths (Princeton, 1971), pp. 58-59.

2. M. D. Gehlen and M. McBridge. "The Soviet Central Committee: an Elite Analysis," in *The Behavioral Revolution and Communist Studies,* ed. Roger E. Kanet (New York, 1972), pp. 103-125.

3. According to Gehlen and McBridge, 55 percent of the full mem-

bers and 60 percent of the candidate members of the Central Committee elected by the Twenty-third Party Congress held no party posts on the central, republic, or regional levels before 1953. Only after 1953 (the period during which increasing emphasis was given to coopting persons into the party leadership positions who had specialized training and experience in some functional service) were many of the members assigned positions, temporarily or otherwise, in various levels of the party apparatus. After 1953, all but 30 percent of the full members held official posts in the party apparatus. Ibid., p. 121.

4. According to the same source, 65 percent of the full members of the 1966 Central Committee had a technical education. Excluded from this account are military officers and scientists. Ibid.

5. Hugh, "The Party Apparatchiki," p. 59.

6. In our opinion, any unrequited exports of goods and services that may have alternative uses in the domestic economy are a burden, at least in the short run.

7. Shelepin's speech as quoted by *Pravda* and *Trud,* 5 June 1970.

8. When Shelepin delivered a speech during the electoral campaign of 1971, its entire section on foreign policy was not quoted in the press, even though it was noted that "A. N. Shelepin dedicated a significant part of his speech to an analysis of the contemporary international situation and an evaluation of the foreign policy exercised by the Party and government." *Pravda* and *Trud,* 3 June 1971. Did these "evaluations" and "analyses" so deviate from the official line that they were censored?

9. Curiously enough, when *Trud* quoted the speeches of foreign guests invited to the Twenty-fourth CPSU Congress, it left attacks on the Chinese People's Republic out of several of them. See, for example, *Trud*'s handling of the speeches of the Mongolian, Bulgarian, and Indian representatives.

10. It is of interest that Suslov, in his speech, took a very similar stand: he criticized the "opportunist and nationalist tendencies" without mentioning the "dogmatist tendency," which is to say that Suslov also refrained from attacking China. Moreover, in the same speech Suslov assaulted the United States as "the policeman of the world . . . , a provoker of destructive wars who kindles armed conflicts in various regions of the globe." Suslov's speech delivered during the 1970 electoral campaign, as quoted in *Pravda* and *Trud,* 10 June 1970. Unfortunately, Suslov's reference to the Middle East was so brief that it is impossible to determine whether his views on this issue fell in line with those of Shelepin and *Trud.*

11. It is interesting to note that Shelepin's ouster on 16 April

1975 and his "resignation" of 22 May 1975 from the chairmanship of the trade unions (he was demoted to junior minister in charge of vocational training on the state committee for professional and trade education) were followed by a discernible convergence in *Trud*'s and *Pravda*'s lines. This alignment, however, might have resulted from changes in the Middle East in general and in Soviet positions vis-à-vis the Arabs in particular rather than from Shelepin's dismissal.

12. For similar references, see *Soviet Military Review,* 1971, no. 4, p. 14; ibid., 1971, no. 5, p. 2; ibid., 1971, no. 12, p. 51; *Morskoi sbornik,* 1971, no. 7, pp. 3-5; *Kommunist vooruzhennykh sil,* 1971, no. 7, p. 16; ibid., 1971, no. 12, p. 39.

13. For a full analysis, see Ilana Dimant, "Die arabischen und israelischen Streitkräfte im Spiegel der sowjetischen Militär presse," *Osteuropa,* no. 10 (1973): 805-813.

14. See, for example, Grechko's essays in *Morskoi sbornik,* 1971, no. 7, pp. 3-5; and in *Kommunist vooruzhennykh sil,* 1971, no. 12, p. 39.

15. Vernon Aspaturian, "Soviet Military-Industrial Complex—Does It Exist?" *Journal of International Affairs* 26, no. 1 (1972): 3.

16. Ibid., pp. 14-15. Ustinov was promoted to full membership in the Politburo and nominated as defense minister following Grechko's death on 26 April 1976.

17. Ibid., pp. 17-18.

18. Ibid., pp. 18-19.

19. Ibid., p. 13.

Chapter 10

1. Zbigniew Brzezinski and Samuel P. Huntington, *Political Power USA/USSR* (New York, 1964), pp. 203-204.

2. See, for example, *Krasnaia zvezda*'s appeal to intervene on behalf of the pro-Soviet faction in Syria; *Krasnaia zvezda* and *Izvestiia*'s joint pressure to issue the "bill of rights" for the Soviet naval presence in the Mediterranean; *Krasnaia zvezda*'s pressure, later supported by the *Izvestiia* group, to proceed from involvement to commitment; *Trud*'s appeals to champion the Middle Eastern Communist parties; the military newspapers' 1973 campaign for recommitment.

3. Anthony Buzek, *How the Communist Press Works* (New York, 1964), pp. 38-54.